Inductive Preaching:
Helping People Listen

INDUCTIVE PREACHING

Helping People Listen

Ralph L. Lewis with Gregg Lewis

CROSSWAY BOOKS • WHEATON, ILLINOIS
A DIVISION OF GOOD NEWS PUBLISHERS

Inductive Preaching.

Copyright © 1983 by Ralph L. Lewis and Gregg Lewis.

Published by Crossway Books, a division of
Good News Publishers, 1300 Crescent Street, Wheaton, Illinois 60187.

First printing, 1983

Library of Congress Catalog Card Number 83-70321

ISBN 0-89107-287-X

Printed in the United States of America

99	98	97	96	95	94	93	92	91		
20	19	18	17	16	15	14	13	12	11	10	9

To

A fine
farm family
now older, grown,
or gone: Mother,
Dad, and
Brothers
Three

Contents

Introduction

How can we help?

Why don't more people listen when we preach?

What implications does our electronic age hold for preaching? Can the new discipline of cognitive science with its most recent discoveries on brain function help us better communicate God's Word?

Modern students of the brain have discovered a clear distinction in function and capabilities between the right and left hemispheres of the human brain. Critical thought, reading and linear logic all seem to center on the left side of the brain. Creativity, visual memory, feelings and imagination are functions of the right half of our brains.

But what does this have to do with a Sunday morning sermon?

Nearly 500 years ago the printing press revolutionized the world. It altered the basis of human communication and thus affected the pattern of popular human thought. Gutenberg hooked humanity on the printed word and corraled much of our cerebral life into a left-brained pattern of linear logic. And for five centuries the bulk of our teaching and preaching has been built on this foundation.

Today the reverberations of a new revolution are shaking the old foundation. The printing press is no longer the primary means of collecting or communicating human thought. Most knowledge is now stored on microfilm or in computer memory banks and communicated by blips on a screen or photoelectronic printouts. And if the communications thinkers are right when they say a culture's means of communicating and storing its basic pool of information and knowledge may be the single most crucial determinant of that civilization's character, then the world of telecommunications promises changes at least as dramatic as Gutenberg's movable type.

We've already crossed the threshold into a new era—the age of visual literacy. If we can't see it, we must have our eyes closed. This year's high school graduates have spent more time in front of their television sets than they have in a classroom for twelve years of schooling. The parishioner who spends fifty hours a year in our pews (perhaps 100 hours if coming on Sunday evening) has the tube turned on in his home more than 2,000 hours each year. Our world isn't just changing; it's already changed.

How does all this impact on our preaching?

Cognitive science's split-brain analysis would categorize traditional sermons, both the preaching of them and the listening to them, as left-brain activities. Homiletics leans hard on analysis, logic and language. Sermons often stress intellectual concepts more than imaginative or inventive ingredients, a sequential instead of a holistic view, facts over feelings, rational rather than relational orientations.

Yet the cultural communications revolution is aiming people in another direction. Today's visual communications are retraining our minds. For the first time in half a millennium the right side of the brain is clamoring for prominence and insisting on involvement in life and learning.

Our listeners are no longer hooked on printed words and linear logic. They are addicted instead to the right-brain sense of action and involvement. And TV is the primary pusher, their main connection if we want to stretch the metaphor.

TV offers cheap involvement. Observers descend from the bleachers and into the action. The microphone puts the ear in the center of the sounds. The camera takes the viewers' eyes into the thick of the fray, the football, the fun. What was once remote, imaginary and unreal becomes instantly vital, vivid and believable through the alchemy of television.

Just as the space age extends the leg by flight, our electronic age extends the brain by computer and word processor, the ear by microphone and the eye by camera. Involvement becomes a way of life, and sensory discovery becomes a primary way of learning.

If we cling too tightly to five hundred years of homiletic tradition, we may soon find an unbridgeable gulf between the daily involvement, discovery and creativity our listeners experience during the week and the comparatively dull, ho-hum routine of Sunday's sermonic decrees. If we don't take drastic steps to turn things around with our preaching, we may soon find that for our listeners the inner dimension of life will seem more and more remote, spiritual reality will appear imaginary and what should be the vivid truth of God's Word may become merely subjective haze. Many of the young, the spiritually uninitiated and the sharp secular go-getters of our empirical society already feel bypassed or patronized by institutional tradition when our sermons depend more on deductive decree than on discovery, when our emphasis is exhortation without concern for exploration or experience.

Why don't the people listen? How can we preach to involve them? What does the Bible have to say? How did Jesus and other great preachers of the Bible involve their listeners? Could their experience in the pre-Gutenberg past hold a key for our preaching in the post-print present and future?

Jesus, the prophets and apostles preached with an inductive accent. But who ever notices? Who pays any attention to Jesus as a preacher? Why do the homiletics texts ignore his example? Who remembers that the common people heard Jesus gladly when he preached inductively, beginning where they were?

Who follows Jesus' example, refusing to speak without a parable, a story, a comparison? Who analyzes the Sermon on the Mount as an eighteen-minute sermon with dozens of examples, visual images, scores of comparisons, and interest-catching devices as diverse as riddles, sex appeal and everyday experience?

Can Jesus teach us anything about preaching? Could other effective preachers from the intervening centuries reveal some simple pattern to help our preaching? Are the hearers only incidental to preaching? Or can the people get involved in our sermons? Can our preaching win their attention and gain their involvement? Can our sermons cross over to use both halves of the brain?

The questions are many, but exciting answers surround us.

Let's look at preaching through a new lens. Jesus and successful preachers since his time show us a simple approach. We can easily see their secrets if we search their sermons. They promise remedy for the feeble, futile sermons so common today. They also demonstrate various methods of achieving lay response to our preaching.

This book is not a study of philosophy, metaphysics or epistemology. Here we study life. We study experience. We study God's Word. And we study common sense and research.

The goal? Keep it simple—simple, but not stupid. Here we strive to seem profoundly simple—as simple as common sense. As common as experience. So common the people hear. They even listen. And they get involved.

1 Need

When Sam Smith drives into the church parking lot with his three-year-old Ford he sees all the new Chevies, Buicks and Toyotas. He remembers his thirty-sixth payment is due tomorrow and the car will be his—just in time to buy another one—a smaller one.

On the way to church, Susan, his wife, has said she needs more money for four-year-old Suzette's day care, for rising grocery costs and the new spring wardrobe she needs for the New York convention her boss wants her to attend. She must have new clothes so she can earn more money to buy clothes so she can work in order to have money to get some dresses so she can. . . Sam bites his tongue and swallows his kidding comment about women's lib.

He watches wistfully as Susan joins a small group entering the side door where the Young Business Women's Class meets. He remembers the *Reader's Digest* daffynition of compatibility as "the couple who both have headaches at the same time."

Proudly he watches sixteen-year-old Steve join the teenage gang rehashing Friday night's game. He wants his oldest son to go to college so he can have a better chance in life. Maybe cashing in on insurance policies will cover some of the rising costs at the university, but Steve seems to be more interested in a used car than college at the moment.

Sally, his fourteen-year-old, walks self-consciously past the knot of high school boys to mix with the girls a minute before Sunday school begins. She must have her teeth straightened and some dental surgery during Christmas break.

Sam wonders whether he should talk with somebody about the pressures—he would if anyone seemed to understand or care. His manager has threatened to let him go if the company doesn't come up with "another million-dollar year." Sales have fallen off and the moguls are head-hunting. Sam's five-year success plan doesn't seem too realistic to him now.

A few minutes later Sam sits in the corner of the Men's Sunday School Class, his mind tuning in and out of the discussion. Mostly out. He reviews the options for the added money his family needs. He could borrow on the insurance, but then he couldn't use that to help pay for Steve's college. He could sell the travel trailer, but he couldn't hope to get anywhere near its value. The idea of a second mortgage brings his thoughts reeling back into the Sunday school room.

He feels a pang of guilt for not paying more attention to the teacher. But he reminds himself that he doesn't really want to be at church anyway. Susan pressures him into it. *And she ought to be happy that I even come*, he tells himself. The guilt passes, and his thoughts again begin to drift.

The final bell eventually signals the end of class. Sam files out of the room, through the educational wing and into the narthex to wait for Susan. When she finds him, they enter the sanctuary together and take their usual place, halfway up, on the right side of the aisle.

The singing of familiar hymns occupies Sam's mind. And for a time at least the raucous sounds of Sam's marketplace fade away in mindless memory. The soft sanctuary music seems more soothing, yet oddly different from the bold beat of the blaring radio speakers he's heard throughout the week. Sam slowly absorbs a subtle sacred spirit; osmosis moistens memories into a mood of solitude, meditation and worship. Limbo seeps up the stalk as the ushers pass the hypnotic offering plates back and forth, back and forth, back and. . .

However, Secular Sam brings all his cultural baggage with him on his trip from his weekday continent called Life to the Sunday island called Church. And his mind refuses to be marooned. His questions, his conflicts, his consternation climb gradually back into his consciousness. Sam is soon back battling his inner wars of family finance and career survival.

When the pastor stands to read the morning Scripture, Sam checks the bulletin for the sermon topic, "The Total Truth for Today's Total World"—a special missions emphasis, according to the order of worship.

While the pastor reads, Sam shifts to his own agenda. He's heard so many sermons in the past decade, he makes it a weekly challenge to construct his own outline. Today he decides to go for seven points— alliterative, of course.

He titles it, "Roaming the Seven C's." Sam suppresses a smile. Cash has to be his point number one. Then Car. Clothes. Compatibility. Career. College. And Current Crisis. Sam is tracing his route through the seven C's a second time when the children's sermon interrupts his journey.

"When I was a boy," the pastor begins and Sam leans forward to watch those children on the front pews and to hear the pastor as he speaks briefly to them.

When the "regular sermon" starts, Sam watches as the restless people squirm in their seats. They shift their weight to find the least painful posture and settle down to think about something or nothing.

After a feeble effort to remarshall his thoughts around his own outline, Sam slowly releases them to wander at random. Memory, imagination and reverie touch base only occasionally with the happenings in the sanctuary. He completely abandons the minister, and his thoughts sail away to mainland Life. He ponders his return to the mad world of Monday morning. *What will I say to the boss? What are my options? Is it worth the hassle?*

Susan leans toward him a little and snuggles under his protecting arm. He remembers: *It's been a good life. We've had our ups and downs. But we get along pretty well—usually. We've had some great times, and then there are the kids. Some things have slowed down a little, but life's pretty good. Sure need more money. Let's see—that's cash—number one in my outline.*

Sam begins to plan his exit about fifteen minutes before the sermon ends. *What's for Sunday dinner?* he asks himself. *Did Susan say chicken? Or was it Spanish rice? Something quick I hope! The game comes on the tube at 12:30!*

Sam eyes the exit and plots his escape during the final hymn. At the last note of the "Amen" chord he makes his move. The direct route takes him uncomfortably close to the pastor at the rear door. Sometimes he can slip out without interruption, but today Pastor Jones eyes him and winks.

Sam is caught. What can he say? "I enjoyed your talk," he blurts out as his mind gropes for a more honest word. He awkwardly shakes the hand the pastor holds out to him. Then Sam hurries through the crowd and out to the parking lot where he slouches down in his car and turns on the radio to hear the noon news—a voice from the real world.

Susan and the kids soon filter out to the car. "The chicken should be done," Susan says as they all head for home.

Secular Sam and his fellow pewmates aren't the only dissatisfied players in the Sunday morning drama. But they'd probably never guess Pastor Jones' squelched feelings of frustration. Here's how the morning went for him:

Pastor Jones' discouragement builds as he guides his congregation like sheep through the passageways of the printed order of worship. Nearly everyone joins in the hymns. They attend to the announcements. But when he stands to read the Scripture aloud, he senses a change. *It's as if an invisible wall rises between us. Why don't they listen? Am I too loud? Too slow? Too fast?* He concludes the reading and sits down again.

During the offertory he thinks ahead. *Maybe I can ring the bell in the children's sermon. Sometimes that seems to rouse them. I wonder why that is? Maybe my sermons are a bit too strong for them. But they should learn to listen.*

After the ushers present the offering to the strains of the Doxology, Pastor Jones calls the children and relates a tale from his childhood, a simple incident when he learned the danger of lying and the value of truth. He wraps it up with a summary of God's attitude toward truth and sends the little ones toward the sanctuary side door and the waiting leaders of the junior church program.

Now the sermon time arrives. As he steps back up to the pulpit, he straightens his tie, clears his throat and waits for silence.

Then he reads the text: "Finally, brethren, whatsoever things are true . . . whatsoever things are lovely, whatsoever things are of good report, if there be any virtue, and if there be any praise, think on these things" (Philippians 4:8).

Why do the people seem to be staring beyond me? I'm the pastor; they should pay attention to me. Why don't they listen?

He breathes deeply and projects his rehearsed tones: "Truth is lovely, dear friends. Truth has a good report. Truth is worthy of our meditation—think on these things."

He defines the truth. He declares the truth. He defends the truth.

His orthodox, well-rounded words ascend to the ceiling, extend to the foyer, and bounce softly off the back wall. He wonders if anyone is really listening.

Some members of the congregation nod in full agreement. But he knows that's a poor gauge because some of those smiling heads slow their metronome nods and let chins rest a moment before they rise again. His discouragement deepens.

Then all eyes open, all heads rise at the midpoint of the sermon when a bit of narration brightens an example. But the encouragement is only momentary as attention lags again and an epidemic of fidgeting spreads through the sanctuary.

By the time he approaches the end of his sermon, he has little enthusiasm left for the emphatic conclusion he'd hoped would inspire his people to respond to the overwhelming needs of the church's mission program. *What's the use?* he asks himself. Half a dozen people steal quick glances at their wrists as he launches into his final example. *What do they care about third-world hunger and medical needs? Any concern for the problems of planet earth fades at five minutes till noon.*

He finally directs the congregation to stand for the benediction. He's halfway tempted to pray an honest prayer from a despairing or perhaps even an imprecatory Psalm. But he resists the temptation to vent his feelings and intones the standard formula of dismissal. Then he retreats down the aisle as the choir offers the choral benediction.

As the last strains of the Amen die away, the sanctuary buzzes with renewed energy. The instantaneous transformation prompts a silent, cynical thought in the pastor's mind. *I wonder if I'll ever awaken the kind of response from a sermon that I always get from the benediction.*

He tries to shake off the feelings of frustration and doubt as the aisles fill and the people crowd toward him. He screws on a smile, shakes as many hands as he can reach, and tries to endure the comments.

"Glad to see you again." "Enjoyed the sermon, pastor." "Have a good week." "Nice talk today." "I always enjoy your little time with the children at the start of the service." The innocuous comments always seem to skirt reality and straightforward sincerity. But at least on this Sunday Pastor Jones hears no bragging about "that good sermon I heard on TV."

By the time Secular Sam and the rest of the congregation finish their chicken dinners and plant themselves in front of the afternoon football telecast, the pastor has concluded his meal and sought out the silence of the manse study. There he replays his frustrations and the morning performance.

What are the people looking for anyway? I preach God's Word—I quote Scripture on almost every point. Why don't they respond? I don't understand, Lord, he says, directing his questions heavenward. *You say your Word won't return unto you void. But every Sunday it seems to. Where's the response?*

It's not as if I don't care or don't try, he tells himself. And he recalls how he has spent his vacations for the past five years visiting some of the country's most dynamic churches, hoping to learn some secrets from successful preachers. He attends all the minister's conferences he can fit into his schedule and has collected enough books and articles on preaching to fill a small library.

Pastor Jones has turned the energies of his youth and the fires of his imagination on the task of melding and molding messages to change the world or at least some part of it. Dedication to the task of ministry has never been his problem. But his high resolve melts into mediocrity every Sunday morning. The people never seem to change. His sermons don't count for much. He wonders if his ministry really matters.

Maybe all the successful preachers are just born speakers, born charismatic leaders, he concludes. *But what about God's promises to multiply human efforts?*

The needs of his congregation are so obvious—personal needs, family needs, human needs. Faith holds the answers. Pastor Jones knows that. He's learned from personal experience. He's read history. He believes the Bible accounts. The needs tower to the skies above him, but sometimes the theological ladders seem too short.

A year ago he seriously considered giving up the ministry. He could serve as a social worker with his undergraduate training. He could spend more time with his family if he had a limited case load and 9 to 5 working hours.

Some of his former university friends kid him about the pastorate. "How does it seem to spend your life telling people what they already know?" They tell him his sermons are good advice. "But advice is the one commodity in the world where the supply exceeds the demand," they say.

Despite the doubts, Pastor Jones has resolved in his mind to stay in the ministry. He's convinced God has called him to the task. And he knows that when Secular Sam and the rest of the congregation head back to their jobs on Monday morning, he will go to his office to begin preparing a sermon for next Sunday. And he will pray that somehow God will bless and use his efforts, his preaching. But the discouragement remains.

The Secular Sam-Pastor Jones scenario is played out every Sunday in thousands of churches across the land. Secular Sam and his counterparts come out of their workaday world burdened and consumed by seemingly insurmountable problems. They come out of a world where they are assaulted by an estimated 600 mass media sales pitches every week—messages they learn to consciously tune out. They come with senses hooked on mass media's electronic input and minds overloaded with very personal troubles. Self-worth, life's meaning and purpose, priorities, security, success and survival all clamor for top billing in their thoughts.

Pastor Jones and a legion of fellow pastors preach more than 350,000 sermons every Sunday morning. They watch and agonize over the struggles of contemporary society. They see the wounds of a family suffering divorce. They see the fear of dying cancer patients. They see the anxiety of middle-aged men thrown out of work. They see the overwhelming uncertainty of youth in a fearful age. And they long to share God's answers—answers they believe in.

But something is wrong. For some reason the answer isn't reaching the needs. Secular Sam and Pastor Jones both come away frustrated.

Perhaps this frustration explains the disturbing trend cited in a June 1978 Gallup Poll. Pollsters asked Americans, "How important is religion in your life?" In 1978 only 53 percent of the people replied "very important to me." In 1952, twenty-six years earlier, 75 percent had said religion was "very important to me." Midway through that time period, in 1965, 70 percent had replied that religion was "very important to me." The series of polls shows a slide of 5 percent over the first half of the period but an alarmingly accelerating decline of 17 percent in recent years.

What are the implications for preaching today? Can preaching help make religion "very important" again?

Few today would question the need for more effective preaching. Just observe the signs. See the symptoms of indifference, aloofness, apathy. Check the deadwood on church membership rolls. Talk to any Secular Sam or Pastor Jones. Consider your own experience.

What's the solution? Is there some unattained goal that could alleviate the frustration surrounding preaching today?

Involvement. That common word is the most promising answer. Involvement has been a major goal throughout twentieth-century preaching. It's what Secular Sam is seeking on Sunday morning. It's what Pastor Jones would like to get.

But how can a minister involve hearers in his preaching? Is there a simple, surefire way?

In recent decades some have tried to capture attention and encourage involvement by using dialogue and discussion. The church has experimented with drama and dance. Sermon content has changed; style and delivery have become more folksy, conversational and direct. But innovation, change and creativity have released little vitality or impact in today's sermon. Despite the creative quest, the dream of getting the people involved seems to be a distant mirage.

Crowds have flocked to hear a few preachers who seem to have found a way to attain the involvement of their hearers. Are there secrets to be learned from these crowd-catchers? They vary so greatly that there seems to be no traceable pattern in their preaching. Close scrutiny of the few giants who have accomplished consistent listener involvement shows no shared format. They evidently navigate by instinct and experience more often than by precept or plan.

Success at winning listener involvement seems independent of training. Pastors without seminary degrees serve most of the growing churches, according to a recent survey of 555 expanding congregations. Apparently education can't promise preaching success. Where can we look for an answer then? Is contemporary preaching beyond the hope of man and the help of God? Is there any biblical basis for a solution? Does Jesus model any hope for our preaching?

Can Pastor Jones and the multitude of ministers with similar frustrations find hope for effective preaching?

Is there any answer to these questions? Is there any solution for the lack of involvement—our primary crisis in preaching today?

There is.

It's as contemporary as our modern problems and as old as the Scriptures themselves. We'll consider that solution in the remainder of this book.

2   A Promising Solution

Randy, a student in one of my preaching courses, waited to talk to me after class. "Why do my people watch the cows outside the church when I preach?" he blurted out with feeling. "I preach the best I know, but some of the people always look out the windows. They can see cows any day of the week. Why do they have to do it while I'm trying to keep their attention on the sermon? What can I do about it?"

I asked, "Why do you think they watch the cows?" We talked about his frustration in the pastorate. I asked him how he started his sermons and whether his major accent was on theology or the people. I inquired about his illustrations with human instances and case studies.

After a few minutes of discussion Randy still sounded desperate. "I'll try anything you say. I really want to get their attention and hold it."

We talked about a number of things he might try. Randy vowed he would work harder to involve the people in his Sunday sermons. He seemed determined as he left for the weekend at his student pastorate.

The next week Randy bounced into class. "Boy, nobody watched cows this Sunday," he beamed. I saw he could hardly wait to recount his weekend.

I asked, "How did you do it, Randy?"

"Prof, I started with this sentence: 'The go-go dancer knocked on the parsonage door on Saturday night at 10:30.'" He grinned as he added, "Those cows really got neglected during the entire sermon. Nobody looked outside; no one looked around. Everybody seemed to stop breathing, just waiting for my explanation.

"What a change to have their undivided attention. They've always been warm and cordial to me, but this was the first time I've ever seen them so engrossed in my preaching."

Randy's experience reemphasizes the preaching problem introduced in the preceding chapter. Involvement problems stalk every preacher—excited young seminarians such as Randy and tired old hands like Pastor Jones.

How can our preaching get the people involved?

Obviously not every preacher could start this Sunday's sermon with Randy's opening sentence. None should try. If you did, how could you top it next Sunday? You'd have to change more than the reference to the specific Saturday night hour!

But we can find the beginnings to the answer in Randy's episode. Broken down and analyzed, this incident with my young student reveals three areas of concern that require our attention if we're serious about our quest for involvement in preaching.

These three areas are not at all new. More than 2,300 years ago Aristotle divided his plan of communication into three parts or proofs: ethical—the speaker's part; emotional—the listener's; and logical—the speech's or message's role. That's basic homiletics, and any fresh strategy for winning listener involvement will have to encompass all three aspects of communication. So let's examine the implications for more effective preaching.

The Speaker or Preacher

Any hope for involvement must start with the attitude of the preacher. He or she has to want involvement. But that desire must grow directly out of the care felt for the people. No one cares how much we know until he knows how much we care.

In my early ministry I knew one rural pastor who became increasingly discouraged by his people's lack of response. One Sunday he got so frustrated he called his congregation of Dutch-American farmers "a bunch of flat-headed Dutchmen," stormed out the side door of the church, and stalked to the parsonage to simmer down. He certainly showed them he cared; but the expression of that frustrated caring ended any hope for an effective ministry in that parish.

Pastor Jones and Randy are better examples for us. They felt some of the same frustrations. But Pastor Jones' compassion and concern for his people kept him from condemning them in a closing prayer. Randy's concern for his people helped him curb the urge to shoot those cows and sent him searching for any help he could get from his preaching prof. Unlike the minister who blew up at his congregation, they were ready to accept some responsibility for the involvement problem.

That's the fountainhead of any hope for involvement in our preaching. Ministry begins in the mind and heart of the minister. Paul spelled out part of this requirement when he said, "Let this mind be in you, which was also in Christ Jesus, who . . . took upon him the form of a servant . . . and became obedient unto death, even the death of the cross."

Jesus added further guidelines for ministry when he said: "Except a grain of wheat fall into the ground, and die, it abides alone; but if it die, it brings forth much fruit. . . . For the Son of man came, not to be ministered unto but to minister, and to give his life a ransom for many. . . . Whosoever would save his life shall lose it, but whosoever loses his life for my sake and the gospel's, the same shall save it."

But how does this impact on preaching for involvement?

It means that if we want involvement we have to be willing to involve ourselves. The true shepherd heart cares enough to identify with the people just as the Good Shepherd lays down his life for his sheep.

Ministry demands sacrifice, and sacrifice is risky.

Effective preaching may mean taking the risk of experimentation. Like Randy, we may need to ask, "How can I be more effective? What can I change about my sermons to get my listeners involved?" Such change is risky.

But meaningful ministry requires more than risking our sermons. It means risking ourselves. It means placing ourselves in the pew with our people, admitting our humanness to ourselves and to them, and preaching with the conviction that we all are "workers together with God."

That personal risk is the price of involvement; the preacher becomes vulnerable. Love and ministry always extract that price.

Comfort, complacency and indifference cannot identify the involved preacher. He has to say, like the Master, "To this end was I born, and for this cause came I into the world, that I should bear witness unto the truth" (John 18:37).

Yet, while hope for involvement in our preaching has to start with the attitude in the mind and heart of the preacher, it can't stop there. Those attitudes of servanthood have to be reflected in his character.

In discussing the effectiveness of preaching, we usually accept the good character of the preacher as a given. But we can't afford to downplay its importance.

Demosthenes ranks the personal appeal of the speaker above all other proofs; the good speaker is the good man speaking well. Ethos or the appeal of the speaker as a person combines with other discussion in Aristotle's teaching; he emphasizes the importance of the speaker's intelligence, character and goodwill.

Both the Bible and Christian tradition amplify the speaker's role by accenting his integrity, sincerity, and desirable attitudes, along with personal morals and behavior. Practicing what we preach involves much more than merely rehearsing our sermon.

Christian thought through the centuries has explored what it means to be a good man. The minister's attitudes, relationships, beliefs and behavior ought to buttress his spoken words. No subject is mentioned more often in the Yale Lectures on preaching than the preacher's personal character.

Today many of our hearers hunger for a listening, caring, growing preacher who relates to the people. Most congregations would rather see a sermon than hear one any day of the week.

If we want involvement in our preaching, we do well to remember Kierkegaard's fourth principle of communication: "Only one who is transformed by Christianity can teach Christianity."[1]

In the September 1980 *Review of Religious Research*, Lutheran pastor William O. Avery and Gettysburg, Pennsylvania professor A. Roger Gobbel reported on two surveys of listening attitudes among Lutherans in south-central Pennsylvania congregations.

In the article "The Words of God and the Words of the Preacher" they said, "The credibility a sender has . . . depends upon the relationship between sender and receiver." Almost 83 percent of the respondents judged warmth, friendliness, and kindness in a minister's sermon just as important or more so than theological expertise or intellectual soundness.

"Laity do not demand moral perfection of their clergy, but they do seek attempted consistency between words and action. . . . They are sensitive to, and influenced by, the personal relationships they have with the pastor.

"When the laity perceive kindness and understanding in their minister, and that the minister has concern for them expressing openness, warmth, and empathy, they consider seriously interpretations of the gospel which may be at variance with their own understandings. When that relationship is positive, the laity are most prone to assert . . . that the Word of God has been spoken. . . ."

This research backs up Scripture and experience. Involvement has to start with the preacher's attitude—an attitude rooted in the mind and heart and evidenced in his character, life and preaching.

But the proper attitude isn't enough to guarantee involvement in

---

[1]Soren Kierkegaard's principles of communication may be summarized: (1) The communicator must take pains to discover the level of the learner and begin at that point. (2) The personalities of the teacher and the learner must be held distinctly apart. (3) The form of communication must be artistic and provide for involvement and self-activity on the part of the learner. (4) The teacher must be what he teaches.

our preaching. The preacher is only one part of the communication process.

The Audience

The involvement that begins with the speaker can only progress with an understanding of the audience. The people are the *only* reason for preaching. Too many preaching books and sermons seem to have lost this focus. Homiletics has often ignored the audience, Aristotle's second concern, as if one message could and should fit all hearers in all conditions and all situations.

The science of market research has transformed the advertising, sales and communication industries of our day. If we really desire effective preaching, perhaps we should listen a little more to what the researchers say about demographics, psychographics and felt needs.

If we're going to have to understand people in order to involve them, there are a number of relevant questions we must ask. Who are these Sunday morning warm bodies—these Secular Sams, these cow-watchers? What concerns them? What moves them to respond? How do they learn? We need to ask and answer all these questions.

Who are those people? In our day it isn't just the philosophers who can't step into the same river twice. Serving many suburban pastorates can be like preaching to a procession. The faces come and go quickly. Even those that stay belong to people who are shaped and changed each week by their experiences as they are swept along by the powerful current of contemporary society.

Who are they? They are the composite of many interacting factors, but primarily they are creatures of our culture.

Consider that culture for a few moments. It's a culture where nearly half the marriages end in divorce. It's a culture where two million Americans live together as couples without the blessing of any marriage rites. Where teenagers earn and spend a couple billion dollars a year. Where more people make more money and have more leisure time to spend it than ever before in the history of the world. Where 60 percent of the women work outside the home. Where transportation has taken us to the moon and beyond. It's a culture where half a million Americans are sacrificed as ransom to the automobile revolution every decade. Where television invades living rooms to demand forty-eight hours each week from the average American family. Where unemployment slowly devours the savings and self-esteem of millions each year. Where millions depend on welfare. Where top athletes make a million dollars a year. Where we have more police than ever, and yet our homes and lives are increasingly threatened by violent crimes. Where a third of the money spent for food fills the tills of the fast-food chains.

Among the countless characteristics of our culture there are many broad traits that play enormous roles in shaping our Sunday-morning listeners. We'll consider just four examples.

First, our culture is undeniably secular. Largely because of the mass communication revolution of the past generation, today's church members grow increasingly secularized. Every night after dinner they sit in front of their TV sets to see, feel, accept and experience the same scenes, emotions, values and experiences as millions of unchurched Americans.

Today's churchgoers absorb the secular environment and in turn are absorbed by it.

The secularization of our culture and our congregations is further emphasized by a second broad trait of our culture, self-centeredness. How many people devote their lives to amassing power and money. How many tear down their barns (and houses and families) to build greater ones in the mad rush for profit and pleasure.

Hedonism flourishes. Security and success are the vaunted goals of life for millions.

Materialism abounds. The good life is measured in terms of things. Values, relationships, loyalties and simple joys give way to money and influence. Family, home and community life have been sacrificed on the altar of the goddess Production. Yet our scores on the happiness scale sag despite the rising GNP.

Some of our self-centeredness is probably a natural self-defense mechanism which enables us to cope in an impersonal world. Individuals have to claw for survival in our computerized age. Millions of lonely people retreat into themselves for shelter from a world where they feel alienated, helpless, afraid and alone. Yet the unseeing stares on our streets speak a strange language to the oldsters who remember a time when people weren't too wrapped up in their own concerns or fears to risk a "hello."

Perhaps the third and most overwhelming trait of our culture is change. Change sometimes seems to be the only constant in our world. We don't have to read students of our culture like Toffler and Sagan to realize it. Experience is proof enough.

I saw cultural change with new clarity when I took my eighty-year-old mother into a K-Mart for the first time. She marveled at the incredible selection and the size of the store. Her surprise amazed me. Then I remembered. She had grown up, married and lived out eight decades of life within a mile of the farm where she was born in a log house built by her pioneer father. She read magazines and books, took an occasional drive around the country roads of Michigan with her husband and family, taught the ladies' Bible class for a third of a century, and reared four sons without ever raising her voice. But her stable, familiar world was largely pre-K-Mart.

I contrast my mother's life with that of mine or my family's. Recently my son, his wife and baby flew to Texas for a business convention. The day the convention concluded they ate breakfast in San Antonio, boarded a plane, ate lunch with in-laws in Atlanta on a two-hour layover, and reached their home outside Chicago in time for supper.

The difference between yesterday and today is mind-boggling. The old saying, "Nobody knows what tomorrow will bring" has never been more true or more unsettling. This is more than a complaint— "The future isn't what it used to be." The Huntsville Computer Center claims the fund of information making up human knowledge has doubled on the average of once every two years since 1960. It's now doubling every six months.

No one knows exactly how this breakneck rate of change affects the individual. But it does. Future shock is more than a theory.

The fourth trait of our culture that impacts so greatly on everyone is partly a result of the previous three: confusion. Paradoxes engulf us. Consider this sampling of cultural inconsistencies:

Unparalleled wealth and income, yet mounting insecurity and poverty;
Expanded information about life and sex, yet soaring teenage pregnancies;
Unprecedented liberties and personal freedoms, yet greater clamor for human rights;
More computers and less compassion;
More welfare and less concern for individuals as persons;
Unequaled mobility and potential in transportation, yet lack of distribution blighting the Third World;
Hundreds of new books each day, yet reading skills decline;
A new book on Shakespeare every twelve minutes, yet increasing sex, violence and soap operas on TV;
Members of the congregation may travel internationally every week, yet concern for world needs fails to increase;
Missiles, nuclear warheads and other military hardware proliferate, yet international insecurities increase;
Food production skills and capabilities increase, yet Americans still give little attention and only one-fourth of one percent of our GNP to world hunger;
Comforts and conveniences crown our achievements, yet polls show most people are discontentented and unhappy about their work;
From 1920 to 1980 the number of millionaires in the U.S. increased from twenty-four to thousands, yet unemployment soared from one million to eight to ten million.

Of course the list could go on. But that's enough to remind us just how troubling and troubled our secular, self-centered, changing, confused (and a lot of other adjectives) our culture really is. Realizing that is part of understanding who our listeners are.

What concerns them? The answer to this question is actually an outgrowth of the first. Without going into much detail (but hopefully not being too simplistic) I think we can say what concerns our listeners is everything that makes them who they are. That means the experiences, the struggles, the cultural influences that directly affect and involve them. Marketing researchers call these concerns *felt needs.*

For example, the secularization of our culture has increased the need many people feel for spiritual meaning. Self-centered people often feel the need for something bigger to commit themselves to. Stability becomes a felt need in a world of change. Order and reason become needs in a world of chaos and questions.

In more concrete terms, a lonely person needs companionship. A victim of insecurity has a felt need for encouragement.

What concerns our listeners depends on who they are. Some problems are almost universal; others are more individual. But as a rule our contemporaries are very interested in answers to their needs— reasonable, relevant, practical, concrete, common-sense answers.

On the flip side, they are not interested in the abstract, the obtuse, the obscure, the irrelevant or the theoretical.

How do they learn? They—we—all learn the same ways. We learn first by our own experience and the model of others. We compare. We contrast. We catalog in our memory bank. Everything filters through our own individualized sieve. We rack it, stack it and file it.

We learn by swatches, snatches and littles. Linear learning is largely lost. We hear the morning news-brief, scan the headlines, read the overnight summaries, check with the secretary and the computer, compare the charts, overhear the boss, lunch with associates, watch a thirty-minute evening news magazine minus ten minutes of Madison Avenue. We learn by computers, by briefs, by summaries, by specialists, by teams, by disparate itemized bits, by unrelated pieces.

We also learn by relationships. We relate to specialists, consultants, the wise, the powerful, the skillful, the shrewd, the advertised, the available, the advantageous.

Actually we all learn by a variety of processes:

1. We learn by listening. . . . . .this involves proclamation.
2. We learn by discussing. . . . . .this involves conversation.
3. We learn by watching. . . . . .this involves observation.
4. We learn by inventing . . . . .this involves experimentation.
5. We learn by thinking. . . . . .this involves cogitation.

6. We learn by remembering ....this involves reflection.
7. We learn by associating ....this involves imagination.
8. We learn by modeling. ....this involves imitation.
9. We learn by attaching ....this involves relation.
10. We learn by choosing. ....this involves decision.
11. We learn by searching. ....this involves exploration.
12. We learn by reading and praying ....this involves revelation.

Ongoing research by psychologists and educational experts continues to enlighten us about human learning. Some of these researchers are now concluding that humans learn only by participation, by involvement. They insist no one learns only by being told; what is learned must be anchored to our reality by experience.

Courses in teacher training for years used a learning pyramid to show the value of human experience and involvement in the educational process:

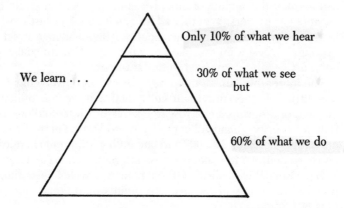

We learn . . .

Only 10% of what we hear

30% of what we see
but

60% of what we do

In a more complex and comprehensive description of learning theory, Dr. Bernice McCarthy discusses eight ways to learn in her innovative book, *The 4-MAT SYSTEM* (Oakbrook, Illinois, EXCEL, 1980). After discussing views of psychologists and educators, she summarizes the work of eighteen researchers. She concludes that listening serves as the dominant ingredient in only one learning style; ideally we should be trained to respond to all learning styles, not just the verbal.

She says 70 percent of students are not analytic learners, the kind who succeed in our school system and always feel good about themselves. She found eight or nine out of ten junior high school students unable to handle formal reasoning. Six out of ten high school pupils prefer concrete experience rather than abstract thought.

McCarthy says traditional education focuses on verbal development and neglects the nonverbal. She concludes that this long-time false dichotomy between these two modes of learning must be remedied. Teaching must become both traditional and humanistic, intellectual and intuitive, content-centered and student-centered, aimed at both the mind and the heart.

Dr. Roger Sperry, 1980 Nobel Prize winner for his brain research, says, "Our educational system, as well as science in general, tends to neglect the nonverbal [right brain] form of intellect. What it comes down to is that modern society discriminates against the right [visual] hemisphere" (*The Psychophysiology of Thinking*, McGuigan and Schoonover, editors, New York: Academic Press, 1973).

Today our preaching often allows for only the listening process, seldom exploring other avenues to the listener's brain. This book is no plea to neglect or eliminate the declaring of God's certain Word, but rather an urging to incorporate additional learning opportunities that can amplify the impact of our preaching by increasing the involvement of our hearers. Whether all human learning or just most human learning demands learner participation, the challenge is set for our preaching. If we want to make a greater impact on our congregations, we must get them involved in our sermons.

The incredible human mind begs for use and involvement. It matters little whether our brain cells total a mere ten billion in the average brain or, as some researchers assert, a tenfold one hundred billion in our two handsful of thick custard housed in the stone case of our skulls. Between 100,000 and one million different chemicals react on these neurons to make limitless interconnections and mental patterns. Using the smallest of their figures, psychologists think these possible variations in the average brain would equal more than 10 plus 801 zeroes.

The number of atoms (one of the smallest units we know) in the known universe (the largest thing we know) equals only 10 plus 34 zeroes according to scientists. The brain possibilities of each member of our congregations outnumber the atomic units of our universe!

This too should be a challenge to our preaching. What are we doing with our sermons to allow for or utilize this unfathomable potential?

But there's another implication of learning research that may shed fascinating new light on our church life as it relates to our preaching. For decades we've known female strengths in verbal skills evidenced by facility of expression and a near absence of stuttering and other speech problems males experience. We've known females tend to tell, males tend to show how. Males teach by doing; females teach by saying.

But now a growing body of modern research is building a case for sexual differences in brain functioning. And that raises some intriguing and disturbing questions.

Does an almost exclusive accent on proclamatory preaching have some relation to the preponderance of women in many congregations? Is our practice of preaching without involving our listeners perpetuating an institutional form of feminine focus? Do we thus discriminate against the male by adding another barrier to his Christian commitment?

Perhaps the key to involvement in preaching holds extra significance for reaching and bringing men into the Kingdom.

Certainly we can't hope to involve or understand our audience if we don't know how they learn—just as we can't understand the audience without knowing who they are, what concerns them and what moves them to respond.

But that knowledge, like the proper attitude of the speaker, is not enough to guarantee involvement in our preaching. The speaker's attitude has to be reflected by, and all our knowledge of the audience has to be included in, Aristotle's third factor of communication.

The Message

Through the centuries preachers and teachers of preachers have concentrated most of their thinking and effort on this last segment of the communication process. Homiletics has focused and sometimes harangued on content, arrangement and logic of the sermon itself. Yet despite all the attention given to the message, few have dared experiment with the basic structure of the sermon. That basic structure is deductive.

In most deductive sermons we state our main point at the outset, declaring where we're going to go in the rest of the sermon. Too many hearers, especially those skeptical of our message, may interpret our opening paragraph this way: "Here's my conclusion, folks, and during the sermon I'll prove I'm right."

That kind of start, whether we mean it or not, certainly doesn't encourage cooperative response or group participation. The hope for involvement fades even dimmer when the thesis seems remote, egocentric, defensive or irrelevant to our listeners.

There have been flickers of hope throughout the history of preaching and in some sermons. An introductory glimmer of life—a go-go dancer, an example, narration, an analogy or a case study—occasionally lights up the porch to the deductive structure of our sermons. But too often the preacher's thesis at the outset slaps the faces of the congregation, and the duel between pastor and people is set for the duration of the sermon.

At first this may seem an overstatement. But consider how deduction defies so much of what we've said we must understand about our hearers. In the marketplace they see, work and struggle with the facts; in the family they feel the facts; they learn primarily from experience and relationships as they're battered on every shore by the problems and realism of life.

Our deductive, propositional preaching, on the other hand, often attempts to take them far from the shores of everyday life on what is more apt to be a solo voyage than a group expedition. Sometimes discovery is finished, exploration concluded when the pastor types up his notes on Saturday night. When he closes the study door en route to the pulpit, he may shut out all chance for mutual adventure. And when he begins his deductive discourse, it can be as if he's saying, "This is my decree. My fiat is finished. The process is ended. Here's my word. Disregard my Jehovah-complex!"

Before we shrug this off as gross exaggeration, maybe we need to ask ourselves some honest questions. Could our longstanding practice of deductive method be part of our problem in winning involvement in our preaching today? Could deduction be a contributor to the feeling many laypersons have that sermons tend to drone along one flight above reality, a country mile from common life? Could a rethinking of our sermon structure provide any help or hope?

Is there some other structure that by its very nature could reflect the preacher's attitude of caring servanthood and declare to the people that we are all "workers together"? Is there an approach for sermons that can speak to cultural experience, emotional needs and real-life concerns while capitalizing on our listeners' learning habits and utilizing more of the potential of the incredible human mind?

Inductive preaching can do those things. So why have we ignored the potential of inductive structure and logic in our sermons?

Induction begins with the particulars of life experience and points toward principles, concepts, conclusions. The inductive course can grow out of the hearer's needs rather than the uncertainty of the preacher. The preacher seeks to lead rather than push. He explores *with* the people before he explains what they find. Inductive preaching is a quest for discovery. It can disarm, interest and involve the people in the exploration and capitalize on the psychological process of learning from experience.

Inductive preaching can't promise to be a total substitute for our existing sermons; it might better serve as a supplement for existing strengths and skills. But an infusion of induction *can* promise to gain attention and involve our hearers in a natural, normal, helpful process. In so doing, induction *can* promise to transform our Sunday morning preaching from a spectator sport into a participation period of growth, insight and cooperation. Induction *can* prevent preachers from leaving the assembled tour group in the terminal while they take a dear saint or two on an 11 A.M. flight to "the heavenly shores and the regions beyond."

But can induction do that without destroying the very foundation of preaching? Does induction demand we throw out everything we've ever known or done in our preaching? Can inductive preaching maintain biblical authority? Where do we start if we decide to incorporate induction into preaching? Is there any practical help for preparing or delivering inductive sermons? Is induction really an answer to the involvement problem in preaching today?

We'll address these and other questions as we continue our quest for the key to involvement in preaching.

3 Old Parts and New Hope

After a seminary workshop on preaching, one of the participants, a Salvation Army officer, came up to talk with me. He said for nine years he'd conducted services along the famous boardwalk of Atlantic City. "But I never heard of 'inductive preaching' until today. 'Inductive sequence' and 'inductive structure' are totally new terms to me," he told me. "But I'll tell you this: I would have never had anybody stop to listen if I hadn't used this method you've described as 'inductive preaching!' "

It's difficult enough to win the involvement of the friendly faces sitting in Sunday morning pews, when we're only competing with cows or the pondering of everyday concerns. How would you like to have to stop an indifferent or even hostile audience on a busy sidewalk and usher them into your church before there was even a chance to preach to them? How would you like to try to get your message across to a marching audience in continuous procession through your sanctuary? How would you like the challenge of winning or losing your entire audience every thirty seconds?

That was the task this Salvation Army officer often faced with his preaching. And he credits any success he has had to inductive preaching—a method he'd stumbled upon and adapted by practical experience in the course of his ministry.

Why does traditional homiletical theory force so many tired and discouraged preachers to wander through such a broad wasteland, only occasionally to happen upon induction by accident or trial and error? Why do the few who become effective preachers usually discover induction after enduring the frustration and failure of deductive homiletics?

Some evangelists with their string of stories and vivid life or death scenes as case studies have unwittingly pioneered one area of induction. For example, D. L. Moody collected stories loosely around a theme as he aimed his simple, basic message at the common people. He felt there was great need for a ministry to those who knew nothing of the Word of God and cared even less for it. So he gathered everyday experiences and stories in envelopes and shuffled these items into various orders as he preached from city to city in evangelistic campaigns. He reached the uninitiated by starting with the experiences of life and guiding his listeners to straightforward conclusions.

Liberal theologians with their problem-solving sermons of the mid-twentieth century scouted out another avenue of inductive accent. They blended biblical and nonbiblical ingredients in an attempt to meet human need. Sometimes assertions were delayed or omitted entirely. The uncertain note of tentative conclusions ended some sermons with no authoritative "Thus said the Lord."

Many fundamentalist preachers make a halfhearted effort at inductive preaching when they cut their sermons down the middle. Half deals with the "then and there" and the second half leaps to the "here and now." Unfortunately hearers often could say, "And never the twain shall meet."

Effective preachers from across the theological spectrum have uncovered some inductive techniques. We'll consider the inductive ingredients in the sermons of many of history's greatest preachers in Appendix 3. Yet despite the dabblers, the trial-and-error explorers and those others who have discovered the effectiveness of induction serendipitously, traditional homiletics continues to ignore the power and the potential of inductive preaching. We've adopted traces of induction without recognizing or utilizing the full potential of the method. Why?

Philosophers have found only two basic structures—inductive and deductive—for all human thought patterns. Why has preaching concentrated on one and ignored the other? Do we expect our listeners to shut down half their brains on Sunday morning? Can't we harness our listener's God-given ability to think for himself, to come to conclusions for herself—and use that ability to involve our hearer in the message we want to communicate? Why don't we?

Perhaps the biggest reason preaching has overlooked the effectiveness of induction is that most preachers don't understand it. Few even know what it is.

In researching this book during a recent sabbatical, I visited a number of theological school libraries. Again and again, when I explained my purposes I received blank looks from librarians. "Inductive preaching?" They'd never heard of it. The longer I searched for material, the less surprised I was by the response of these professional researchers. At one point, a computer search of a million and a half titles in an inter-library pool turned up only one dissertation on the subject.

But what was even more surprising to me than the dearth of writings on induction was the response of seminary preaching professors I visited and contacted. Some of the responses I got from them were as uncertain as those I'd found among library staff. Most were interested in the idea of inductive preaching, but it became clear as we talked that few had done much thinking about induction.

It's really not surprising then that most preachers don't practice or understand inductive preaching. There's no connection made between inductive method and preaching in most seminary training or in homiletics texts. So induction is seen as some suspicious, complicated and abstract theory, unrelated to the high calling of addressing a Sunday morning congregation.

That's a great and tragic misunderstanding. Great because the strength of inductive preaching is that it is practical, not theoretical. And tragic because the result of an inductive approach is the same as the often unrealized goal of every preacher delivering a sermon— involvement of the listener.

I keep coming back to the word *involvement* because it's the key to explaining and understanding inductive preaching. It gave me my best response to all the blank looks given me by theological librarians. "Inductive preaching is the means of getting listeners involved in the sermon," I'd say.

That simplistic explanation was usually met by an understanding nod or grin and some telling remark such as: "Now that's a worthy goal," or "My minister could sure use some help there." The need for involvement is something we all can understand and appreciate.

But just how is that involvement achieved? How does the inductive process apply to sermons to insure involvement? What is inductive preaching?

Perhaps the first step in understanding inductive preaching is to consider a sampling of common ingredients. Even to those for whom inductive preaching is a strange new term, some of those ingredients should be surprisingly familiar.

Narrative. I knew one flamboyant preacher who jumped on the pulpit and rode it as a camel for 800 miles to find a bride for Isaac. "Whumpf! Whumpf! Whumpf!" He lunged up and down over desert dunes, imitating Eleazer in quest of Rebekah. Others have stood on the velvet upholstered pulpit chairs to show how the giant Goliath towered over the boy David.

But narrative doesn't need such dramatics to hold listener interest. Theatrics may make memorable impressions, but imaginative, realistic story format doesn't demand fireworks and melodrama to win pleased attention.

All the world loves a story. And throughout the centuries good narrators usually have preached to above average crowds. Narrative invites involvement. It seizes interest and postpones the punch line until speaker and listener reach the conclusion together. Thus a story can inductively lead the hearer toward a cooperative conclusion without having to defensively protect or prove the speaker's proposition. Instead, attention resides inherently in the narration as hearers listen and accept the message couched in story form.

Did you ever notice what happens when a story is interjected into a sermon? There's almost always a discernible change in the congregation. Eyes focus, ears are tuned, fidgeting stops. Stories almost always involve people. Yet how little of the story element can be found in most sermons.

Perhaps a recent spate of books about "the story" in preaching bodes well for the widespread rediscovery of narrative. The declaration that "the story *is* the sermon" squares with much evidence in Scripture, as we'll see in Chapter Five.

Eugene L. Lowry, in his excellent little book, *The Homiletical Plot: The Sermon as Narrative Art Form* (Atlanta: John Knox Press, 1980) gives a dozen helpful hints in his chapter on biblical narrative preaching.

1. Attend to every "insignificant" line.
2. Look between the lines.
3. Catch every encounter and imagine the scene.
4. Bring data from your own experience and imagination.
5. Move behind behavior to find mixed motives.
6. Move behind facts to prior dynamics.
7. Utilize the senses.
8. Switch identification with the agony and grief included.
9. Utilize active grammar with strong nouns and active verbs.
10. Break into first and second person singular form. Show it; don't tell it.
11. Move from the subjective to the objective, from particular to general—and back again.
12. Set the stage by foreshadowing major turns of events.

Questions. More than one pastor has rhetorically boomed out a question, "Who did . . . ?" only to have some child's big little voice fill the sanctuary with a response: "I don't know, but it wasn't me."

Rhetorical questions have long been suggested as attention-getters in sermons. Some messages lean heavily on this device to confront and involve the hearers. "The deafening question," said Father Regis Duffy in *Liturgy* (May 1974), can only be answered by the listener; so silence appropriately follows this kind of probe by the caring preacher. The daring use of this technique, says Duffy, demands the "preacher's deep and unconditional acceptance of and respect for each of his listeners," as well as personally grappling with the answers himself.

Whether questions are direct, demanding a verbal response, or merely rhetorical, they defer to the listener, allowing him or her a place to jump in and take part in the sermon. Questions involve the people.

Unfortunately some preachers seem never to have a question about anything. And thus they fail to capitalize on an effective inductive element in their preaching.

Parables. These are always inductive by their very nature. Parables represent a message in and through a scenario. Listeners discover the point and its implications for themselves as the parable is told.

Too often when we think of "parables" we think only of biblical examples, Jesus' stories and others such as Nathan's parable of the sheep which he told to ensnare King David. But "parable" is a much broader term. It can be a fictional account which represents deeper meaning (C. S. Lewis's *Narnia Chronicles* are extended parables). Historical human instances and even contemporary experiences can be used parabolically.

What distinguishes a parable, according to Donald Capps in *Pastoral Counseling and Preaching* (Philadelphia: Westminster Press, 1980) are these features: (1) *altered relationships*—something happens in the story to permanently change the relationship between two or more of the characters; (2) *story details communicate meaning*—the message of a parable is woven into the descriptions and events of the story itself; (3) *open-ended*—a parable symbolizes life's ambiguity and allows the listener to draw at least some conclusions on his own; (4) *emphasizes insight*—lives are changed as story characters and listeners gain insights about themselves, God and the world; (5) *transforms perception*—a parable seeks to help the listener see through different eyes and restructure his or her viewpoint.

So even a case study or the simple recounting of an everyday activity can take on parabolic meaning if it incorporates some of these features.

Analogy. Every preacher knows both Testaments include many examples of analogy. The Bible explains many theological concepts with such images as a tree, bride, building, cornerstone, sheep, shepherd and water. Reasoning by analogy is very common in any type of communication, argumentation and investigation where unfamiliar ideas must be clarified. It's an inductive technique in the sense that it explains the unknown by the better known and it allows the general implications to be drawn out of the specific idea.

A warning is required though. Analogy ran amuck for centuries, plaguing the Christian church with wild excesses. Legitimate Bible analogy slid to absurd depths when preachers allowed their imaginations to race without restraint, reason or responsibility.

Such dangers of misuse have long been recognized. In the early days of Christianity Clement and Origen tried to construct scientific canons to govern analogy and allegory, but they failed to create a viable methodology. Even Augustine erred when he allegorized the Garden of Eden, adding imagined flora, fauna and action that in turn became the basis for questionable doctrine.

Such excesses led to the basic exegetical principle of the Reformation insisting every Scripture passage has but one meaning. John Calvin championed the cause against allegories. Luther too said, "Origen's allegories are not worth so much dirt."

The conflict in the church persists with one group maintaining that the essence of Christianity is found (and confined) in its original verbal frameworks, while others feel preaching is inferior unless expansive "spiritualizing" ornaments Scripture, interpretation and sermons.

It's true that freedom to expand meaning has often become license to distort truth with illusory fancy, fiction and figments. Yet scriptural models suggest there must be a legitimate use of analogy. While the ministerial record warrants caution with this technique, analogy can be another effective inductive ingredient in sermons.

Dialogue. One of my pastor friends began a regular program of dialogue with his people. Once each month he scheduled a talk-back discussion in the morning worship service to encourage involvement.

He had just finished the Scripture reading one Sunday when a man stood quickly and said, "Pastor, I've often thought about the question these verses raise. What do you think Jesus meant, and how does that carry over for us today? I'd surely like to hear what the folks have to say about . . ."

A lively discussion filled the next thirty minutes. Then the service concluded with the benediction and organ postlude.

The minister greeted his congregation at the door when he saw the clouded face of the man whose question had sparked the morning's discussion. "Oh, pastor," the troubled parishioner blurted out, "I'm so sorry and embarrassed. I just realized this wasn't the Sunday we were supposed to have discussion. What about the sermon you planned for today?"

The pastor grinned and tried to reassure the man. "If the message I had planned to share today won't keep until next Sunday, it must not have been too important, John. We had a good session today. So whatever you do, please don't worry about it." Obviously dialogue can get people involved. But isn't it just another term for discussion? How does dialogue fit into an actual sermon?

Sometimes the dialogical sermon has been a running dialogue between the pulpit and some representative in the pew. On other occasions two preachers have carried on a conversation the congregation could overhear. But both these methods tend to be stodgy and artificial unless special precautions guarantee a realistic feel.

Some effective preachers during the centuries have created a dialogical effect with the entire congregation. Many of the prophets bargained and bantered with their hearers. Street-corner evangelists often learn to mix conversation and direct discourse in response to heckling from their crowds.

But how can we make dialogue work for us in our day of staid and silent congregations? How do we then keep the worship service from becoming another Sunday school discussion hour?

One way might be to reserve a time near the end of the sermon for listeners to add their comments. Or a pastor could call for examples from the congregation to lead into a topic. For instance, in a sermon on the will of God the preacher could ask for two or three volunteers to give an example of the Lord's leading in their lives, and maybe even ask them a few follow-up questions to clarify their comments before going on with a sermon on the subject.

Sometimes dialogue doesn't have to be actual; even a dialogical attitude can help get listeners involved. What would happen if every preacher preached as if he were engaging his people in conversation? Imagined dialogue that asks and answers hypothetical questions the congregation might have is another promising technique.

True dialogue, actual or attitudinal, may seem risky at first thought. But it can be a token of genuine Christian love because it indicates a real and obvious desire to include listeners. It strives to listen through their ears and see through their eyes. And while the results may sometimes be a little unpredictable, as was the case of my friend whose entire sermon got preempted, too many of our typical contemporary sermons leave nothing to be said.

Experience. Modern sermons often impinge on our hearers' lives only on the cranial level of doctrine, belief and thought. We can talk in orthodox terms such as "regeneration" or "sanctification." We can even issue the call to be "born again" every Sunday and yet never see our listeners' lives changed if our doctrine remains an abstract idea.

For the faith we preach to make any difference, believing and behaving have to bond in common life. The head and heart have to unite in life experience. And our sermons need to show how this happens; our theology must tie into everyday life.

The most typical response to this need has been the two-part sermon, where the ideas, the doctrine, the theology are discussed at the outset. Then the conclusion attempts to relate it all to the lives of the congregation.

"And this week when we face the trials and temptations of the marketplace, we need to remember what we've been saying about Paul's admonition to the Corinthians. . . ."

"If we think about the implications of the message this morning, if we thoughtfully consider Jesus' words, our family and work relationships would be transformed. . . ."

While such references to our listeners' experience are far better late in the sermon than never, the sudden sermonic jump demands a quantum leap from our listeners—if they're still listening. They may not be.

As Fred B. Craddock writes in *As One Without Authority* (The Phillips University Press, 1974): "The plain fact of the matter is that we are seeking to communicate with people whose experiences are concrete. Everyone lives inductively, not deductively. No farmer deals with the problem of calfhood, only with the calf. The woman in the kitchen is not occupied with the culinary arts in general but with a particular roast or cake. The wood craftsman is hardly able to discuss intelligently the topic of 'chairness,' but he is a master with a chair" (page 60).

Our listeners live every day in the realm of experience. Experience determines their view of reality. They pragmatically judge every new idea they face by asking, "Will it work? Does it square with experience?"

So if we're going to keep experience-centered listeners with us until the conclusion of our sermons, we must keep all parts of the message closely tied to their experience. But how?

Instead of starting with abstractions such as "mankind is mortal," we can begin with a concrete experience and say, "Deacon Adams died of cancer last month." We can give illustrations from the family or work life of our congregation. We can use common experiences such as birth, eating, walking, fishing to illustrate points or make analogies.

Human experience doesn't become the basis of our message, but it can validate what we're saying; it can punctuate the Word in a way our people will readily understand. Such references to common life become more than application points at the end of the sermon; they serve as guideposts along the way, all pointing to the truth at the end of the road.

We'll talk more about how this affects the structure of the sermon in a later chapter. But reference to experience merits initial mention here as one of the most fundamental elements of inductive preaching.

Other potential elements of induction could be enumerated, but this is a logical place to depart from a summary listing because "experience" is more than just one element of induction. Experience is the very foundation of induction. And grasping this is as crucial to understanding inductive preaching as knowing the elements that can make up an inductive sermon.

Induction can be simply described as the reasoning process by which particular instances of experience lead to the forming of general concepts. For example, based on specific previous experiences, say with pencil sharpeners, telephones, or vending machines, we draw general conclusions about such items and determine how to respond to and operate other—sometimes very different—pencil sharpeners, telephones and vending machines.

Machines aren't the only things we learn about by inductive experience. We also use induction with people and ideas. Our specific previous experiences with medical doctors influence our attitude toward any doctor we meet and greatly determine our general opinion of the medical profession or even the science of medicine.

Our previous personal experiences with mathematics, say in a high school geometry class or balancing a frustratingly muddled checkbook, greatly affect our attitude toward a whole body of knowledge.

Such induction is a human habit. We casually use it in daily life every time we respond to a situation or solve a problem by comparing it to previous situations or problems we've encountered. Induction is the process by which life teaches us. We all learn much from living.

Of course we know learning from life isn't foolproof. Experience can't promise perfect predictability. For that reason philosophers may insist that our almost innate belief in inductive inference based on experience has no basis in reality. They may write books about the chasm between experience and prediction, between yesterday and tomorrow. They may insist life affords no absolutely predictable inference, and therefore induction is not truly logical.

Yet induction persists as a deep-seated human habit.

Inductive process contributes to all of contemporary life. Being more than trial and error, induction serves technology as well as natural and social sciences. It also serves us all directly on a daily basis. For even amid our sophisticated modern technology, people today depend largely on experience (more sophisticated experience than in the past to be sure, but experience nonetheless) and common sense.

We gamble our lives on inductive experience every time we trust the brakes in our car to prevent us from plowing into the rear end of a stopped semi or proceed through a green light without checking to make sure the cross traffic will stop. From the mountains of life's minutiae we constantly seek patterns, principles, generalizations, truths that will enable us to confidently decide present action, predict the future and build an improved life. Thus induction constitutes the very basis for our daily living. It serves as the primary means of arriving at knowledge required for human survival.

It's no wonder then that induction is a human habit. We have come to believe in induction because of our inductive experience with it. We know it works well for us in everyday life.

Even though the philosophers may scoff at induction as illogical, we believe in it as we believe in our experience. In real life, concrete experience overshadows our abstract logic. Our induction outweighs our deduction. Thus we prefer a reasonable sermon to one with airtight, abstract logic. Reasonable induction from experience carries more clout for contemporary listeners than the fail-safe propositions of an ivory-tower mind. Induction after all is an old and trusted friend.

Yet most preachers depend totally on deductive approaches. That's all they know, all they're taught. Inductive alternatives are only faint tracings dimly etched in the sand.

How then can this inductive process of reasoning from particulars to general conclusions be applied to the preaching of sermons?

Again the key is involvement.

An inductive sermon is one that starts where the people are, with particular elements—the narrative, dialogue, analogy, questions, parables, the concrete experiences—and then leads to general conclusions. In fact, what distinguishes inductive preaching is not so much the ingredients as the use of those ingredients.

Deductive preaching starts with a declaration of intent and proceeds to prove the validity of what the preacher says is already determined to be true. Inductive preaching, on the other hand, lays out the evidence, the examples, the illustrations and postpones the declarations and assertions until the listeners have a chance to weigh the evidence, think through the implications and then come to the conclusion *with* the preacher at the end of the sermon.

Such a process involves listeners by giving them a part in the sermon process. It enables them to think along with or even ahead of the preacher. It involves them. Thus the sermon itself becomes part of their experience, part of their familiar inductive learning style. The conclusions that are reached, the assertions made at the end of the sermon bear the mark of personal conviction, arrived at and tested by personal thought and experience. The conclusions reached are personal conclusions; thus the implications for the listener's life are clear, in fact inescapable.

Obviously any communication process that allows people to work through and accept truth for themselves holds real advantages over just telling them what to believe. It better enables truth to become personal—the ultimate goal of all of us who preach God's Good News.

An added benefit of induction is that it represents an aggressive movement of the mind. The passive intellect is converted by inductive inquiry into the active reason when seeing becomes looking. The mind is stirred from mere receptivity and becomes inquisitive, prayerful and persistent. In induction the hearer joins the process to inquire, to venture forward, to incur risk, to gaze into the unknown, to synthesize, to test.

Induction as the logic of discovery permits humanity to become as questing little children instead of slaves to the past. The excitement of exploration replaces the dutiful drudgery of doing what tradition dictates. So while experience, the raw material of induction, has to do with the past, it does more than merely bind us to tradition. Inductive inquiry progressively reaches forward to fresh truth—to fresh knowledge of truth. It moves toward growth, from the known to the unknown.

Basically induction is mere discovery by utilization of, not invention of, facts. Submission to facts stands as the glory of the inductive method. And that's why inductive conclusions ring so believably true. They square with the facts and the reality of human experience.

But understanding inductive preaching demands more than a knowledge of inductive elements, a basic grasp of inductive process or an appreciation for the benefits of induction. We can't possibly fully understand inductive preaching until we recognize and accept the attitude inherent in inductive preaching.

We talked briefly about the preacher and his attitude in Chapter Two, but attitude's role in inductive preaching needs to be reemphasized here. A preacher can't preach an inductive sermon without an attitude of tolerance, charity, respect, trust, cooperation and patience toward the hearers. All those things shine through when a preacher allows the listener to become involved in the sermon process, when the preacher confidently preaches with the belief, "When you see, you'll believe and do."

By the use of an inductive approach the minister says, "Come, walk with me. Together we'll find generalized concepts and conclusions as we look at some vital, representative instances. We'll begin where you are. We'll use evidence common to our everyday experience. We'll go at your pace and follow your interests, face your problems. And ultimately we'll find the answers to your needs in God's Word."

The stature and character of the preacher—his compassion, humility, his serving heart—enable him to defer his assertions, delay his advice, postpone any declaration until he and his listeners reach common ground. He doesn't cling to any elevated position of authority, but by the attitude evident in the inductive process he descends to become one among his listeners. He puts aside pride to be a worker together with his hearers. He serves as a player-coach, not as a loud voice admonishing from a platform above the field. He sits not as a sovereign monarch, or even as the king's representative looking down on a vast domain, but rather carves out a common niche, a place to stand among the people.

Inductive attitude encompasses such a wide range of attitudes there's only room for a sample list here. But for the preacher or the sermon to be truly inductive they must both be:

Inductive Attitudes

accepting .... not approving
accommodating .... not acquiescing or accosting
asking .... not demanding
beckoning .... not badgering or bemeaning
compassionate .... not compromising
cooperating .... not coercing
courageous .... not conflicting
dialoguing .... not dictating
directing .... not driving
encouraging .... not insulting
engaging .... not opposing
humble .... not hard
inquiring .... not insisting
investigating .... not imposing
involving .... not evading
probing .... not "preaching at"
respecting .... not renouncing

The title of Fred Craddock's book on induction, *As One Without Authority*, tends to alarm evangelicals, but it summarizes the inductive attitude. The inductive preacher becomes the group leader of an exploration party. He doesn't profess either to know everything or to know nothing of the territory or tribal problems the listeners face in daily life. He only seeks to guide them from where they are to where they need to be without any great show of authority or coercion.

I cite neither Craddock nor Soren Kierkegaard, whose third principle of communication holds that a true teacher teaches without authority, to argue for the abandonment of any and all authority. (In fact we'll discuss authority's role in induction in Chapter Nine.) But the abdication of dogmatism and the resultant "I'm-with-you" attitude of the preacher is an inductive requirement.

The cultural milieu of our day pleads for such an attitude from preachers. Our hearers demand a piece of the action, a part of the process. Today's listener is no more likely to let someone else chew and describe his Sunday dinner for him than he is to allow the preacher to do his thinking for him in the Sunday sermon and then calmly swallow the pastoral pronouncements.

Today's preacher needs to understand the meaning and the implications of inductive preaching because today's hearers demand to be involved. And involvement is the promise of induction.

4   The Story of Induction

Why does Secular Sam sit in his Sunday pew and worry about his financial struggles instead of following the pastor's sermon? Why did Randy's rural congregation contemplate the cattle and ignore his words? Why does a Salvation Army officer have to struggle to get the attention of Atlantic City boardwalkers? Why can't any listener just take the preacher's word as the law of the Medes and the Persians? Why does the mind stray from the spoken word?

The simple answer is people want and need to be involved. But how did we get to this point? How did humanity get so hooked on induction? How did the habit develop?

The Garden of Eden started the struggle against authority. Since then humankind has become increasingly discontented, unwilling to accept assembly-line uniformity and anonymity. Down through history human nature has protested, "I'm different. Respect me. My opinions count. I gotta do my own thing."

Human willfulness begins to surface before a toddler can say the word "no." Long before children reach rebellious adolescence they chafe at arbitrary authority. And we never seem to outgrow that desire for self-determination. Today Adam's independent offspring around the world protest against being swept into one inert pile of dust by any of the world's large authoritarian brooms. In our humanness we have continued to exercise our independence not only against parents, institutions and earthly powers, but we flaunt our independence in the face of God.

Then is it only human perversity pushing us proudly toward involvement and induction?

No.

Induction is part of our nature. "Made in the image of God" has to mean more than docile, sheeplike follow-the-leader behavior. Our Creator intended life to be more than a dumb, circular circus parade of elephants clinging to the next tail in an endless, unthinking line.

How else can you explain the incredible complexity of the human mind? In Chapter Two we stated that the number of possible mental patterns in the average human brain is almost countless times greater than the number of atoms in the universe.

The potential for unfathomable creativity has existed in the human mind since creation. It's part of the divine imprint stamped on Adam. And induction is one of the two ways the incredible human brain works.

The inductive pattern of thinking apparently was first identified by Plato in his quest for answers. The *method* seems to be his coinage; it first appears in his *Phaedrus,* where Socrates is advocating an art or technique of rhetoric as opposed to the devices of the Sophists. The word *method* suggests a "path" or "route," being derived from *meta* and *odos,* indicating a movement according to a road.

To think or argue clearly and effectively it is necessary to understand the route along which our thoughts progress. He who has such a route, such a direction, possesses method.

The logic of deductive reasoning has been systematically studied for 2,000 years. The logic of inductive or empirical inference has also been a major preoccupation of philosophy for centuries.

Logic and method are not the same thing. Logic is, of course, indispensable to method. Logic is the inner machinery conducting us along the path; it provides us with the tactics we use.

Aristotle devotes more attention to deductive logic in his writing than to the inductive method of analysis. But in his *Physics* he says of human learning that it is clear "we must follow this [inductive] path."

God certainly uses the inductive path in his communication with man. We'll see in subsequent chapters how many elements of inductive process are found in the Bible, and how Jesus stresses induction, including many of the elements and techniques mentioned in Chapter Three.

In contrast to Jesus' new accents and practices, the scribes and Pharisees deductively revered the traditions of the elders and declared them as ironclad rules. Early Christians struggled with this inherited Jewish accent on legalism and the development of growing doctrinal concerns. They built a corpus of regulative dogma to protect the young faith.

Through 600 years the Dark Ages preserved in monasteries the Latin residue of these basic beliefs. Scholasticism during the Middle Ages blended the deductive accent of Aristotle with the teachings of the Roman Church. These long centuries lacked the conditions that demand inductive approach to learning from experience rather than from dogmatic decree. Authority was respected, tradition revered, deductions fully accepted. So for hundreds of years not much happened to stimulate development of the inductive accents of the Old Testament story as practiced by Jesus. His accents on learning from experience, freedom from tradition, the importance of the individual and other flexibilities were largely obscured by the rigidities of legalism and theology.

The inductive milieu of our day hasn't risen in a vacuum. Many historic pressures have shaped our attitudes, dictated our needs, affected our tolerance of decrees, decided how much autocratic influence will restrict us and determined how open we are to learn from our experience.

Erratic progress in inductive experiments slowly moved culture away from total dependence upon the past as various courageous innovators added their insights to the reservoir of human knowledge. In the thirteenth century Roger Bacon's *Greater Work (Opus Majus)* broke with tradition by accenting experience as more important than reasoning in arriving at "useful knowledge." The work of this founder of modern science led to his imprisonment when authorities discovered "suspect innovations" in his writings about anatomy, optics, philology and alchemy. He may be called a pioneer of the modern scientific method.

Later Francis Bacon's self-appointed role was to stress experience and inductive experiment. He insisted on collecting facts and then drawing theories from them. While not a great scientist, his writings helped scientific progress. He became ill and died while making an experiment on the use of snow as a food preservative.

But induction is more than ill-advised experiments with electricity, lightning, gunpowder, human flight, magnetism, sugar, paper, germs and snow.

In philosophy Kant believed the mind is actively *involved* in the objects it experiences and organizes experience into definite patterns; but he refused to claim absolute knowledge. His turning to inner experience led many philosophers and theologians to discuss intuition and religious experiences.

However, inductive experience is more than the slippery, short-lived religious experiences called to the witness stand to verify the existence of God.

Thousands of pages of civilization's record flow from hundreds of years of study; still they have produced no satisfactory general history of inductive methods. Therefore it would be helpful to trace the progressive development of induction in the history of ideas.

When and where is inductive movement most apparent? What events and broad trends contribute to its growth?

Renaissance (1350-1600)

Induction came to new light in the Renaissance. This movement spread over Europe as a cultural wave, beginning in Italy. Rebirth of literature and arts, with an upsurge in science and commerce, led to "the discovery of the world and the discovery of man."

Petrarch and others dreamed of cultural awakening as the printing press fostered the flow of information, culture and education. The Renaissance inspired a desire for adventure, a love of classical knowledge, a surge in philosophical reflection and a resurgence of economic activity. Copernicus, Galileo and a multitude of others advanced the causes of science and technology. Humanism sought "universal man," lionized "knights of the pen" and pushed to free humanity from the past. The revival of Platonism and Neoplatonism led to an otherworldly and religious tone.

Francis Bacon applied the neglected inductive aspect of Aristotle's rhetorical method to nature, and all Europe joined in a wishful flight from the complexities of urban life to simple pastoral pleasures. Skepticism spawned in the less hostile climate of pleasure and utility. Occult tradition and wisdom from Egypt, Chaldea and Palestine floated in on the tide of new learning. Greek and Latin flourished.

The period saw a shift: from scholasticism to the secular accent, from superstitions to scientific explanations, from religious orientation to a human center, from the serf's bare survival to scholarship, culture and commerce. Architecture changed from cathedrals to houses; art from religious to nature and human form; armies from swords to gunpowder; society's accent from group to the individual. Skills, trades and merchandising flourished.

A multitude of mariners plied the seven seas, circled the globe, claimed new continents. Self surfaced; the individual, freedom, personal worth and independence rose to highest values. Tradition and bondage to the past lost their grip. Authority weakened. Experience, exploration and experimentation thrived as prime movers in the human arena. Induction had found a favorable climate. The individual surfaced; the institution was no longer the only hand on the helm. The people began to be involved.

Reformation (1500-   )

The Reformation of the sixteenth century sought to bring the Renaissance back to God as center. But the name *Reformation* refers more to the aspirations than to the achievements of the age.

For more than a thousand years after the fall of the Roman Empire, the church had held Europe together. It boasted the supreme position as the center of culture, defender of Christianity and mainstay of the people. The church served as the framework uniting the various states of Western Europe. Church authority, strong and almost universal, dictated human life. In 1200 A.D. all European leaders accepted the Pope and his supremacy. From 1300—1500 political struggles, religious schisms and corruption within weakened the church. Demands for reform and the pressure of heretical sects also depleted its influence. Other factors included rising nationalism, revival of learning, fracture of feudalism, poverty of peasants, growth of commerce and an increasing middle class.

In 1517 Martin Luther nailed his ninety-five theses on the Wittenberg door, and the fires of Reformation ignited all over Europe. Accent on the priesthood of each believer set the stage for respecting human experience; the common people were involved. Aided by the printing press, these new ideas spread rapidly. The inductive method had found more fertile soil.

Science and Technology (1600-   )
Empirical method spilled over from nature study to other realms of investigation when Galileo, the Italian physicist, launched his experiments in 1600. Kepler, Newton, Jenner, Darwin, Mendel, Pasteur, Einstein, Fermi, Salk, with a long train of other men and women, share the honors as pioneers of the empirical method. Astronomy, anatomy, nature, medicine, mathematics, chemistry, mechanics, physics, geology, electricity, energy, magnetism, nuclear theory and space travel—all these fields of science rely heavily on inductive method. Cumulative facts exert inductive pressure; deduction seeks patterns and application.

Scientific induction constitutes only one form of this universal practice, but it has provided the forum or arena for developing inductive methodology. Technological progress has included much more than windmills, buttoned clothes, compass, spectacles and the mechanical clock. The explosion in communication, transportation, computers and other aspects of our daily life springs from the inductive fountainhead.

Revolution (1775-   )
Revolt against government rule rises early and continues late in human experience. Mutiny, betrayal and disloyalty assume new luster when we speak of the American Revolution and the French Revolution.

In 1776 worldwide attempts were launched to achieve liberty, constitutional government and human rights, beginning a century of revolution. America's Revolutionary War in several ways became "the shot heard round the world." Its place in human history was far more than an eight-year war spawning a new nation; it was far more than an uprising for individual rights and democracy. As Thomas Paine declared, the Revolutionary War "contributed more to enlighten the world and diffuse a spirit of freedom and liberality among mankind, than any human event that ever preceded it."

The umbrella term *revolution* has come to include industrial, technological, scientific, cultural, sexual, institutional, educational, transportational, communicational, ethical, moral, racial, economic, generational and political uprisings. Just to think of the expansive possibilities of the word helps us see the shift away from authority and deductive pronouncement toward freedom, experience and the inductive method.

Authority, deduction, tradition and force of all kinds faced new challenges during this period when democracy and self-rule arose. Inductive method actively allied itself with this quest for human freedom, individual value and universal involvement.

Education

Popular education in schools and academies eventually grew out of the Renaissance's awakening interest and emphasis on knowledge and learning. No longer was education the lonely bastion of the clergy. Laymen wanted to learn. The European universities begun during the Middle Ages became popular centers of learning. The American university system that grew out of the old-world model began to boom with a shift from strictly traditional, classical education to include practical learning. And universal education soon became a cherished right of democracy, universalizing the need, demand and opportunity for individual involvement and inductive accent.

But it wasn't just the popularity of education that made such an impact. The methods of learning also greatly contributed to inductive emphasis. American educational life in the inventive nineteenth century began to take on a distinctively empirical-inductive flavor. The case method approach to legal education was introduced in the 1870s at Harvard's School of Law. It derived legal principles from the study of past cases. The Harvard School of Business later adopted the case study method when a Law School graduate became professor there. Case-study techniques have since found popularity in almost all areas of education, including seminary courses.

Progressive educational theory, especially in the twentieth century, began challenging tradition, threatening the unknown and clamoring for complete answers. Stress on greater freedom, activity, informality, group and project learning, along with individuality, brought new opportunities from diversified experiences, both past and present. And induction took another irresistible step forward.

Humanism
Humanism shifted from its initial focus on the classical literature of Greece and Rome to a primary stress on humanity as the center of the universe. Christianity's call for God-centered life here and hereafter was often silenced by the siren sound of the race's primal cry at the dawning of a new day. The lust and luster of new freedom even today make many forget life's source, sustenance and mission.

Cultural, religious and political scenes all spawned a sense of personal power and worth. Flexing newly discovered muscles, the reaction against authority expanded to include claims of independence from traditional culture, classic language, catholic religion, church and institutions. In this new era mankind stood in the middle of all research, all production and all truth.

The new humanity assumed the role as measure of all things. Induction became a common way of life. Let experiment and experience reign!

The ebb and flow accent in human history undulates from idyllic ancient Greece to a Middle Age stress on sin and suffering. The focus shifts to the joy of living, on to the physical world and back to the practical aspects of human life. Lately the movement has come to the scientific humanism seeking to solve all human problems. Spinoffs from the space age raise the level of living in other areas too. Humans now believe they can solve all human problems, meet all human need. Induction is come of age.

Television
Few will argue that television has not transformed our culture. Its impact is obvious on family life, leisure time, standardization of American speech and many other areas of our lives. But its relevance to a discussion of induction is more subtle.

The content of television gives viewers a false impression of personal involvement in an incredibly wide range of situations and experiences, strengthening the urge for action and involvement in real life. In addition to this, the physical act of TV viewing becomes, in a sense, an inductive process. This occurs because a television "picture" is nothing more than a series of electronically flashing dots. The screen never shows a completed picture. To "see" an image on a television screen, the human eye must receive the stimulus from a few dots of light every millisecond. The eye transmits these impulses to the brain, which has to record them, recall the previous impulses and predict future impulses in order for the mind to visualize the picture. The brain has to fill in or recall 99.999 percent of the image at any given moment. In essence, the brain is processing particulars and proceeding to its own generalized conclusions. Thus, thousands of hours of TV watching every year train our brains in the inductive process, whether we realize it or not.

Miscellaneous Factors

Many other assorted factors add fuel to the fires of induction. Contributors include: freedom movements; labor and reform movements; equality crusades; women's liberation movements; youth revolutions; situational ethics; laissez-faire government; black, gray and gay rights, along with other assorted minority powers; increasing esteem for common sense, personal experience and involvement.

Perhaps we can better understand the background of induction if we also consider a related concept, a joint strand interwoven with induction throughout history. That strand is *authority.* If you look back through our summary, you'll see the story of induction is also the story of authority and human attitudes toward authority.

For example, after the Reformation authority was transferred from the institution of the church to the document of the Bible. In time, revolt against documentary authority became as intense as earlier rebellion against institutional authority. Modern liberal theology transferred authority to living experience. Biblical criticism tended to so reduce Bible authority it became for many only a "repository of religious experience." So today's minister often preaches to hearers for whom the Bible has lost much of its old authority.

Deduction exerts a strong sense of authority in its propositional dictums. On the contrary, induction allows a listener to assume a measure of authority in the process of reaching conclusions. Deduction stands on traditions and the authorities of the past. Induction accounts for the pressures of the present.

Considering this connection between induction and authority not only gives us insight into history, it says much to us about our world today. Authority (and human response toward it) continues to be a dominant issue in the last years of the twentieth century. Authority has lost much of its clout in recent decades. In home, family, government, church, creed, the weight of authority is slipping. Tradition, power, prestige no longer dictate either belief or behavior.

Blame for this present state of affairs has been attributed to a wide range of causes: Dr. Spock, parental and juvenile delinquency, the antiwar movement of the Vietnam era, modern education, materialism, institutional insensitivity, the mass media, government oppression, communist plots and numerous other popular targets of contemporary criticism. Whatever the causes, authority has lost much of its influence in our culture.

Often people seem unaware of their innate skepticism or their "show me" attitude with its dependence upon the inductive proofs of human experience. Their demand for involvement has become a sometimes unconscious cultural need. But that's part of the inductive drive within us all.

Today's fabric shows the warp and woof of yesterday's loom; the past has guided us to this point. But our inductive tendencies aren't solely the result of humanity's willful, wandering path through history. Our innate creative nature, like a shuttle, also has shaped subtle patterns in our esteem, our individual sense of adventure, our desire for novelty, our endless quest to be free, unfettered, truly individual and involved in the processes of life.

Every one of us who is a part of twentieth-century culture walks the path of induction every day. We all share a creative need to be involved. It was born in the Garden and drummed into us by thousands of years of human history.

Then can we expect our congregations to get involved, or to even listen, if our preaching ignores this crucial characteristic of human nature?

It seems unlikely.

Can we find scriptural precedent for appealing to our God-given, historically nurtured inductive nature and seeking involvement with our preaching?

That's the question we'll consider in the next two chapters.

5 God's Way?

A seminary professor's life seldom calls for serious head to head confrontations. And the rare teacher/student rumbles in my twenty-year experience have never reached Richter scale proportions. So I was surprised one recent semester by a student's reactions in my "Pulpit Communications" course. As the term progressed I sensed that reluctance was building slowly into resentment. He walked glumly into class every day, spoke only when called on, and even then his feelings of discontent glared through.

Despite my personal attention, private conferences in my office and other attempts at communication, I just couldn't seem to get through to this young preacher. He wouldn't open up and admit what was eating at him—until his final exam when the truth came gushing forth.

He wrote in part: "I personally think deductively and most of the great preaching I have heard is deductive. Before I rest any confidence in inductive preaching, I will have to witness its effectiveness. I'm assuming a 'wait and see' attitude toward inductive preaching.

"I was distressed because the course didn't major on expository preaching, the most important kind of preaching. I have been sorely disappointed and disillusioned by the course content. I have been very disturbed because I so much wanted to learn how to preach convincing expository sermons.

"Rarely in my educational experience have I finished a class not knowing what I have learned or why I have learned it. This course has filled me with a sense of frustration and disappointment because my expectations have not been fulfilled. I wanted to learn how to preach Bible exposition—I don't now and never did classify sermons as either inductive or deductive. I have been most disappointed by class discussion of induction and deduction instead of giving us some good Bible expository sermon outlines."

My inability to get through to this student so disturbed me that I determined to make one more attempt. I gave him the first draft of Chapters One to Four of this manuscript and told him I'd pay him to read and react to it. But when he returned the manuscript to my office he refused any pay. He offered no real response to what he'd read, and I felt reluctant to press for his reaction. When he closed my office door behind him I felt more frustrated than before about our inability to communicate.

What bothered me most about this young preacher's final exam was the clear but unspoken implication of his attitude: "What the world needs is authority, an inerrant Bible and preachers with enough courage to preach the truth without compromise." In his mind my call for understanding, consideration and adaptation to listeners was a compromise—a faithless abandonment of God's high calling to confrontational, biblical preaching.

As I considered my experience with this student, I realized many readers would share his questions. Am I really advocating a gutless compromise? Can an inductive approach, adapted to our listeners' needs and interests, be biblical?

After much careful and prayerful examination and reexamination of God's Word, I wrote this chapter and the next, my response to those questions.

Let's begin by opening our Bibles and starting where God's Word begins. Watch for the story element in the Scriptures. Read the list slowly: creation, Eden, the first man, woman, the first baby, sin, the first murder, the Flood, the Tower, the Promised Land, flight to Egypt, test of faith, man's plan for God's promise, the Covenant, Lot's folly, Sodom, child of promise, family trouble, twins, conflict, conflict and flight, ladder at Bethel, love delayed, wrestling with an angel, brothers at peace, sold into Egypt, fury of a scorned lover, forgotten in jail, delivered by a dream, brothers in a bind, feast or famine, shepherds in Egypt.

All these stories and more are included in the first book of the Bible. Many more follow as we continue more quickly through the Old Testament with the following broad reminders: baby in a basket, baby-sitter for hire, bricks without straw, flight out back, the burning bush, the plagues, the Exodus, wandering, the Law, the manna, the census, the rules, the Tabernacle, crossing the Jordan, possessing the land, the judges, the kings, the Exile, the return, the prophets.

The stories continue as we turn to the New Testament, as these headlines remind us: voice in the wilderness, Lamb of God, followers, fourfold life of Christ, death and resurrection, ascension, Pentecost, The Acts, first martyr, apostle to the Gentiles, missionary journeys, letters to churches, Apocalypse.

As we consider this quick survey, scores of other Bible stories crowd to mind. Faces in that crowd include: Tamar, Miriam, Saul, Esther, Naaman, Ruth, Bathsheba, Simeon, Nicodemus, the woman at the well, the rich young ruler, Judas, Thomas, Demas, "Prisca," Onesimus and literally countless others. Who could exhaust the list of stories in Scripture?

That raises other questions for those of us who seek to communicate God's Word to our world today. Why is there so much narrative in the Bible and so little in our sermons? Could God's extensive use of narration, perhaps the most inductive of potentially inductive elements, say something about God's basic communication philosophy?

In Chapter Three we listed a variety of other common inductive ingredients. Let's do a quick check of Scripture for them.

Questions play a continuous role throughout Scripture—from God's first query, "Adam, where are you? Why did you hide?" to those many Psalms composed of heart-wrenching questions with desperate calls for answers: "How long, O Lord, how long? Will you forget me forever? How long must I wrestle? How long will my enemy triumph? Why have you forsaken me? Whom shall I fear? Lord, what do I look for? Where is God? Where can I flee? When foundations are being destroyed, what can we do? What is man that you are mindful of him? Who may dwell in your sanctuary? Who is God besides the Lord?"

God himself uses questions to counter Job's accusing questions. And the questions of God's prophets echoed throughout the hills and plains of Israel: "Why do you persist in rebellion? What are your sacrifices to God? What do you mean by crushing my people and grinding the faces of the poor? What do you see? What fault did your fathers find in me? Where is the Lord? Where are the gods? Why do you bring charges against me? Have I been a land of great darkness? Why do my people say, 'We are free to roam'? Does a maiden forget her jewelry? Why do you go about so much, changing your ways? Would you now return to me? How long will you harbor wicked thoughts? Lord, will you completely destroy Israel? What does the Lord require of you? Will they not return? Who is wise? Who can endure? Who will not fear? Are you better than those kingdoms? How can Jacob survive? Will not the land tremble for this? Will I not destroy the wise men? What have you done? Is the Spirit of the Lord angry? Does he do such things? Why do you now cry aloud—have you no king? Has your counselor perished? Who can withstand his indignation? How long must this go on? Who despises the day of small things? Why do we profane the covenant of our fathers by breaking faith with one another? Who can stand when he appears? What did we gain?"

Jesus silenced his questioners not with dogmatic, airtight defenses, but with questions: "Whose likeness and inscription is this? What do you think? What did David do? What did Moses say? Which was neighbor?" He urged his disciples toward truth and commitment using questions: "Who do you say that I am? Peter, do you love me? More than these?"

Dialogue is another tool of induction. And again a quick thumbing of the Scripture shows us a book laced with dialogue between man and God, Satan and man, Satan and God and man and man. Conversation is a big part of God's bigger story. Some of the Bible's most basic theological messages are made memorable by recorded conversations. The fall of man is presented through Eve's conversation with the serpent. The issue of God's sovereignty is nowhere presented so graphically as it is in the argument Job had with him. The crux of the gospel is perhaps most clearly expressed in the discussion between Jesus and Nicodemus. Again and again God uses and records dialogue to communicate his message.

There is no need to remind ourselves of God's attitude toward the use of the inductive element *parables*. And in Chapter Three we pointed out God's extensive use of *analogy*. Many of his most crucial teachings are dependent on such analogies as father-child relationships, vines and branches, bride and groom, sheep and shepherd, buildings and cornerstones.

Imagery, which could be considered a subelement of analogy, merits mention here as we survey the Bible for inductive elements. Despite the fact that the Old Testament Hebrew language is limited to about two thousand root words and ten thousand vocabulary words (compared to one hundred thousand in Greek and about a million in our English today), descriptive imagery thrives in the Old Testament. The short book of Hosea alone includes more than four hundred images and inductive figures. This poetic prophet leans heavily on the imagery of his own experience to express his nearly incoherent, unbroken sob.

Amos plunges into the darkness to pursue the growling lion as it gnaws on one of his lambs. Then he draws an analogy, asking, "The Lord has roared from Zion; who can but prophecy?" as he compares his personal experience with the national scene.

This analogous image of Amos' actually incorporates another one of those potential inductive elements mentioned in Chapter Three—*common experience*. Within the framework of the Bible's narrative—stories of human experience—are countless further references to everyday human experience. The Bible confronts readers with the reality of every basic inescapable human experience from bodily functions to taxes and death.

Can an inductive approach be biblical? A look at the raw ingredients of Scripture would seem to indicate that it can. Indeed, if you delete from Scripture the elements of narrative, questions, dialogue, analogies and imagery, and references to common human experience, you would reduce Holy Writ to a few scattered shreds.

But as we said in Chapter Three, it's not merely the inclusion of inductive ingredients that defines the inductive process; it's the use of those ingredients. So we must not jump to the conclusion that induction is biblical or that the Bible is inductive just because the ingredients are there. The more important question is, "How does God use those ingredients?"

God doesn't just tell a story in order to get our attention for the main part of his message. The inductive elements we've mentioned aren't just clever little gimmicks dropped into the Bible to dress up dull truths; they aren't a sugar-coating to make the instruction more palatable. These ingredients are central to the entire God-to-man communication.

Narrative bears the weight of the biblical record from the Garden to the New Jerusalem. The structure is that of a story, from first to last. The Old Testament is a story which leads up to the Gospel stories in the New Testament. Plot and counterplot, subplot and parentheses—stories and *the* story carry the record of human faith and folly down the stream of time.

Of course the Bible includes deductive treatments for the instruction of believers. But any essays of doctrines, words of wisdom or theological treatises are landscaped amid a multitude of persons and their experiences.

Where would you look in the Bible to find an abstract discourse on failure? There is none. Yet from Adam's abandoned Garden to those left outside the city walls in Revelation 22, one case study after another illustrates human failure and God's gospel of the second chance. See the failure theme in Cain, Noah, Abram, Jacob, Esau, Samson, David, Solomon, the prophets, Judas, Peter, John Mark and many others.

Basic to all biblical revelation comes the stated or implied importance of experience, learning from experience and teaching by experience. In fact, human experience—real people, specific and concrete instances—forms the central framework of the Bible. How different this is from most sermons today.

Preachers make note of and use God's inductive particulars in their study and preparation to draw their conclusions. But come Sunday morning they usually start with the conclusions it took them all week to reach. And those conclusions become the bases (and too easily the baseball bat) for drilling dogma and doctrine into the listeners. Thus preaching too often becomes didactic, dogmatic and deductive as preachers share the results of their research, but not the process.

God's method of communication is altogether different. He doesn't start his Bible message by saying, "I'm going to prove my loving faithfulness by presenting the world with a means of salvation from sin and death." Instead, God begins by recounting his specific acts in history and tries to sustain their intensity in ever-increasing scope. The message unfolds through five historic events from the Old Testament that stand as basic to faith: the call of the patriarchs, exodus from Egypt, the Sinai Covenant, the promise of Canaan fulfilled, and the establishment of a kingdom. Three New Testament events form the foundation for the new covenant: the life and teachings of Jesus, his death and his resurrection. These historical acts of God in human experience lead the reader inductively from specific facts toward the conclusion—God's declaration of help and hope for the world.

But God doesn't start with the answer. Generally in the Bible the concrete comes before the abstract, the particulars before the general, the data before the rule. While some decrees and dogma may be found in Scripture, they tend to follow experience, examples and cases in an inductive way, rather than precede them in a deductive, authoritarian manner.

Inductive structure and principles abound in Scripture: observation before reasoning, facts before principles, evidence before conclusion, movement from the familiar to the unfamiliar, use of suggestion without drawing inferences, careful and gradual progression from one stage to another.

God teaches two ways: by revelation and by reason. He combines highest authority and greatest freedom of investigation. He reveals himself and his truth gradually. Progressively he shows mankind his will and his way. He prepares the way; he awaits human readiness.

He reasons with his slow-thinking creatures from the particulars of our experience. We are to learn from the examples of others. Models good and bad parade before us as God's reasonable appeals build stronger reasons for our obedience.

After the Garden of Eden scene, God's reasoning unrolls like a carpet in the narrative of the human story. Commands, assertions and decrees blend softly into the narrative format of the Bible.

God's purposes are achieved not by dogmatic authority, but by induction, as humans learn from the experience of others. God's preferred method of teaching is by grace rather than decree. His inductive method builds toward the truth from the indirect teaching of facts. His usual style is not dogmatic but indirect. It is designed to provide a process of moral discipline, not a reservoir of easy theological, creedal answers.

Not only do we find induction in the overall structure of the Bible; it can be seen in individual books. In fact my colleague, Dr. John Oswalt, a Bible scholar, says Proverbs is the only deductive book in the Bible. It's the exception in that its broad general principles stand as universal decrees, not as responses to particular instances.

All the other sixty-five books, insists Oswalt, should be identified as inductive in approach, accent and/or format. Even Paul's writings and the other epistles are inductive in that their general principles are a response to particular situations and experiences. The doctrine in the book of Romans, for example, relates directly to the people at Rome, with their background, culture and history. The teaching in Thessalonians on the hope of the Second Coming is in response to the specific hardships they were suffering at the time.

Other books in the Bible demonstrate more clearly their inductive format. For example, the Gospel of Matthew is constructed with eight narrative parts as artistic segments with similar structure. For purposes of analysis we can say the first Gospel account would equal a two and a half hour sermon with its 23,684 words in the Authorized Version.

These eight sections of narrative give the life and ministry of Jesus. Five of these story portions precede didactic segments of his teachings which grow out of and are based upon the narrative of his incarnate life. Concepts flow out of the inductive processes of life.

The Interpreter's Dictionary of the Bible (Volume 3, page 304) outlines these alternating sections of Matthew with the following mix:

    I Infancy Narrative—chapters 1, 2
   II Discipleship—chapters 3—7
        A. Narrative beginning of Jesus' ministry—chapters 3, 4
        B. Discourse—Sermon of the Mount—chapters 5—7
  III Apostleship—chapters 8—10
        A. Narrative—Jesus' ministry of healing and teaching—8:1—9:34
        B. Discourse—mission of Jesus' disciples—9:35—10:42
   IV Hidden Revelation—11:1—13:52
        A. Narrative—growing opposition to Jesus—chapters 11, 12
        B. Discourse—hidden teaching of eight parables—13:1-52 (narrative)
    V The Church—13:53—18:35
        A. Narrative—Messiahship and suffering—13:53—17:23
        B. Discourse—church administration—17:24—18:35 (narrative)
   VI The Judgment—chapters 19—25
        A. Narrative—controversies in Jerusalem—chapters 19—22
        B. Discourse—criticism of scribes and Pharisees—chapter 23
            Doctrine of *parousia*—chapters 24, 25
            (three parables and judgment narrative)

VII The Passion narrative—chapters 26, 27
VIII The resurrection narrative—chapter 28

This arrangement lists nineteen of Matthew's twenty-eight chapters as narrative, and most of the remaining discourse chapters include much story element.

The book of Mark runs along as a boy's account of the gospel with much narrative, concrete human experience and rapid movement. Inductive process unfolds on center stage.

Luke amplifies experience viewed through the eyes of a physician. Feelings and emotional impact reflect the author's sympathy, and Jesus' contact with women and children, the sick, handicapped, and outcasts as subjects of human and divine compassion.

The so-called theological fourth Gospel as recorded by John is viewed by some as abstract, theoretical and almost otherworldly. Yet note the narrative element highlighted by ticking off the titles of his chapters:

1. The Baptist and others follow the light
2. Wedding at Cana
3. Nicodemus
4. Woman at the well
5. The man healed on the Sabbath as a witness
6. Feeding the 5,000 bread from Heaven
7. Jesus at the Feast
8. Free to be stoned
9. The blind man healed
10. The sheepfold and the Shepherd
11. Lazarus raised
12. The triumphal entry
13. Upper-room footwashing and Last Supper
14. Last will and testament
15. The vine and branches
16. The Comforter
17. The high-priestly prayer
18. The garden of Gethsemane
19. The trial and crucifixion of Jesus
20. The resurrection
21. Fish for breakfast by the lake

In this fourth Gospel John presents inductive evidence to reach his goals. Fourteen signs—six words (the "I am's" of Jesus) and eight works of Jesus—attest John's theme as representative instances. He cites experience, cases, narrative with objective accent—see, hear, know, do, say—all these so "you might believe." Thus he seeks to achieve a quiet authority, calling on life as witness (John 20:31). His method is strongly inductive. He aims at human involvement.

We've looked for evidence of induction in the basic structure of the Bible and in individual books. But what if we look even closer—at the preachers and sermons in the Scripture?

People in the Bible preach. Some preach well. If human nature remains basically unchanged, then the Bible affords us an unexplored gold mine for concepts to help the preacher in our day. Both Old and New Testaments could provide us with case studies in preaching techniques. The prophets preached, and in fact many books of the Bible were preached long before they were written.

In the New Testament, Gospel writers record sermons, talks and experiences. Apostles and authors of other New Testament books record their messages in an oral preaching style. Even Paul's thirteen letters can be analyzed helpfully as sermons sent to be read to the various congregations.

Seeing the method, the style, the appeals and the concepts employed in the Bible should help contemporary preaching. What are the lost principles? Where have the changes come? What did the early preachers know about preaching that we have lost in the shuffle?

We tend to look at men and women in the Bible devotionally rather than realistically. We glamorize them as saints without learning their techniques or principles.

Homiletics books tend to ignore the prophets and preachers of both Testaments. Our sermons follow Greek rhetorical patterns rather than Bible models.

The book of Ecclesiastes, the recorded words of one referred to as "the preacher," stands out as an example of induction by elimination. One college Bible professor told me he urges students never to read the book unless they read it all. "It leads to suicide," he says.

Particulars are gathered to illustrate the "vanity and folly of life" until "the end of the matter" when "all has been heard." Then with the crack of his whip the writer of Ecclesiastes uses only the final two verses to draw out the concluding concept, summarize it and apply his proposition to life. How different from traditional homiletic advice and structure.

Reference to experience and the use of thirty questions in the book get hearers involved in this real-life sermon. While he does begin with a text in the first two verses, the preacher draws listeners into the drama of life by his blanket coverage of human experience from birth to burial, from the womb to the worms. He advises by a few scattered sayings, but his primary preaching is encapsulated in the thirty-one-word conclusion of this forty-minute sermon.

ECCLESIASTES OUTLINE

See vanity and folly.
Where is meaning?
   not in wisdom
   not in withdrawal
   not in weeping
   not in wine
   not in wind (14 times)
   not in works
   not in words
   not in worship without obedience
   not in wickedness
   not in weapons of war
   not in writing.
But walk uprightly.
Conclusion (12:13, 14):
   Fear God.
Keep his commands.
   All the duty of man
   God will judge—
   nothing hidden.

The Book of Malachi, a twelve to fifteen minute sermon of 1,782 words, stands as a model of a preacher seeking inductive participation by his hearers. "The messenger" gets them involved by running dialogue, direct discourse and more than twenty-five questions to confront the listeners. He makes repeated reference to history as experience, case studies, personal and family life, basic relationships, continuing responsibilities, corporate and individual activity, speech and action, belief and behavior.

Undeniable love: God's love for Israel—1:1-5
Unacceptable sacrifices: corrupt offerings by corrupt priests—1:6-14
Unkept obligations: the priests' neglect of the Covenant—2:1-9
Untrue husbands: rebuke for idolatry and divorce—2:10-16
Unexpected judgment: the coming of the Lord—2:17—3:6
Unmeasured blessing: God's promise if tithes are forthcoming—3:7-12
Unwarranted assertions: sure meting out of justice—3:13—4:3
Unforgettable farewell: an admonition, a promise, a threat—4:4-6

We'll consider Jesus' examples in the next chapters, but many other famous sermons in the Bible could also serve as inductive models. Stephen's sermon to his executioners is a masterpiece of induction. Paul's address on Mars Hill and his testimony before the Jews in Acts 22 and King Agrippa in chapter 26 also show skillful use of the inductive process.

Can the inductive approach to preaching be truly biblical?

The preachers in the Bible and the very structure of the Bible and its books say yes. In fact, each of the 2,930 different characters in the Scriptures shouts one message. Each stands as a monument to one chief idea: we can learn from experience.

The divine story comes wrapped in human history. Even the Incarnation is inductive. The Word becomes flesh and dwells among us (John 1:14), so we can see, so we can hear, so we can know.

It seems the inductive process is God's primary instructional method. He seems to be saying in his Word, "Stop, look, listen and live. Then you can hear the Word of the Lord."

When God wanted to deliver a message, he didn't drop a twenty-four-volume set of theological works out of the clouds. He told a story. Maybe we should learn something about our preaching from God's communication style.

Can inductive preaching be truly biblical?

If we want to be truly biblical, there may be no better way.

6 Master Model

One day a pastor friend and I got into a discussion about an inductive approach to preaching. I shared a few of the basic concepts I planned to include in this book. After we talked, unknown to me, he decided to try an inductive sermon on his rural congregation.

In the midst of a sermon series on Matthew's Gospel, he shifted to an inductive approach one Sunday morning without saying anything to anyone about his experiment. Because he wanted to give the test a fair try, and because he's also a purist, he preached a sermon that was, in his words, "pure induction without alloy, without mix or letup from beginning to end."

The next time we talked he related the results to me with a mixture of excitement and consternation. "It nearly ruined my day," he said. "The lights started coming on all over the congregation. You could see the interest and involvement grow as those farm people began to get insights—a new grasp, a new awareness. They began to lean forward, and you could almost hear the reactions showing on their usually stoical faces. 'So that's what Jesus meant.' 'O yes, that relates to . . .' 'I've always wondered about that. . . .'

"It was as if the spectators had come out of the stands and down into the arena," the pastor reported. "But I was so intrigued by their reaction that I just couldn't concentrate on my sermon."

The next Sunday he went back to his familiar deductive approach so he could concentrate on teaching his people. "There's just so much about the Bible they don't know," he reasoned.

I tell this story here because it's an example of what I think could happen in thousands of congregations if ministers would experiment with inductive-style sermons. But I also recount this experience because of my friend's rationale for sticking to his old deductive habit.

"There's just so much about the Bible they don't know" is a concern more ministers would do well to embrace. God's Word holds the answer to every problem our people are facing in our tumultuous twentieth-century world. And too few preachers today are relying on the strength of that Word to enrich their ministries and empower their preaching.

And yet I'm convinced the Bible also offers solutions for the problems of twentieth-century preaching as well as for the everyday problems of our people. And when we insist on the traditional evangelical style of deduction as our prime channel of conveying God's Word to our people who don't know it, I think we preachers show there's just so much about the Bible we don't know either.

Why are preachers so slow to check primary sources for examples of the craft? In the last chapter we took a quick overview of God's communication style in the Bible. What about the example of his Son? Why is Jesus so seldom listed in the index of preaching books? Why do we use Christ's life and words as the bricks and mortar to construct our theology, our systems of ethics, our theories of philosophy and then neglect to study his method and concepts for preaching? Probably because Jesus doesn't fit our traditional homiletical mold.

However, since Jesus' words comprise approximately 20 percent of the entire New Testament (36,450 of the total 181,253 words) we ought to be able to learn something of his speaking style from closely examining his recorded words. And since God's Son is the supreme example of all that is Christian, it seems reasonable that his example should have a measure of impact on Christian preaching today.

Jesus' Message

Let's start with Jesus' sermons. What does he talk about?

Time and again Jesus trips the memory banks of his hearers. He triggers interest and involvement with constant appeals to universal human desires, needs and experiences. His sermons are neither academic exercises in intellectual regimentation nor mere ethical advice. He digs into life. He ferrets out feelings. He probes into his hearers' deepest relationships. Life and experience—normal, healthy, common life and experience—seem to dominate his talks with the people. Note the breadth and relevance in this partial list of his subjects.

Adultery, anger, anxiety, avarice, death, debts, doubts, eternity, faith, fasting, fault-finding, giving, greed, honesty, hypocrisy, joy, kindness, knowledge, law, legalism, life, lust, marriage, money, oaths, parenthood, prayer, pretense, respect, responsibility, reward, rulers, sex, slander, speech, stewardship, taxes, trust, unkindness, virtue, wisdom, zeal.

Just reading this list of subjects from our pulpits would no doubt create a stir in our sanctuaries next Sunday. A series of sermons based on a sampling of topics from Jesus' hit-list would probably do more than three cups of fellowship-hour coffee to keep our dozing deacons awake and listening. But it's not just Jesus' treatment of relevant topics that kept the crowds coming back for more.

We might call Jesus the Master Storyteller. He wouldn't preach without a story, and most of those were *parables*. The New Testament records thirty-three to seventy-seven parables of Jesus, depending on your definition. He doesn't use them merely as teasers, light introductions to get his hearers listening for what he really wants to say. They are often the primary expression of his message.

Jesus' little stories are tied to very big ideas. The story of the good Samaritan forms a sermon on compassion. The prodigal son teaches forgiveness. The parable of the talents instructs us about personal responsibility. When Jesus preached, *narrative* carried much of the weight of his message.

Analogy is another favorite technique in Jesus' speaking. He talks about light and salt, houses on rock and sand, shepherds and sheep, yokes and burdens, living water, chiefs and servants, bosses and employees, vineyards, vines, branches and doors. And within those and many other analogies Jesus compares and contrasts familiar images: wise and foolish builders and virgins, sheep and goats, light and darkness, the broad and narrow, rich and poor, younger and elder.

Jesus repeatedly returns his listeners to common experiences by his references: forty-nine times to sheep, twenty-seven times to sowing, twenty-two times to reaping and harvest and ten times to water imagery. All are everyday, crucial parts of the agrarian culture he lived in.

Familiar, concrete terms are Jesus' vehicles for conveying abstract concepts. He uses the common lily as an object-lesson in trust. A beam and a splinter symbolize large and small faults. The concept of service is represented by a cup of water.

Scripture records 153 questions Jesus asks of his listeners. And he is in constant dialogue with the people who gather around to hear him. In fact, all of the inductive ingredients mentioned in Chapter Three—narrative, parables, analogy, dialogue, questions and reference to common experience—are constant, common ingredients in Jesus' preaching.

His 2,320-word Sermon on the Mount serves as an ideal model for studying Jesus' preaching style. In this sermon, which could be preached in about twenty minutes and might be titled "The Happy, Satisfied Person," Jesus probes a strong felt need of his hearers: "How can a person be happy or satisfied?" He walks around that universal question, pulling out examples as beatitudes and analogies—some subtle, some sweeping, but all simple, common and powerful in their impact.

Tradition has tended to overlook Jesus' use of inductive elements in the Sermon on the Mount. Too often we read the Beatitudes as fiats, decrees and pronouncements of authority. A closer look would indicate Jesus didn't deliver them that way.

Instead, he asks nineteen questions in this sermon, giving it an overall feel of dialogue and involvement on the part of the people. And the entire sermon is chock-full of analogies and references to experience the people could easily relate to. Broken apart and analyzed, the sermon shows this:

    I Analogies—5:3-16
       Poor, mourners, meek, merciful, pure, peacemakers, persecuted, salt, light in human experience.
   II Attitudes—5:17-48
       Self-righteousness, hate, lust, respect, honesty, revenge, love, giving, prayer, fasting, greed, anxiety, judging, faith, choice.
  III Actions—6:1—7:23
       Give, pray, fast, work, serve, don't worry.
  IV Alternatives—7:24-29
       Gates, fruits, trees, foundations.

Words............................ 2,320 (18-20 minutes)
Images, pictures, examples, illustrations 348 or 1/6⅔ words
    (Wolves, sheep, fruit, light, rock, sand, storm, build, etc.)
Comparisons .... 142 or 1/16 words
Verbs for energy, action .... 404 or 1/6 words
Pronouns to clarify and relate......... 320 or 1/7¼ words
Second person pronoun for directness.. 221 or 1/10 words
Present tense—relevance, realism..... 65% approximately
Future tense .... 30% approximately
Past tense......................... 5% (149 words KJV—
                                  not tradition
                                  not authority)
Varied viewpoints.................. 42 different aspects of happiness

Jesus doesn't start the Sermon on the Mount with a declaration of the importance of listening to his words or with a threat for those who don't listen. He doesn't start with his declared conclusion, but leads his hearers with the reasonableness of his beatitudes and analogies, his comparisons and contrasts to a place of choice. At the end of the sermon he offers them a decision, to heed and be wise or to ignore his words and be foolish. And once that point of decision is reached, Jesus allows the people to draw their own conclusions.

Jesus, here on the Mount and in other teachings, begins with the known, the concrete, the personal to guide hearers to the unknown, the abstract and the universal.

Again and again throughout his ministry, he uses what is an inductive, progressive logical sequence in his teaching which begins with the simple and proceeds to the complex. The steps could be outlined like this:

1. Introduce idea.
2. Explain—illustrate simply.
3. Reason—appeal to the mind.
4. Apply—"go and do."

"Come," "see," "hear" stand in front of "think" or even "believe" when Jesus preaches. Add up the ingredients and the structure of his messages and the evidence seems overwhelming. Jesus preaches inductively.

With almost infinite variety he raises issues and involves hearers in his messages. "Do you know this parable?" "Go tell John what you've seen and heard." "What is this generation like?" "Do you see this woman?" "Who is that faithful and wise steward?" "Were these Galileans the worst sinners because they suffered?" "See the fig tree." "Who is greater, he who sits at meat or he who serves?" "Did you lack anything when I sent you out without purse, scrip or shoes?" "You seek me because you ate the loaves and were filled."

But if you recall what we talked about in Chapter Two, you'll remember the *message* is only one-third of the communication process. If we want to fairly judge Jesus' inductiveness, we need to examine his role and attitude as a speaker and his relationship and that of his message to his *audience*.

Jesus and the People
The Sermon on the Mount says a lot about Jesus' understanding of and relationship with his audience. While the Pharisees and other religious leaders of the day demand that people come to them, Jesus goes to the people—physically as well as attitudinally through his message.

He goes to the Mount with the masses. Yet he tries to personalize his sermon. In addition to the dialogue-creating questions in the Sermon on the Mount, the words "you" or "your" are stated or implied 221 times. Jesus speaks directly to his audience.

Perhaps it was Jesus' style of going to and speaking to the people that brought them thronging to hear him. Jesus' listeners didn't seem to sit silently on the back pew either. The Gospel accounts record some 125 incidents of Jesus communicating with others. And about 54 percent of those encounters were initiated by his hearers.

It's interesting that the Son of God, who came to earth to convey the most important message of all time, who had the clearest channel to God and the deepest understanding of the message, let the audience determine his communication agenda more than half the time. Instead of standing up and proclaiming the message he knew the people needed to know, he responded to his audience's questions, objections and doubts. He allowed and welcomed their involvement at the outset.

Untutored Jesus and his unlettered twelve turned the towns upside down with their preaching. Religious leaders entangled in their ancient lore and endless footnotes never could understand why the common people heard Jesus so gladly. "Where did he get his learning?" they asked.

Much of his relevant learning came from time spent sharing and living with the people. He knew and respected the common people and their experience. He met them on their own turf. He related to their personal needs and interest.

I've heard some preachers rationalize a lack of involvement and responsiveness of their congregations with a martyrlike observation: "Jesus' listeners rejected his message too."

But that's just not true. Time and distance have distorted history.

The fact is, the common people flocked to Jesus with their diseases, their doubts and distresses. Religious people resisted him.

The common sinners crowded around him. Entire cities emptied as the populace streamed into the wilderness where he was preaching. The "good" people were offended.

Religious "sinners" were distressed, embarrassed, miffed at Jesus. They accused Jesus of being a friend of publicans and other sinners. The unsophisticated ones gathered around to hear his stories, his parables, his intriguing sermons.

True, the rich young ruler went away sorrowfully, but open hostility came from professional religionists. Resistance, rebellion, rejection came from them. And they were a very small minority.

We might claim the sinful people were offended by Jesus because they were "sinners." But if we offer that as a defense for our own offensiveness, for the lack of response to our "God-given" message, we're missing the truth of the broader picture. Go back two thousand years and look again.

The vast majority of sinners—the rabble, the untutored, the unsanctified—throng to hear Jesus. They climb trees, they sneak through the press, they cry out to him without fear or embarrassment.

The elite are incensed, the privileged are put out at him; the chosen few protest his proletariat policies. The religiously sophisticated snub him. But the masses nearly mob him in their excitement to hear him preach.

The sinners come to him. The so-called saints want him to be dogmatic, deductive, doctrinal. Instead he tells stories. He relates parables. He holds them spellbound with enigmatic comparisons. He reserves his doctrinal decrees for the believers and any dogmatism for the religious.

He relates to sinners as friend and companion. He goes to weddings, funerals, feasts to share with the people. His sermons begin where the multitudes are—in common experience.

He can preach with confidence. He trusts the people to learn from experience, from induction, rather than from decrees. He leads the hearers to their own conclusions, and his. He doesn't drive them to agree whether they choose to or not. When they have reached conclusions, proclaimed their agreement, *then* he proclaims application and consequence of these concepts. His message is molded to the audience.

Jesus the Preacher
In Chapter Two, when we discussed the speaker as one of Aristotle's three elements of communication, we said a preacher's inner attitude of servanthood needed to be reflected in his life and his preaching. Such an attitude put into practice becomes an inductive message in its own right. It shows rather than tells.

Jesus the speaker is inductive by the very nature of his being. The Incarnation itself is clearly an inductive idea. Instead of just saying he loved us, God came in human form to live out his message.

Paul described this inductive attitude and act in Philippians 2:5-8 when he said:

> Let your attitude to life be that of Christ Jesus himself. For he, who had always been God by nature, did not cling to his privileges as God's equal, but stripped himself of every advantage by consenting to be a slave by nature and being born a man. And, plainly seen as a human being he humbled himself by living a life of utter obedience, to the point of death, and the death he died was the death of a common criminal. *(Phillips)*.

Jesus "made himself of no reputation" (KJV). His ministry, when you stop and think about it, was a very inductive procedure. The identity, authority and purpose of Jesus as the Son of God (the abstract message he came to deliver) is only gradually, progressively revealed by the acts and events of his life (the concrete illustrations of that message).

God didn't start his great Incarnation sermon to the waiting world by spelling out his thesis. He didn't say, "This is what I'm going to do when I send my Son into the world" and lay out the details about mangers, rejection and crosses. No, instead God allowed the concrete to come before the abstract. The specifics preceded the general application; life experience preceded the theory in true inductive fashion.

As illustration, consider the unfolding revelation of Jesus' authority. You can see this in any one of the Gospel accounts, but for the sake of simplicity and chronology let's skim through Mark and see how the authority of Jesus as God (the central thrust and message of his coming) is progressively revealed through his life experiences.

Occasion	Authority Revealed	Reference in Mark
Call of disciples	To draw men	1:16-20
Teaching in synagogue in Capernaum	Teaching authority	1:21, 22
Casting out demon	Over spiritual world	1:23-28
Healing Simon's wife's mother	Over disease	1:29-31
Accusation for not fasting	Over customs	2:18-20
Plucking corn on the Sabbath	Over Sabbath	2:23-28
Healing "withered hand"	Over Sabbath	3:1-5
Choosing the twelve	To choose whom he will	3:13-21
Teaching via parables	To choose method of teaching	4:1-34
Stilling storm	Over nature	4:35-41
Raising Jairus' daughter	Over death	5:35-43
Sending out twelve	To delegate power	6:7-13
Feeding 5,000	Over material needs	6:32-44
Unwashed hands	Over traditions	7:1-23
Blessing children	Parental authority	10:13-16
Riding unbroken colt	Over animal kingdom; ownership authority	11:1-11
Cleansing Temple	Priestly authority	11:15-19
Olivet discourse	Prophetic authority	13
The crucifixion	Over his death	15:24-41
The resurrection	Over the grave	16:1-8
Great Commission	Over world evangelization	16:15-18
The ascension	Exaltation to all authority	16:19, 20

Jesus doesn't try to impress anyone by declaring his authority or deity. He lets his example speak. He doesn't tell; he shows his power. Experience is the proof he lays out for the people around him.

However, Jesus not only inductively withheld his authority until it was proved in his life. Jesus the speaker refrained from leaning on his own authority when he preached to the multitudes. We've already seen how he cited human instances, referred to experience and shared relationships. We've noted his use of narrative, parables, dialogue and questions in his inductive attempt to avoid exhorting his listeners as one more authority figure from the religious community. Furthermore, Jesus didn't even lean on traditional authority. The primary reason the religious, educated elite resisted and resented the simple preaching of Jesus was because he didn't buy into their system. He didn't rely on their respected footnotes. He didn't cite their authorities. He didn't shrug off common experience as irrelevant or unimportant for life and learning.

It seems Jesus recognized in his preaching what God understood when he dreamed up the incarnation concept: experience carries the persuasive authority inductive human beings need to comprehend and believe the truth. Incarnational preaching, whether in the first or the twenty-first century, demands the word become flesh. And that happens best when the authority of the speaker and the truth are fleshed out for the audience with the proof of experience.

Some readers may be thinking, "Yes, but doesn't the Scripture say 'Jesus taught them with authority and not as the scribes!' " It does. Yet I'm convinced what Matthew meant with that observation is that Jesus exuded real authority, not the artificial brand supported by the position, tradition or institutions of the religious leaders of his day. Even when Jesus cited Scripture with a posture of authority, he did so only to the proudly religious who claimed to adhere to it and when he was instructing those who already believed. John quotes Jesus as saying, "I do not speak on my own authority."

A thorough study of everything Jesus said in the New Testament will show a definite pattern that should have important implications for our preaching today. Jesus used two distinct styles of communication, depending on the situation and audience. He did sometimes use a didactic, deductive approach—but only when speaking to his disciples and other believers. When he spoke to the public, to the multitudes, his approach was *always* indirect and inductive.

For sake of clarity let's distinguish between these two styles by designating one preaching and and the other teaching. When you analyze the two, you find a long list of interesting differences.

His Preaching Is Largely Inductive	*His Teaching Is Largely Deductive*
1. For "the people"—the many	1. For disciples—the few
2. Sometimes to multitudes, public	2. Demands small growth groups; private

3. From life—parable, experience, story, analogy, examples, Bible
4. Based upon experience, life
5. Relates primarily to hearers
6. Leads to faith, Bible, God
7. Leads to belief and teaching

8. Accents narrative elements
9. Examples precede argument
10. Examples prior to faith

11. Needs several examples
12. Points to probability; reasonable

13. Leans on common sense and life

14. Begins with hearers' questions
15. Begins with hearers' interest, then leads to mutual conclusions

16. Clamors for attention and interest
17. Seeks common ground and rapport
18. Seeks to gain respect, authority
19. Leads to faith and teaching base

20. Primarily evangelistic
21. Primarily for unbelievers, youth
22. Begins where hearer is without faith
23. For outsiders, uncommitted
24. More descriptive
25. Publishes announcement
26. No strict rules—reasonable
27. Provides analogies from history

28. Compares and contrasts experience
29. Accents the concrete
30. No authority but life, experience
31. Not reinforced with proofs

32. Nonadversary stance
33. Prophetic accent on change
34. Demands decision
35. Allows no postponement
36. Preacher doesn't tarry
37. Preacher wins converts to faith

3. From Scripture, text, biblical base
4. Based on biblical faith
5. Relates primarily to truth
6. Builds on faith in Bible and God
7. Prepares believer to preach inductively

8. Accents didactic element
9. Examples follow argument
10. Examples follow assertions, assumptions

11. One example may suffice
12. Assumes agreement, faith, belief

13. Leans on formal logical sequence

14. Begins with answers, solutions
15. Begins with speaker's conclusions, then pushes to application of them

16. May assume hearers' attention, interest
17. Assumes rapport and common faith
18. Assumes respect and authority
19. Leads to service and more preaching

20. Primarily educational
21. Primarily for the faithful
22. Begins where speaker is—with faith
23. For insiders, believers
24. More hortatory
25. Pushes assertions
26. Accents logic, order, sequence
27. Leans on logical dictums, tradition

28. Follows speaker's conclusions, assertions
29. Abstractions are common
30. Assumes authoritative posture
31. Leans on logical proofs, authority

32. Defensive, adversary stance
33. Priestly accent on status quo
34. Assumes agreement
35. Teaching takes time
36. Teacher repeats and perseveres
37. Teacher enables converts to serve

38. Prepares people to receive teaching
38. Equips believers to preach inductively
39. Calls to choice, obedience
39. Calls to growth, maturity

Preaching and teaching may be carried on side by side as in Matthew 5:1, 2 and 7:28, 29. But later Jesus makes a distinction as his teaching becomes secret with small groups of believers. His teaching ministry equips his followers for their individual inductive preaching, thus perpetuating the Christian program in endless sequence—preaching, teaching and service.

The preaching style of Jesus shown on the preceding chart was what earned the enmity of the scribes and Pharisees. Their approach was just the opposite:

They	*He*
Past tense	Present tense
Theoretical	Practical
Institutionally oriented	Individualistic
Explained by defining	Explained by showing, doing
Relied on tradition	Relied on present facts
Stressed abstract thought	Stressed inner feelings
Relied on authority	Relied on experience
Impersonal	Personal
Trusted rules	Trusted relationships
Ruled people	Respected people
Conclusions set	Evidence before conclusions
Programmed to a set pattern	Individualistic
Rigid	Flexible
Rationalistic accent	Relational accent
Accented words of others	Accented his own words and works

I think we as twentieth-century preachers need to thoughtfully consider the differences both between Jesus' preaching and his teaching and between Jesus' preaching and that of the religious leaders of his day. We must choose our model of authority in our preaching—Jesus or the scribes: the ring of experience or the singsong of repetition.

For the scribe, the Good News seems neither good nor new, more a decrepit code of prohibitions than a vigorous hymn of liberation. The scribe and his tribe do not announce, but enounce; do not proclaim but declaim; do not incite but recite; do not enkindle, but extinguish.

Whose example do we follow in our preaching? We have a choice to make. If Jesus, with all his authority, chose to preach inductively in a nonadversary manner rather than by fiat, who are we to cling to authoritative, deductive pronouncements? Let's consider again his example as a preacher.

Jesus does not clamor or claw for his place in the sun. He lets his stories carry his message without fanfare or pompous declarations when he preaches to the populace. He does not declare with unquestioned certainty as much as he shares, guides and walks in the way with the people. He aims to lead rather than drive. He accompanies more than he accosts. He counsels instead of confronting, compelling or contending.

He trusts his stories to gently shepherd the flock toward the fold. He denounces the wolves in sheepskins. He attacks the hireling. He, the Gentle Shepherd, warns against thieves and robbers. The sheep know his voice and his mild manners as he guides them to safe and abundant life.

Jesus trusts the people and the inductive process of learning from experience, accenting common life, accepting the people with respect, assuming the role of guide, friend and confidant. He is no autocrat, no pompous boss, no proud proclaimer of his own conclusions, no declarer of personal decrees without the quiet proof of experience.

Jesus shares the process with them. He never pushes the people. He doesn't push his propositions. He gently guides. He instructs, teaches, trains them.

We could sum it all up by saying Jesus respects his hearers as if they were created in the image of God. Can we do any less? If Jesus is our example, shouldn't we too trust his mild method of induction?

His enemies shook their heads in amazement and admitted, "Never man spake like this man."

Maybe it's time we tried.

7 Web and Flow

I once saw a preacher begin his sermon by acting out the loading of God into a "cosmic wheelbarrow." He then wheeled him to the edge of the universe and unceremoniously booted Deity off the platform and into oblivion with a swift kick.

I knew another preacher who dreamed up a novel idea for gaining attention at the beginning of his sermon in a sleepy Quaker college chapel. The plan was to strap his son's toy cap pistols under his suit coat and surprise everybody with some Quick-Draw McGraw antics, firing the smoking guns above the stunned students.

"You're a liar," another minister bellowed as he stepped to his pulpit one Sunday morning. There was a dramatic pause as he waited for his flabbergasted flock to crawl out from under the pews. Then he shouted again. "You're a liar!" A second time he paused before asking, "Does that sound like Jesus?" Another pause. "Well, that's what I heard a member of this church say one day this week." And for the next twenty minutes, while he preached, the mind of every man, woman and child in the sanctuary replayed the events of the preceding week, trying to imagine who it was their pastor had heard.

One Easter Sunday a pastor in a small county-seat town put an American Standard toilet stool in the chancel of his church and "potted" a lily in it. The shocked congregation called the bishop, and the repentant pastor was ridden out of town on an ecclesiastical rail—the Methodist appointive itinerant system.

Billy Sunday shattered chairs, ranted and raved against John Barleycorn, disrobed to show his BVD's and slid into second base in the chancel to illustrate a point.

One flamboyant young student pastor told of dramatizing the felling of a giant redwood in the midst of his sermon. As the crashing monster came down, he reported, "The congregation moved over in the pews to let it fall."

But aren't there more appropriate, less outrageous means than these for getting our listeners involved in our sermons?

The elusive goal of involvement has inspired a great deal of creativity throughout the course of preaching history. And perhaps no other time has presented such a challenge to the preacher who wants to get and keep the attention of his listeners.

We've talked earlier about the demands and expectations of contemporary listeners. They want to begin where the action is. They are impatient with point to point structure. Television and movies have conditioned them for dramatic action, concrete content, a moving message, rapid movement, human interest and constant variety.

Preachers of a hundred years ago were often allowed an hour or two to complete the logical process of a sermon. But today's listener won't stand (or sit) for that. For those accustomed to the ten to fifteen minute segments of the broadcasting business, a twenty- to thirty-minute, commercial-free time slot on Sunday morning strains the attention span.

For the minister facing these problems, the sort of dramatic, theatrical, attention-seeking stunts mentioned above can seem terribly tempting; sometimes such extremes may look like the only hope for breaking into a congregation's consciousness. While they may very well make a lasting impression, such antics can overshadow the essence of what was meant to be communicated. Shocking introductions may serve to get attention, but keeping that attention and, more importantly, keeping the attention focused on the message is a bigger matter. Unless you have a three-ring circus lined up to illustrate your three main points, theatrics will seldom carry an entire sermon. They are more apt to be mere flash in an introductory pan.

Like the big splashy introductions, induction aims for the attention of our listeners. But it hopes to do more than shake the saints out of their sleep so the preacher can talk at them for a few minutes. As we've emphasized a number of times already, the goal of induction is not just to get attention, but to keep it in such a way the people take part in the thinking process of the sermon, staying with the preacher until preacher and people reach the sermon's conclusion together. Induction attempts to transform our congregations from observers to participants.

Some people have tried to liken inductive preaching to an extended introduction. But it's really more than that. Induction can be woven into and comprises all of an inductive sermon—the parts and the whole.

In an inductive sermon, from beginning to end, listener attention and agreement is courted by design—not demanded by decree. We can't fully understand inductive preaching unless we understand that design—the structure which makes a sermon inductive.

We've already discussed extensively the characteristics of induction and many of the differences between induction and deduction. But it might be well to review some of those findings that impact on the design of a sermon.

Inductive preaching begins with the particulars—facts, illustrations, experience, examples; deduction starts with assertions, conclusions, propositions, generalizations or principles. Induction builds with and bridges beyond the particulars it starts with. Deduction defines, delimits, diminishes, dissects or defends its first premise. Inductive examples precede and lead to assertions; deductive examples follow and bolster assertions already made.

In an inductive format any propositions, assertions, declarations or exhortations follow or flow out of the illustrative material in the course of the sermon process. Deductive sermons begin with the preacher's conclusions that are a result of sermon preparation—conclusions offered as *givens* to listeners who may or may not be ready to accept them and go on from there.

The difference may be summarized this way. The deductive preacher begins with truths and then sets out to prove them. The inductive preacher seeks to help listeners see the truth in such a way that they are ready to accept, agree with and respond to that truth at the end of the sermon.

But how does all this affect the practical business of how a sermon is designed or outlined? One general rule of inductive outlines is this: an inductive outline normally begins with instances that serve as cumulative evidence leading up to any subdivisions. That's in contrast to a deductive outline that starts with points or divisions followed by examples and evidence.

In his book *Preparing for Platform and Pulpit* (Nashville: Abingdon Press, 1968), John E. Baird offers a sample inductive outline. It's presented here alongside a typical deductive structure.

INDUCTIVE	DEDUCTIVE
Illustration	I. Introduction
Statistics	II. Central Idea
Main head A	Main head A
Illustration	Statistics
Instance	Illustration
Instance	Main head B
Main head B	Instance
Quotation	Instance
Instance	Illustration
Subhead 1	Main head C
Illustration	Subhead 1
Subhead 2	Illustration
Main head C	Subhead 2
Central Idea	III. Conclusion

Body { ... } ... } Body

As you can see, the most obvious difference between these outlines is the order of the illustrations in relation to the main heads they support. But there are more differences as well.

A separate sermon introduction often is unnecessary when the inductive structure begins with concrete illustrative material. The initial instance serves the functions of an introduction and also bolsters the cumulative evidence in the inductive process.

A separate conclusion is not usually needed if the inductive arrangement leads to a central idea or basic point of the sermon. For instance, simple inductive movement consists of illustrations leading to the concluding central point or idea in this manner:

> Illustration A
> Illustration B
> Illustration C
> Therefore: Central Idea and Conclusion

Traditional parts of the sermon thus tend to melt into a holistic unit in any inductive arrangement. A sermon moving inductively sustains interest and engages the listener, but it may not have points any more than a narrative, a story, a parable or even a joke has points. That does not mean the preacher preaches without a point, however. (I'm afraid there is enough pointless preaching already; that's not what we're advocating here.) Every inductive sermon needs a point; it's the discipline of this one idea, this point which gives focus to a sermon's preparation, its delivery and its hoped for reception. The point of an inductive sermon is the place we want our listeners to reach at the conclusion of our sermon.

For years, in trying to explain these ideas about induction to my students I've used the image of a whirlpool to try to get across the idea of a sermon drawing listeners into our conclusion. Often when we discuss this point in class I draw a simple illustration to portray the idea visually.

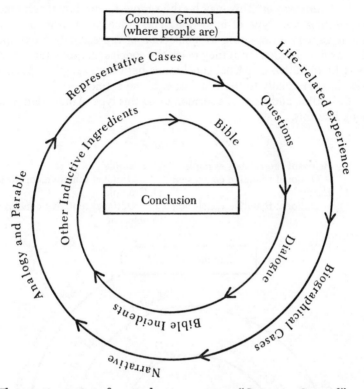

The starting point of any inductive sermon, "Common Ground" on this diagram, could be a life-related experience, a problem, a question, a need, a conflict or some other tension point But it always begins where the people are and draws them, by means of any number or combination of inductive ingredients, into the conclusion that is the scripturally-based focus of the entire sermon.

The specifics-to-the-general, evidence-leading-to-conclusion movement we've emphasized here is the most basic principle behind inductive structure. But there are a number of types of induction (they also might be called inductive arguments, inductive thought processes) which could be used for an inductive sermon. Each of these types of induction can achieve the inductive sermon's goal of congregational involvement—of drawing the people into our conclusion. All of them meet the requirements of and exemplify the characteristics of induction we've discussed throughout this book. And all of them fit the basic whirlpool pattern just mentioned here.

For your help in understanding the possible structures of an inductive sermon, we'll detail eight types of induction in this chapter and the next with outlines, charts and comments.

1. *Enumeration.* This may be the simplest (certainly it's the most straightforward) type of induction. The inductive, whirlpool movement gathers momentum as a selection of representative examples build on each other until they reach the conclusion. Sometimes there may be tentative or partial conclusions between examples. But they also lead gradually to the conclusion of the sermon.

An outline and chart of a sermon using this type of induction would look like this.

OUTLINE

A. Relevant life-related example
   Optional tentative conclusion
B. Example
   Optional tentative conclusion

C. Example
   Optional tentative conclusion
D. Example
   Optional tentative conclusion
Conclusion

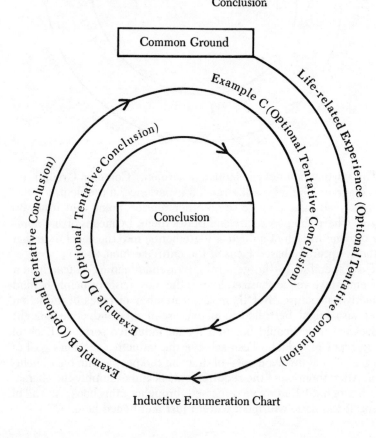

Inductive Enumeration Chart

The number of examples (this includes anecdotes, cases, Bible incidents, references to experience and other inductive ingredients, possibly even quotes and facts—in short, any supportive evidence) enumerated in this type of induction will vary, depending on time factors, subject and sometimes the audience.

The more hostile and unresponsive an audience is to the conclusion we want to make, the more and the smaller steps we may need to take to get them there. The examples we select could incorporate any or all of the inductive ingredients we discussed in Chapter Three and could include any combination of historical, contemporary and scriptural references. One good rule of thumb in selecting examples is to begin with the *most* contemporary, the one closest to our audience, then progress from there.

2. *Exploration.* A more complex approach, one which uses more extensive, more deliberate enumeration as its means of movement could be termed inductive exploration. In this type of induction a broader selection of examples from many different sides of a subject are purposefully brought together to give a well-rounded picture.

The process is not unlike that of an explorer who on sighting a new land tries to sail around it to determine whether it's an island or a peninsula. Or a land-bound explorer who in coming upon a new landmark walks around it to determine its extent and nature. The examples, the vantage points from which the subject is seen, may vary depending on the subject matter. And as in simple enumeration, those examples may be followed by optional tentative conclusions. But the sermon picks up its inductive momentum as the preacher walks entirely around the topic, exploring and learning by gathering examples that finally lead him and his listeners to a better understood discovery and conclusion at the end of the sermon.

An exploration type sermon could be outlined and charted pretty much as any sermon using enumeration, just with more deliberate and inclusive steps.

For example, let's suppose you wanted to preach a sermon on the concept of redemption, titled "The God of the Second Chance." In keeping with the walk-around idea and our basic whirlpool structure, the following diagram may provide additional understanding.

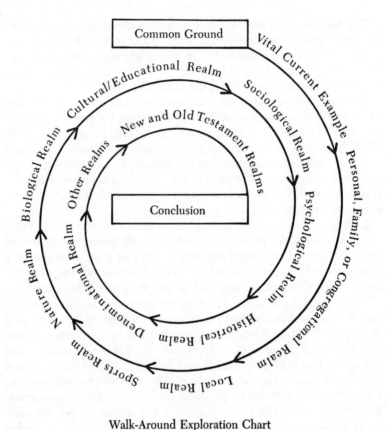

Walk-Around Exploration Chart

Suppose you start your sermon on redemption with a vital illustration you've seen in the paper recently about a young woman who fell onto the tracks in a crowded rush-hour subway station in New York and was pulled to safety just moments before an express train roared through the station. Then you share one or more examples from personal, family, congregational or local experience of someone whose life, career, family or whatever was spared, someone who received a second chance. You might include a sports account illustrating the second-chance idea.

An example of some creature in nature where the mother risks or even sacrifices her life to protect her young could make a valuable subpoint. More material drawn from other areas can then combine with Bible content to offer additional insight to the idea of redemption until you are led to the conclusion you want your listeners to reach.

You would not need to include all the steps shown on the diagram above. Nor is the walk-around format restricted to the realms of experience mentioned on this chart. In fact, the same subject could be treated with a walk-around sermon which explores all sides of the subject of redemption by trying to answer journalistic questions (Who? What? Where? When? Why? and How?). A sermon that moves around the subject asking and trying to answer those questions with stories, illustrations, quotes, Scripture, etc. could present a broad view of redemption. And the basic idea of an exploration type of sermon is to present a well-rounded, organized view of the subject on the way to the basic, logical conclusion.

3. *Biography*. Presented as a case study, a biographical sermon on the life of a Bible character could be inductive in its movement. The accumulated factual material can gather momentum until it reaches a conclusion that spells out logical principles, propositions and applications drawn from the study.

An inductive biographical sermon on the life of Moses might be outlined and charted like this:

Introduction for attention, interest, relevance and focus
a. Birth
b. Bulrushes
c. Private-paid tutor
d. Pharaoh's grandson
e. Court and school in Egypt
f. Identity crisis
g. Hero's reward
h. 40-year flight
i. Burning bush
j. Back to Egypt
k. Ten plagues
l. Exodus
m. Wilderness
    Principle, application conclusion

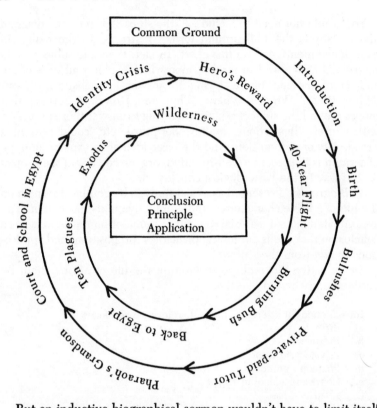

But an inductive biographical sermon wouldn't have to limit itself to one Bible character. Not long ago my esteemed colleague Dr. Charles Killian preached a three-pronged biographical sermon based on the oft-repeated biblical phrase, "the God of Abraham, Isaac and Jacob." This sermon could be outlined like this:

Biography No. 1
a. Call
b. Confidence
c. Covenant
d. Career
e. Characteristics
   I Abraham

Biography No. 2
a. Content
b. Confident
c. Coexistence
d. Compromise
e. Confused
   II Isaac

Biography No. 3
a. Cheater
b. Cheating
c. Challenged
d. Cheated
e. Changed
   III Jacob

∴ IV Conclusion

Each one of the three biographical cases could form a distinct and separate whirlpool pattern that could be shown on our basic whirlpool diagram. But to show how the three parts fit into one sermon, it might be best to diagram them from a different, third-dimensional perspective.

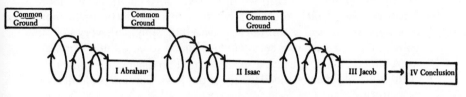

Combination Biography Chart

The three cases highlight the characteristics of each man. Without emphasizing the differences as the biographies are presented, the obvious contrasts build to the conclusion that is spelled out only at the close. The conclusion: *If God claims these three diverse characters as his own, if he can be the God of Abraham, Isaac and Jacob, he can be our God too.* The sermon thus includes implications on grace, hope, God's favor, and an especially strong message on the Christian concept of acceptance. The applications are many.

It just so happens this sermon used three biographical cases. The number could vary. And not all the cases would have to be Bible characters for the sermon to be inductive or to be biblical.

4. *Narrative.* A sermon structure that relies primarily on storytelling can be very inductive if propositional material is withheld until the story or stories make the point. And the Bible contains a wealth of stories that deserve to be retold.

The books of Esther, Ruth and Jonah could each be preached in a story sermon that leaves any sermonizing until the conclusion of the story. Great historical events in the Bible provide additional grist for the narrative sermon mill. The Exodus, the taking of the Promised Land, the fall of the kingdoms, the nativity, events in the ministry of Jesus, and Passion Week could all be developed as narrative sermons.

Narrative can be used to present a survey of broad movements within the Bible. For example, an Old Testament narrative history of the children of Israel might include six scenes (a true narrative doesn't have points): (1) The example of Abraham; (2) the Exodus; (3) the Exile; (4) near extinction; (5) extension and rebuilding; and (6) expectancy.

Simply postponing any propositional material until it was illustrated in the story or until the conclusion of the sermon would make our "History of the Jews" sermon inductive. But it could be doubly inductive if after each scene (or at the end) we used the inductive ingredient of comparison to compare the experience of God's chosen people with our experience today.

The narrative examples mentioned thus far have all been simple, single-narrative ideas that could make up the entire sermon. But just as the biography structure we discussed above could include more than one biography, the narrative sermon could incorporate more than one story. And as was the case with biography, not every story in a combination narrative sermon would need to be a Bible story.

A simple, single-narrative sermon could be diagrammed like this. (The story of Jonah or the "History of the Jews" sermon could fit such a pattern.)

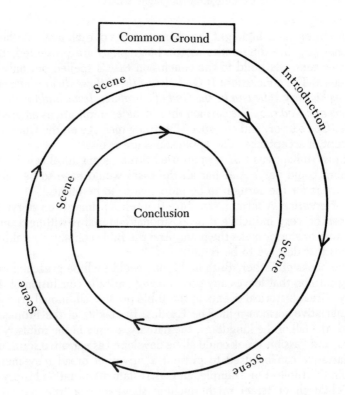

Simple Narrative Chart
(one basic story)

A combination narrative sermon, say on God's providence, could combine one or more biblical stories with one or more nonbiblical stories to illustrate different aspects of that providence. The consecutive whirlpool movements of the sermon could be reflected in a diagram like this:

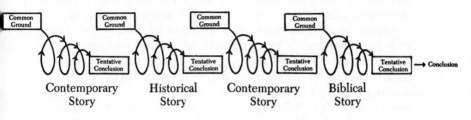

Combination Narrative Chart
(two or more stories)

In a narrative sermon, an introduction may or may not be necessary to set the stage. Sometimes the opening scene is relevant and strong enough to become common ground for the sermon. Optional tentative conclusions may be made (preferably after each scene in the simple narrative or after each story in the combination narrative). But as with any inductive sermon, all tentative conclusions must lead to the final conclusion at the close of the sermon, and all conclusions (tentative or final) must be preceded by illustrative material that brings the listeners to that point.

A few cautions need to be raised concerning narrative sermons:

First, a sermon that relies entirely on the telling of a story or stories is perhaps the most difficult type of inductive sermon to pull off. To do it effectively, a preacher needs a creative imagination and strong storytelling skills. Since storytelling is usually a learned skill, most ministers would do well to practice and gain confidence telling a story as only one part of another type of inductive sermon (as one element of a sermon using enumeration, for example) before they risk an entire sermon to their storytelling abilities.

A good book on storytelling could be very helpful for anyone wanting to sharpen storytelling skills. A good practice for preachers would be to check each story in a sermon against the four basic elements of any good narrative:

1. The beginning
2. Succession of events and conflict
3. Climax
4. The end.

The second caution for narrative sermons relates specifically to the use of biblical narrative. Even an inductive, well-told Bible story with assertions delayed until the conclusion may fail to involve some listeners for whom the Bible seems remote or irrelevant to life. So it can be especially helpful to intersperse Bible stories with contemporary stories in a combination narrative structure. Using a strongly life-related introduction to a Bible story is also recommended.

Another option, one that can and should be used in conjunction with the other two is to incorporate within any noncontemporary story (whether it's biblical or historical) some comparisons to contemporary experience. For example, Esther's selection as queen could be compared briefly to a modern Miss America contest. Jonah's feelings about going to Nineveh could be likened to the imagined response of Jimmy Carter, had his advisors suggested he undertake a secret, personal diplomatic mission to visit the Ayatollah Khomeini in Tehran during the Iran crisis. The children of Israel griping about the manna in the wilderness could be compared to the grousing about food you can hear in any high school cafeteria.

Countless comparisons can be made in relating Bible stories to our people today. We need only to use our imaginations to better involve our listeners.

Narrative is the fourth type of inductive arrangement. We'll detail four more in the following chapter.

8   More Web and Flow

One February, during a class discussion in a course on inductive preaching, one of my students shared his experience with a Valentine's Day sermon on God's love which he'd preached the week before. "As I prepared my sermon," he said, "I was struck by three major characteristics of God's love that seemed analogous to human love. So, starting with the human love idea, I found examples to illustrate and tie the concepts together."

Then the student pastor shared this example from his sermon:

"The day before Valentine's Day my wife told me she was running into town to do a little shopping and asked if I wanted to come along.

" 'No, I'm too busy today. Too much studying to do yet,' I said.

" 'Don't you want to pick up some candy or flowers or anything?' she asked.

" 'I'm sorry, honey. I just don't have time today,' I said as she reluctantly retreated out the door.

"When she returned from town sometime later, she looked me in the eye and said, 'For the five years we've been married you've always remembered Valentine's Day. Tell me,' she smiled accusingly, 'you already have something, don't you?'

" 'Yes, honey,' I said, 'I remembered Valentine's Day.'

"On Valentine's morning I confessed what I'd done. I told my wife, 'I bought a whole package of cheap Valentines, wrote little messages on them, and hid them around the house. You'll be finding my little love notes for weeks.'

"At that point in the sermon," the student reported to the class, "my very staid congregation burst into spontaneous applause, the first time that ever happened in the church as far as I know. And then

I drove home the point I wanted to make that even before we see how, God's love has made careful and loving provision for us.

"After seeing how induction drew my people into the sermon, I'm impressed with the inductive approach. My wife is sold on it too."

An analogy such as my student used could be just a means of making a single point in a sermon, or analogy could be the fifth of eight basic inductive arrangements and form the structure of an entire sermon.

5. *Analogy*. We can, by examining Scripture, find that God makes use of four kinds of analogy: *relational* (father-child, bride-groom, shepherd-sheep); *comparative* (dogs, swine, wolves, treasure); *spatial* (highest, deepest); and *functional* (fruit, walls, body, head, door, roots, salt, light).

But how could analogy be used in the structure of an entire sermon?

One answer could be seen in the example of an expository sermon based on Psalm 1—a sermon that expands Scripture's analogy of the righteous life being like a tree. You could begin the sermon quickly with the question in your mind (or spoken to the congregation if you wish): What is a Christian life really like? This could set the common ground for the sermon.

You might relate an anecdote about some strong Christian who got away from his regular supportive fellowship and saw his spiritual life take a downward turn. At the close of the illustration you could make the tentative conclusion that the Christian life requires nourishment.

You could proceed with a series of additional illustrations (anecdotes, quotes, facts, Bible examples, Scriptures or whatever) to lead to additional tentative conclusions. The Christian life is like a tree in that: growth should be continuous; as a tree gives out oxygen, the Christian life should also result in a giving process; it becomes more and more stable as it grows; it receives constantly; it provides shelter and comfort to those around it; it reproduces. The possible tentative conclusions are many. But each needs to be illustrated before it is stated if the sermon is going to maintain its inductive movement.

After a number of tentative conclusions have been made, the sermon can conclude by drawing all the tentative conclusions together and answering the question: What is the Christian life like? The Christian life is like a tree. And the comparisons can be reemphasized to close.

This same kind of inductive movement could be used for many of the basic analogies God uses throughout Scripture. How is God like light? What does it mean for us to be Christ's body? How are Christians like salt? In what ways is God like a shepherd or a father? The list could go on and on. Diagrammed, they could all look something like this:

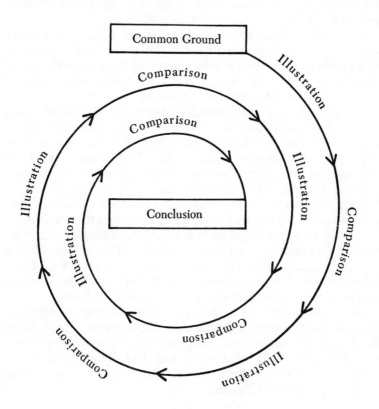

Analogy Sermon

As noted in the discussion of analogy in Chapter Three, there are dangers in stretching analogies too far. Remember Luther's judgment that "Origen's allegories are not worth so much dirt." For that reason, when analogies are used as the primary message of the sermon we might be safest to confine ourselves to the analogies God uses in Scripture. There are more than enough to choose from.

But there's another way to use analogy as the basic structure of a sermon without making that analogy the primary message—only using it to get across the message. For example, sermons on "The Seven Keys to the Kingdom," "The Four-Sided Foundation of our Faith," and the like use analogy to make their message more concrete. Such sermons could be very inductive if they utilize inductive ingredients and delay assertions until after their illustrative material.

6. *Causal relation.* Any sermon that examines or searches for a cause or an effect could be adapted to an inductive structure. And in our pragmatic, questioning day the cause and effect approach holds real potential for involving our congregations.

There are two basic approaches to a sermon using causal relation. One begins on common ground with the apparent effect and asks, *What is the cause or what are the causes that bring about this effect?* The entire sermon becomes a quest for reasons which are not asserted until the conclusion of the sermon.

For example, you could preach a strong inductive sermon using causal relation as a funeral message for an exemplary Christian in your church. You could begin with an illustration or a summary of the man's admirable Christian character (the effect). Then you could set the stage for the quest of causes by implying or actually asking a question such as, "How do we explain how _____ _____ became the man we knew, respected and loved?" You could then examine some of the potential ingredients or causes that made up the man's life. One way might be to illustrate the different fruits of the Spirit he exemplified and then conclude with the assertion that _____ _____'s kind of Christian maturity resulted from a careful cultivation of those fruits of the Spirit. Such a sermon could be a challenge to Christian maturity for everyone at the funeral.

Or instead of using the fruits of the Spirit, you might illustrate the man's commitment to family; his profession; other people; to his Lord; and then conclude with the proposition that a significant Christian life results from a balanced life including all those areas.

Such an inductive funeral sermon with its use of causal relation could be diagrammed like this:

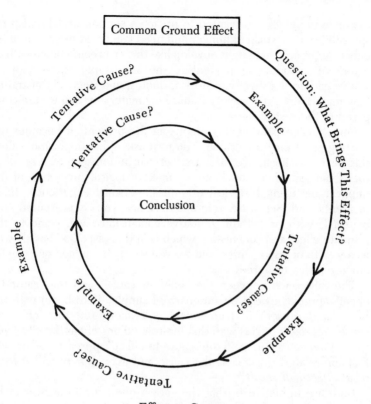

Effect-to-Cause
Sermon

For this kind of sermon to be truly inductive, a true quest, the introduction of the tentative causes should be more illustrative than declared. That's the reason for the question marks after the "causes" in the diagram. You may want to make tentative or partial conclusions after examining each potential cause, but any dogmatic assertion about the ultimate cause should be deferred until the conclusion. The quest for the cause should continue until near the end.

For further understanding of this "effect-to-cause" approach to causal relation, it should be made clear that the effect you start with doesn't have to be a person's life. It could be a concept such as "the mature Christian life" presented in a life-related manner. Then you could proceed with a question and a quest for the causes, much as you would with the funeral sermon example.

The second basic causal relation approach in a sermon would start with the causes and ask, *What would the effect be?* This approach lends itself best to sermons that are predictive or prophetic in nature.

For example, if you wanted to preach a sermon on Christian responsibility in a world of hunger and need you could use a "cause-to-effect" approach that might develop like this. You could begin with an extensive introduction presenting the *status quo*. Let's suppose you've gathered a variety of stories, quotes, and facts, all illustrating how materialistic our society is and how materially rich we are compared to the rest of the world.

Once you've painted this picture of the present, it becomes the starting point for this sermon. You next ask, What implications does this have for the future? What effect can be foreseen as a result of these causes? Then you begin to make a logical projection of the implications using historical examples, personal experience, Bible incidents and Scripture references. Once you've presented that material, with or without tentative conclusions, you come to the ultimate effect and conclusion, which is in this case: God has allowed us a wealth of opportunity, and we will surely be judged one day for our use of his resources.

The difference between the "effect-to-cause" and the "cause-to-effect" approaches can be summarized simply. Both begin with the life-related present in true inductive fashion. But the "effect-to-cause" approach begins with that life-related present as the effect and asks, *What caused it?* And the "cause-to-effect" approach begins with that life-related present as the cause and asks, *Where will it lead, what effect will result?*

Both are inductive in that they are a quest for an answer to be reached at the end of the sermon. And both are effective whirlpool structures for involving listeners in a mutual quest with the preacher.

7. *Problem-solution* or *Question and Answer*. These two names both fit one basic type of inductive sermon structure. So they really belong in the same category.

John Dewey's problem-solving became a popular format during the 1940s and 1950s. But its weakness lay in the fact that unlike true induction, it didn't necessarily lead to a firm conclusion. Often this type of sermon only pointed toward probability. The result was a rash of weak-kneed sermons that never really said much of anything. That's not what is being proposed here.

To get the feel for the problem-solution type of induction, suppose you wanted to preach a sermon tackling the problem of human suffering. You might start with a life-related example close to your congregation—say a fatal accident in your community. Such an illustration could pose the problem/question: Why does God allow suffering? You then use additional illustrative material (anecdotes, quotes, scriptural incidents and/or verses, etc.) to lead to some tentative, partial or previously attempted solutions/answers. You might want to build the heart of the sermon around the Book of Job, using contemporary examples and comparisons to parallel the answers Job's friends tried to give him. Not until you've finished presenting the evidence do you reach the final conclusion. Due to the subject matter in this example you won't be able to reach any simple solution/answer to the problem/question; but in the conclusion you can emphasize the response God gave Job.

Such a problem-solution or question-answer sermon could fit our basic inductive, whirlpool movement diagram something like this:

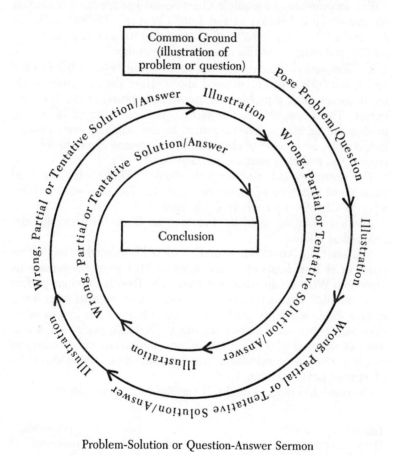

Problem-Solution or Question-Answer Sermon

Any sermon seeking to answer a single question or solve a single problem could easily fit into this kind of inductive structure. Does God answer prayer? The problem of evil. How do we align God's sovereignty and human choice? Such sermons very naturally begin where people are, at "common ground," and beg for inductive treatment; the quest for understanding automatically takes on an inductive, seeking feel if in the sermon the preacher can keep his answers in check until the people also reach them by way of his illustrative material.

As in earlier types of inductive movement, there are variations on the single-question, single-problem approach. You could preach a very inductive sermon using a combination of problems or questions, each leading to its own conclusion.

For an example of a mutiple question-answer approach (a sermon on the seventh petition of the Lord's prayer, "Deliver us"), see Appendix 1. There you will find a complete sermon text as well as an outline and diagram of this sermon by the author.

8. *Elimination.* This type of induction is somewhat related to the problem-solution idea mentioned above. Here the inductive movement comes after a problem or question is posed at the sermon's outset. The remainder of the sermon is a checking off of wrong, inadequate or incomplete responses to the original issue. Finally, inductively, by process of elimination, the sermon comes to the conclusion the preacher wants to get across.

The sermon which makes up the Book of Ecclesiastes is a good example of this type of inductive structure. You may want to refer again to Chapter Five where Ecclesiastes is outlined.

Another example could be a sermon on Christian perfection developed as follows:

You start on "common ground" with a life-related example that poses or at least leads up to the question that gives the sermon its direction: What is Christian perfection? Or, How is Christian perfection possible? Then using additional illustrative material (anecdotes, quotes, Bible incidents, Bible references, etc.) you one by one introduce and check off a number of things Christian perfection is not. After eliminating all or at least the most common misconceptions, you finally reach your conclusion(s) which in inductive fashion should be illustrated before stating.

Outlined and diagrammed this sermon might look like this:

Life-related example
Question or problem:
  What is Christian perfection?
    Not angelic perfection
    Not Adamic perfection
    Not perfect body
    Not perfect knowledge

Not perfect performance
Not perfect judgment
Not perfect relations
But:
  example—perfect love
  example—perfect motives
  example—perfect attitudes

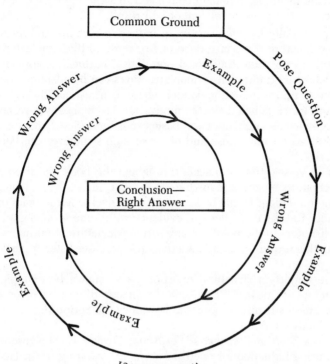

Elimination Sermon

The preceding discussions of eight basic types of induction illustrated how each type could be used through the structure of an entire sermon. But the possibilities for variety in inductive sermon structure certainly are not limited to the outlines and diagrams offered here; these eight basic types of inductive movement can be adjusted and adapted an infinite number of ways.

Different types of induction could be used even within the same sermon to provide inductive movement to different parts of the sermon.

Another variable could be the degree of induction used. A sermon could use (1) an inductive introduction; (2) an inductive study of the Bible; (3) an inductive arrangement of one or more parts of the sermon; (4) an inductive argument from particulars to generalization, or (5) a combination of 1-4 in what would be a totally inductive sermon. While any use of induction would improve the chances of involving listeners, I remain convinced that the more extensive the induction, the more involvement will result.

A potentially broader variety of inductive sermon structures becomes apparent if we introduce one or more of these eight types of induction into some traditional homiletical outlines or approaches. The following traditional sermon structures can be adapted easily or altered to utilize induction: ladder, chase, contrast, antithesis, cable, mousetrap, Hegelian dialectic, motivational sequence, yes-response, barbed-wire entanglement and basic expository. (See Appendix 4 for suggestions on how these and other sermon structures can become inductive.)

As we've said time and again throughout this book, the strength of induction, its means of involving the listener, in fact the real measure of true induction, is that it doesn't start by declaring the point of the sermon. But the examples and evidence within the sermon gradually lead listeners to the point. So any sermon structure or outline which meets this requirement is inductive and increases listener participation.

One important structural question we've shown by example but haven't really dealt with specifically in our discussion of possible arrangements is this: Where and how does the Scripture text fit into an inductive sermon?

In *The Biblical Preacher's Workshop,* Dwight E. Stevenson suggests using induction for doctrinal sermons exploring truth. He says the sermon should move inductively through the use of analogy and example to the climax of the sermon which should be the pronouncement of the text. He likens induction to a nominating speech which concludes by unveiling the text, standing center stage in all its glory with floodlights aglow. Such inductive movement toward the text can be "authentic, biblical preaching," he says.

Craddock disagrees with a description of inductive preaching as *leading to* the text. He feels the text can be incorporated earlier in an inductive sermon. And he argues that biblical narrative, biography and story in the sermon can be very inductive.

From what we've seen in this chapter and last, they could both be right. The placement and amount of biblical material could vary from one inductive sermon to another—depending on subject matter, audience and type of inductive structure used.

But whether the text is presented at the starting point of the sermon or the conclusion, the Bible can and needs to be the foundation of authority for the entire sermon every time we stand up to preach. This biblical role is so crucial, its authority so vital to anything we plan to preach that we'll examine this issue more extensively in the following chapter.

9 Unbeatable Combination

When I think of dogmatism in the pulpit I think of some incidents I've encountered. The first comes by way of a professor friend of mine who teaches in a seminary known throughout the world as a strong evangelical center of training.

During a class discussion about preaching, my professor friend noticed an increasing agitation in the movements and on the face of one restless student. At the end of the hour this young preacher, his features flushed, rushed to the professor's desk. "You're wrong!" he blurted out. "It's not that way at all. I've seen good preaching back home and I know how it is! You're all wrong! They told me I'd have to fight heresy here! And they were right!" With that explosion he stormed out of the classroom, leaving the open-mouthed professor aghast.

Within a month of that outburst, that student pastor split his little rural congregation and reported proudly to friends in the seminary hallways: "That's the third time I've had to stand up and be counted. After three church splits people ought to believe me when I say I'm no compromiser. They either straighten up and do what I say or I kick 'em out. This is no time for preachers to straddle the fence or stand in the middle of the road."

I cringe every time I think of that young preacher and the poor people in his congregations. I can easily imagine the kind of sermon that dogmatic young man preached.

I don't have to imagine anything about the next example. I clearly recall every word of the message—the shortest sermon I ever heard. The dean of a small, strict Bible school preached it with blazing intensity in one of the school's regular chapel services. This administrator walked to the pulpit when he was introduced. He stood for a

moment and sternly surveyed his student audience. Then he suddenly pounded on the pulpit and bellowed his six blazing words. "GOD
HATES THE SIN OF PETTING!" He paused dramatically, then
abruptly dismissed the assembly. The startled students twittered and
giggled their way out of the auditorium with an added layer of guilt
and an extra thirty minutes in their day.

It's not surprising that the dogmatic attitude of the hard-nosed
seminary student or the dogmatic approach of the tough-talking
dean cost these preachers any hope for maximum effectiveness.
These men, after all, represent extremes.

And yet I wonder. Is there more of their style of dogmatism in most
of us, in most of our preaching than we're willing to admit? How
many millions inside (or outside) our sanctuaries every Sunday morning fail to respond to the gospel primarily because they aren't ready to
accept our opening declarations: "This is the way it is," or even "This
is what God says!"

I think of some people I've known.

Heading to a Little League baseball game, I stopped and offered a
ride to an old man with flowing white hair, a full beard, bare feet and
wearing bib overalls. As he slid into the seat, he carefully maneu-
vered a large walking stick in beside him. "Helps me handle unruly
boys and ugly dogs," he explained. He told me he was on his way to
the next town for a horse show, but my ballfield destination suited
him fine. He'd be that much farther down the road.

As we talked, I listened for a natural point to witness to my passen-
ger. When I found it, I began to share. But as soon as the old man
realized the direction of my words, he interrupted me with a stream
of profanity. The explosion was only indirectly aimed at me. His
primary target was Christian broadcasting and one Christian broad-
caster in particular whom he vehemently vilified. This old man said
he didn't believe in all that blankety-blank talk about a person's need
to be changed. Then he added proudly, "I belong to First Church in
_____ (He named a town not far away). And we don't have to put
up with that kind of nonsense there."

I contrast the memory of that old man with another man I knew
years ago. John was so conscious of moral implications he refused to
drink pop out of a bottle or can for fear some youngsters would see
him and think he was drinking beer. I never heard him utter a word
of slang—never a "gee," "golly" or "gosh." He regularly spent his
spare time waiting on shut-ins around town. He was a respected
businessman, known and loved by the entire community for his concern and service to others.

For twenty-five years this devoted family man, father of nine,
attended church regularly. Yet time after time I watched as he en-

dured evangelistic invitations and altar calls. His chin would tremble, his knuckles would turn white as he gripped his hymnal or the back of the pew in front of him. He continually refused to make his own decision to accept Christ.

It wasn't until he lay on a hospital bed, eaten away by cancer, that he finally surrendered his life to God. I went to visit him as he was dying. He looked up through his tears to lament, "If I'd only known years ago how much better it is to be on the inside looking out than on the outside looking in."

I once stood in a yard and talked with another man, a fifty-year-old father who told me he finally had enough money from his machine shop and some real estate to retire in a warm climate. For years he'd worked ten- to twelve-hour days, six or seven days a week with one goal in mind—early retirement. He'd had no time for church and little for his family. His materialistic dreams had engrossed him. As we stood and talked about spiritual questions, he said sadly, "Do you think I want to die and go to Hell? I want to go to Heaven as badly as anyone you ever met, but I tell you the truth when I say I've never met anyone whose life has been turned around by any dramatic new birth."

In the years since that man's retirement and sudden death in the South, I've thought often about how to reach such people—those who are so deluded by materialism they don't feel God can do anything for them. I've thought of my moral friend and wondered, How can we reach those who think they're good enough on their own? Or those who sit in our congregations every Sunday and still fail to respond? I think, too, of the old hitchhiker and ask myself, How can we reach those who have become embittered against the gospel by years of experience and prejudice?

Clearly it is not enough to bolster our messages merely by increasing the frequency or the volume of our "Thus saith the Lords." Dogmatism nearly always fails with such people.

Peter Berger in *The Precarious Vision* (Garden City, N.Y.: Doubleday, 1961, p. 184), has gone so far as to say, "a claim to religious authority, carried into a dialogue, however polite, is a club held under the table. A claim to authority always projects the point at which coercion will replace communication."

I certainly don't want to imply that we should preach without any real authority. It is absolutely essential that what we preach be firmly grounded in the authority of God's Word (as we'll see as this chapter unfolds). But we must recognize Berger's point. There are multitudes of people in our age who react against our most reasoned and reasonable appeals to tradition, institution and even God's revelation as ominous, authoritarian threats.

Then how can we preach the strong message of gospel truth without having them feel we're flicking the whip of authority from our pulpits? How can we break through the barriers of contentment, resistance and hostility to help listeners realize their need to change or to grow? How do we get them from "common ground" to the Good News?

Perhaps the beginning of an answer is found in another pastoral experience I had calling on a couple with grown children. In the course of our conversation the wife expressed the unhappiness and emptiness they both felt about their middle-aged lives by saying, "It would be hell to go on living like this."

The husband was scheduled for surgery a couple of days later, and I visited him in the hospital every day for a week. We continued to talk about his unhappiness, and I shared the gospel with him. The last day before he was released I finally said to him, "You know, you could go home tomorrow as a Christian."

He paused a minute and nodded. "Yeah, Reverend," he said, "but you gotta wanta!"

He went home the next day without making that decision. A few years later I heard he'd died in an automobile accident in California. I'm not sure he ever did accept Christ.

But his words "you gotta wanta" have helped me crystallize a lesson I've learned from years of experience with many other people who have refused or been reluctant to accept the gospel message. The lesson is this: We never *convince* others with our preaching; we can only help them to convince themselves. An old saying expresses a similar idea: "A man convinced against his will, is of the same opinion still."

Before I go any further I ought to make clear I'm not trying to exclude the Holy Spirit from playing his role in any decision process. But he won't circumvent human will either; that's a limit God placed on himself from the beginning. In order to make the lesson more theologically complete, however, perhaps we should restate it this way: We never convince others with our preaching; we can only help the Holy Spirit help them to convince themselves.

The best way I know to do that is to involve our listeners in the thinking and deciding part of the preaching process. For many that requires an inductive approach.

Despite the disturbing failure of the church and our preaching to reach millions of lost and needy people, despite sagging church attendance, and despite the undeniable epidemic of listlessness, daydreaming and boredom plaguing the pews of countless churches, most preachers have been slow to embrace inductive preaching as a viable strategy for communicating the gospel.

Part of their reluctance no doubt arises from a lack of understanding of what inductive preaching is, how it works and what it can accomplish. That's why we've gone to such lengths thus far in this book to lay the footings and the foundation for the inductive structure in preaching. A basic understanding needs to be built.

However, I'm sure some have gotten this far who are understanding the concept of inductive preaching in a new way, but who are still hesitant to embrace inductive preaching as a valid, basic approach to the preaching ministry.

I've had some students and colleagues raise a number of concerns over the years. So I'd like to face the most common concerns here.

"Isn't induction a little dishonest? Aren't you manipulating your audience when you don't say where you're going at the outset?"

"Doesn't induction's emphasis on a common-sense approach to communication neglect the intellect and the intellectual?"

The next three concerns are often closely related in a questioner's mind.

"Induction just doesn't sound forceful enough to me. It sounds as if it coddles and tolerates listeners in their sins. God calls preachers to be strong and forceful. People today need a healthy dose of solid biblical doctrine. We can't afford to be weak-kneed compromisers."

"With such a heavy emphasis on contemporary and life-related material, don't you run the danger of basing your authority on human experience rather than the Word of God?"

"Induction just doesn't seem to be scriptural enough. Certainly we have to relate our sermons to the real lives of people, but not at the expense of a balanced exposition of Scripture."

Basically this chapter is my response to such concerns. And I'm sure after reading the preceding seven chapters many readers will anticipate some of that response. However, most of what is said in the rest of this chapter may come as a bit of a surprise since it may seem to be a drastic turnabout.

First, a reaction based on a very quick review of where we've already been:

"Isn't induction manipulative? Doesn't it neglect the intellect?" To those two concerns I'd say this: One of the chief characteristics of inductive preaching is the attitude of honesty and transparency. It explores rather than exploits. Rather than being pushy, it allows interaction and involves the listener's intellect at every step. It doesn't ask listeners to buy assumptions for themselves without first displaying the evidence. As far as it being deceptive, we don't consider Jesus' parables deceptive just because his listeners didn't realize where he was taking them until he reached the end of the stories.

"Induction isn't forceful enough!" To that complaint I'd respond with a number of points made earlier. First, there is simply no evidence to show that force ever really convinces anyone of anything—unless you're talking about brainwashing. Induction can and should lead to strong principles, assertion and doctrine; it just doesn't start with them. It leads to the discovery of truth rather than declaring propaganda. The inductive approach respects listeners as individuals and in so doing earns the rapport and credibility for making a strong stand a little later. There need not be any compromise in waiting to make a point until the greatest number of people are willing and ready to accept it. Of course, there is a danger in an inductive sermon that the preacher may never come to any strong conclusions or may not clearly communicate any basic doctrinal message. But that's a problem with the preacher, not the inductive process. The deductive approach doesn't preclude the possibility of pointless preaching either—as millions could testify every week.

"But induction just isn't scriptural enough. It's based more on human experience than on the Word of God." In response to this I reintroduce a number of points summarized from earlier chapters.

With the evidence presented in Chapters Five and Six, induction seems to be much closer to the communication model presented by the Bible as a whole and the preachers within it, than does most of the deductive preaching practiced for centuries. Jesus' approach was undeniably inductive and incompatible with our usual traditional homiletical teaching and structure. If there's a question about the amount of Scripture content or expositional opportunity within inductive preaching, Chapter Seven's outlines of the various inductive sermon structures should have shown ample opportunity for as much reference to and exposition of Scripture as time and intent of a sermon allow.

Concerning the "authority" question, I'd like to make a few additional comments. While I would never want to equate contemporary human experience with Scripture itself as the source of authority for our sermons, the Bible which God inspired and ordained as his own Word is a record of humans' experience with God. Accounts of human experience can and must do in our sermons what they do in the Bible—that is, introduce, illustrate, prepare for and lead to God's ultimate truth and authority. The preacher by attitude as well as emphasis can and should always make it clear it's God's truth that the sermon is about; it's God's Word that is tested by and applied to human experience. Experience is the medium—not the authority of theology.

Again, this is the role of the preacher, whether choosing to preach deductively or inductively.

While I've tried to discount the above criticisms by retracing the path we've followed thus far, while I think most of these concerns could often be raised about traditional deductive preaching, and while I'm convinced these dangers can be avoided, I will concede that inductive preaching may present unique dangers in the areas criticized.

So here's where we're going to proceed on a path that may at first seem to contradict everything we've done, said and seen so far in this book.

We've contrasted induction and deduction with charts like this showing their potential differing characteristics:

Contrast Chart

INDUCTIVE	DEDUCTIVE
Accumulative	Assertive
Achieves authority	Assumes authority
Asks questions	Asserts answers
Assembles facts	Asserts concepts as facts
Builds on facts to find causes	Binds facts into categories
Constructive	Constrictive
Creative	Cognitive
Defers assertions	Declares answers
Diagnoses reasons	Defends reason
Discovers causes	Declares conclusions
Expanding	Contracting
Explores, exposes	Explains, exhorts
Flexible, elastic	Firm, set
Intuitive	Intellectual
Invites participation	Imposes principles
Involves listeners in question	Imparts answers
Open	Closed
Prophetic	Priestly
Practical	Prescriptive
Progressive	Protective
Reasonable	Reasoning
Relates	Restricts
Relational accent	Rational accent
Seeks causes, concepts, conclusions	States effects, conclusions
Seeks reasons, evidence, principles	States results, proof

In an attempt to explain and build a case for the less familiar method of induction, we've offered an admittedly lopsided view. We've proceeded as if everything about deduction was dangerously wrong. Yet it's not. In fact, any one of the deductive characteristics in the above contrast chart could be a very positive factor in preaching—given the right situation and the proper preparation.

Let me further add that for years I have urged young ministers to combine inductive and deductive strengths in their sermons. I've said, "No evangelical can be content to preach only inductively. The gospel preacher holds truth in such high esteem he must declare God's message deductively after he's explored inductively."

Too many preachers are like poor hunting dogs; they sniff out a trace of truth but stop short of treeing their quarry. The question mark is not the last word of inductive process. Induction leads to conclusions and beyond!

By trial and error in our daily lives we employ inductive process to find workable solutions, then we implement our results in tomorrow's living. Today we discover. Tomorrow we incorporate, apply, amplify and advocate. In electronics, space, biology, computers and other areas, we first discover, then we declare. Induction leads quite naturally to deduction.

Our preaching must include declaring, proclaiming, urging, sharing! Truly effective inductive preaching goes from quest to discovery and then presses on to advocate, to urge. The completed sequence is sensibly, scientifically and scripturally sound.

As we've already seen, the Bible generally presents the concrete before the abstract, the data before the rule. But decrees and dogma can be easily found—following inductive questions, experiences, examples and cases.

Contrary to common opinion, Paul in his epistles involves the people inductively. He refers to experience, he witnesses, he asks questions, explores, cites examples, uses biography, analogies, parables, comparisons and contrasts. For example, in the Galatian epistle he leads with eighteen questions; he narrates his own life; he allegorizes Abraham, the covenant and his two wives; he compares with similes and metaphors as he leads to inductive conclusions about Christ, freedom and the gospel.

Even when he writes to the "saints" in Ephesus Paul refers strongly to experience: "you," "I," "we," "he," and "us"—remember! He resorts to analogy: aliens, strangers, walls, covenants, sojourners, citizens, cornerstone, foundation, temple, heirs, old man, new man, etc. Thirteen times he refers to the analogy of the body. Though he makes no use of inductive questions here, he does involve the people in his analogical induction.

Paul uses seventy-five questions in the early chapters of Romans to involve the people inductively. These queries spawn his answers. Exhortations seem smoothed into these answers. On the basis of the particulars in chapters 1-11 Paul now stands on the conclusion:

"Therefore, I appeal to you by these mercies of God to apply these principles in life."

Only four questions appear in his final five chapters of the Roman epistle. He has dialogued with questions until he gets the Romans involved in cooperative inductive conclusions; then without equivocation he declares his gospel assertions by applying the truth to daily life in a deductive, propositional manner. Only after eleven chapters of seeking to achieve authority does he assume the right to proclaim so deductively. He cites examples, particulars and human instances; he witnesses, he questions and answers questions. But he reserves his strongest exhortations and assertions until after he has firmly established authority in the earlier chapters.

Jesus' example is further evidence in favor of a balanced inductive/deductive approach to our preaching.

To the multitudes his message is like a "missionary theology" in a foreign land. Jesus doesn't dictate or demand at the outset, but uses induction and diplomacy to build goodwill, agreement, acceptance and accumulated authority. He doesn't assume authority at the start; rather he seeks to achieve acceptance first.

When he speaks to his committed followers he seems more authoritative. He assumes he already has agreement, authority and common ground.

These differences I had noted for years, but only recently have I seen a continued process here. Jesus begins his incarnate message at ground zero—where the people are. But his disciples have already come partway—they have agreed to the principles of faith growing out of his earlier sermons to the people. Taken together, his preaching and his teaching combine to complete a process moving from inductive particulars to principle and on to his pronouncement of practical deductive application—a continuing process from induction's discovery to deduction's declaration.

For years I charted three processes: (1) inductive, (2) deductive and (3) combined inductive-deductive. But I viewed the combination as a union of two very different processes, when in fact induction and deduction are two equally vital parts of one process—a process we could call full-orbed induction. And like Jesus' teaching of his followers, this process includes deductive declaration and application of the discovered principle disclosed by the earlier induction.

Let me try to clarify what I'm saying here with a little imagery. So far in this book we've viewed deduction as the visible part of a tree, starting with the trunk (the general truth) and branching out to smaller applications. We've presented induction like the root system of a tree, starting with tiny rootlets (specific examples and evidence) that gradually draw together into larger and larger roots and finally converge at the trunk (the general truth). Taken separately, the root structure and the branch structure of a tree seem to be opposites. One finds and accumulates sustenance, and the other spreads and dispenses it. But actually they are equally necessary halves of the same whole. The root system would be useless without the branches. The branch system couldn't survive without the roots.

So it is with induction and deduction in the overall sermon process. The two methods dovetail. The one complements and prepares for the other. Where induction ceases, deduction commences. Induction discovers new knowledge; deduction clarifies it. Induction accumulates the particular facts; deduction asserts the resultant general concepts.

To use a different analogy, Jesus' example seems to say to us that preaching, like a bridge, needs two pillars. Effective preaching serves as a cooperative venture between God and man, one pillar grounded in eternal truth, the other rooted in human experience.

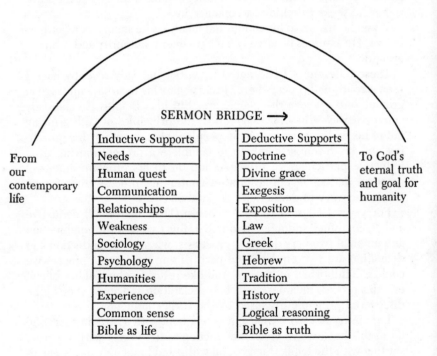

SERMON BRIDGE →

Inductive Supports	Deductive Supports
Needs	Doctrine
Human quest	Divine grace
Communication	Exegesis
Relationships	Exposition
Weakness	Law
Sociology	Greek
Psychology	Hebrew
Humanities	Tradition
Experience	History
Common sense	Logical reasoning
Bible as life	Bible as truth

From our contemporary life

To God's eternal truth and goal for humanity

The-Two-Pillars-for-Preaching Bridge

Jesus emphasizes what traditional Christianity has sometimes repeated only in muffled and muted tones. He reminds us of a truth we so easily forget: *both and* is most effective. *Either or* sometimes perhaps, but often *both and*.

Preaching needs both yesterday and today. The Bible stands as solid basis, and today's relationships keep the sermon vital, alive, relevant.

Preaching must present God and his eternal truth. But human need, experience and relevance constitute crucial factors of the sermon too. Without God's eternal truth and the tradition of history, the strong security is missing. Without the contemporary human dimension, what earthly good will there be? What interest? What significance?

Combined Steps
The full-orbed inductive sermon could be divided into these twelve steps. The first nine reflect the inductive concentration of this book thus far. But the last three steps, which are equally important, would usually require deductive development.

1. Accepting listeners with respect	
2. Aligning with listener needs	
3. Asking key questions	
4. Arousing attention	
5. Amassing representative instances	Basically Inductive
6. Ascertaining assumptions	
7. Assessing assertions	
8. Achieving authority	
9. Accepting conclusions	
10. Applying to personal life	
11. Advising from experience and revelation	Basically Deductive
12. Advocating, asserting, recommending	

When we begin to think in terms of a full-orbed inductive sermon, we see some new implications for the inductive whirlpool patterns in Chapters Seven and Eight.

What we're saying now is that those diagrams really only represent the first part of the combined inductive-deductive approach. The full-orbed approach would be better diagramed like this:

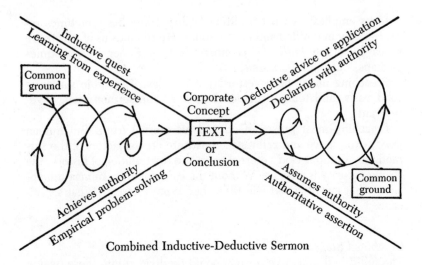

Combined Inductive-Deductive Sermon

Any one of the inductive structures in Chapters Seven and Eight could be inserted in the left side of this combined structure. And any traditional deductive outline could be inserted in the right side of this diagram.

You will note that a full-orbed sermon not only begins on "common ground," where the people are; it also ends on "common ground." Whether a sermon's final focus is invitation, application or challenge, the implications need to come back to the everyday life of the people. The message has to reach them and move them where they are.

The placement of the *text* at the midpoint does not imply that we ought to avoid Scripture until the sermon reaches that point. If you recall the various inductive structures diagramed in the preceding chapter, you will remember many possible ways to incorporate Bible content into an inductive flow. You could even introduce and use the *text* of the sermon earlier in the inductive side of the process. But any use of Scripture in the inductive flow of the sermon is primarily illustrative, evidence presented to reach the corporate conclusion at the midpoint. By that time, authority should be achieved and can then be assumed throughout the rest of the sermon. Once the people and preacher have reached the midpoint together, the *text* can be asserted with authority and the applications and declarations can develop deductively from there.

You might conclude from this combined structure diagram that the inductive portion of the sermon serves much the same function as an introduction does in a traditional homiletical structure. However, that's only partly true.

Induction introduces, but it aims to do much more than merely introduce, just as Jesus' parables do more than arouse interest. They foster involvement. They convey truth. They delay assertions. They engross. They involve. But they also instruct.

Jesus uses parables and human instances as process material. These help invade the consciousness, the thought patterns, the behavior and habits, the lives of listeners. For Jesus, the parables and other inductive ingredients become part of the designed communication process. So our sermons need process material to get the people "into" the sermon itself.

Some preachers have been satisfied with content material only. Truth may be all that matters for them. Not Jesus. Process and content both count for Jesus. He must *involve* the people and he must *inform* the people. He plans for *both* involvement *and* instruction to result from his preaching. If we want both results from our preaching, the full-orbed inductive approach offers the best combination.

The two sides of a combined inductive-deductive sermon can telescope to fit the needs and commitment of listeners. For instance, a sermon to youth needs more induction than does a study of faith directed toward the old saints. On the other hand, the old-timers will be glad for some examples before the deductive teaching. Some situations may call for a 50-50 division; but most occasions will demand that the amount of time and content alloted to each accent be adapted to fit the hearers.

Whatever the length of the two parts, the combined ingoing-outgoing whirlpool structure would always look like a horizontal hourglass—flowing inductively into the conclusion and then moving deductively to application and declaration:

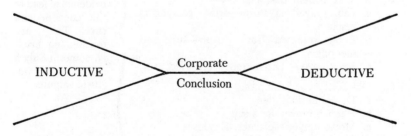

INDUCTIVE   Corporate Conclusion   DEDUCTIVE

But one valuable variation on the combined structure might be to use a multiple hourglass approach within the same sermon to discover and then apply a series of points. This could prove especially effective for imparting a heavy dose of deductive teaching by breaking the sermon into a well-paced series of smaller doses. Such a sermon could be charted like this:

There may be times when you think your audience would be so reluctant or unprepared to embrace your major premise or when you feel the implications of the inductively discovered truth are so clear you can stop the sermon at the midpoint and allow the Holy Spirit to take the listeners beyond that. But as a rule effective, full-orbed inductive preaching needs to incorporate deduction too.

When it does, all the concerns about induction raised at the start of this chapter can be easily erased. For it's in the deductive "half" of the full-orbed sermon the preacher can be forceful. It's here he can reemphasize the authority of God's Word as the basis of the message. It's here the preacher can best include exegesis and any verse-by-verse exposition.

Here is a sample sermon outline that could fit the basic combined structure diagrammed above:

Does It Pay to Pray?

A. Contemporary Examples:
  a. Specific recent answers to prayer in personal, family or local church life.
  b. Specific recent answers to prayer in national, denominational, world church.

B. New Testament Examples:
  a. Paul prayed in storm—crew, passengers rescued.
  b. Peter released from prison—surprised meeting.
  c. Jesus prayed—Lazarus raised, 5,000 fed, *et al.*

C. Old Testament Examples:
  a. Daniel in lions' den.
  b. Hannah prayed for a son.
  c. Moses prayed—plagues, Exodus.
  d. Abraham—on Mt. Moriah, in life.

CONCEPT: Life and the Bible can show us many examples—God answers prayer.

TEXT: "Pray without ceasing."
"Men ought always to pray and not faint."
"The effectual, fervent prayer of the righteous man avails much."

> All these inductive supports serve as evidence to lead to the concept and text. They are touched on briefly, some in only a sentence or two. (10-15 minutes)

I   Reasons for Praying

II Requirements for praying

III Results of praying

Conclusion: Application and Challenge to Pray

} Can include subpoints, more examples and any other ingredients common to typical deductive sermons. (10-15 minutes)

Any sermon, whatever the subject, whatever the intent—evangelistic, doctrinal or basic expository—can and must incorporate a combined approach if it's going to achieve maximum effectiveness and involvement. As Merrill F. Unger says in *Principles of Expository Preaching* (Grand Rapids: Zondervan, 1955):

"In dealing with Scripture, no premise ought ever to be used in deductive reasoning that cannot be sustained by sound induction. The question is not whether the inductive method should be cultivated less, but how . . . the deductive method can be employed to supplement [induction]."

Unger, like most preachers and almost all homiletics writers, stresses deduction much more than the inductive side of preaching. Yet he clearly recognizes the necessity of induction for balanced, effective preaching. Such a balance requires *both* inductive ingredients *and* the inductive process we've spelled out here in this book.

For D. L. Moody and many other great crowd-catchers, this combination structure became an effective preaching pattern. Moody consistently led his listeners to personal involvement by his anecdotes and narrative references to experience. Then when they were ready to accept his decrees, he proclaimed the deep unswerving beliefs of his fundamentalistic faith.

Many contemporary preachers have also found success with the combined approach.

Billy Graham often pounds his hand with Holy Writ as he shouts, "The Bible says . . ." But he repeatedly refers to human examples, life experience and narrative content.

Leighton Ford, Graham's brother-in-law, combines induction and proclamation with good insight. He has made significant study of preaching effectiveness and communication principles. For example, returning from our extended family's celebration of Thanksgiving we heard a broadcast of Ford's memorable sermon "Entitled or Entrusted?" He begins with strong, personal, inductive thrust: "She lives in New Orleans."

Jay Kesler, president of Youth For Christ and tremendously effective as a youth speaker, combines induction with proclamation as skillfully as any preacher on the horizon today. He holds thousands of teenagers spellbound as he shares with dramatic detail the experiences of youth he knows. After he's given his listeners life examples, he gives them the gospel—straight.

Louis Hadley Evans, Sr., long-time Presbyterian leader, incorporates much inductive content into his popular sermons. His format may be deductive or inductive.

Leslie Weatherhead, British Methodist spokesman, constructs genuinely inductive sermons. For example, his sermon "The Real Thing" begins with an "ebony" elephant table, speaks of jewelry from the "early Woolworth period," and after involvement with common experiences proceeds to Jesus, the gospel and our shared Christian faith.

Donald Soper, British street-preacher, understands the need for interest and involvement more than most. The demands of the street have spawned inductive insights and usage.

Increasingly, Catholic preachers identify with experience in their more inductive approach to sermonizing.

Clement Welch and others at the Episcopal College of Preachers in Washington, D. C., have sponsored seminars on inductive preaching to spur preachers toward involving their listeners via induction.

Many effective Baptist preachers have abandoned dull, deductively doctrinal sermons in favor of an inductive accent on experience until they have won their listeners' involvement. Then they proclaim. Then they declare. Then they assert. Then they "preach."[1]

The most effective preachers in nearly every generation have stumbled onto this unbeatable combination. Appendix 3 cites many other examples of successful preachers throughout Christian history who united induction with their deductive declaration of the gospel.

Just as full-orbed induction, the combined inductive-deductive sermon process, answers the questions about induction posed at the start of this chapter, so it also corrects the concerns this book has raised about deduction. The following chart illustrates:

---

[1]Dr. Glen Stassen, professor at Southern Baptist Seminary in Louisville, tells how the Methodists saved the Baptists. He says in the days of George Whitefield the Baptist preaching was deductive, dry, dull and doctrinal. The number of converts and members declined. Wesley's revival preaching spurred Baptist preachers to accent experience in their sermons, and the doom of the declining Baptists was averted by preaching on both experience and doctrine.

Deductive Preaching Process Corrected

Objections to Deduction Alone:	*Solutions Offered by Combining with Induction:*

1. Begins with speaker's:
  a. generalizations
  b. assertions
 	
  c. conclusions (propositions).
	1. a. Begins with particulars leading to conclusions.
	   b. Seeks cooperative conclusions, corporate concepts.
	   c. Delays assertions until agreement is achieved.

2. Begins where speaker is—not always where hearer is.	2. Begins where hearer is—not just where speaker is.
3. Tends by its nature to be subjective and prejudiced.	3. Lets facts, particulars and life itself speak.
4. Sometimes gives unwarranted, unwanted advice before establishing any common ground.	4. Saves advice, exhortation and proclamation until hearer has reached by induction the cooperative concepts leading to mutual conclusions.
5. Authoritarian.	5. Achieves authority. Doesn't assume authority early.
6. Assumes an adversary posture either defensively or aggressively.	6. Proceeds from nonadversary stance. Shares experience. Shares the process.
7. Accents rational exercise rather than relational experience.	7. Accents relational experience—not rational exercise alone.
8. Tends to be irrelevant, remote or impersonal.	8. Relates to life and experience. Shares human instances.
9. May show no respect for hearers or their opinions.	9. Respects hearers and their opinions.
10. Subject-centered instead of person-centered.	10. Accents hearers' needs and brings the sermon to serve hearers' best interests.
11. Tends to keep a set format, structure, content.	11. Adjusts representative instances, varied experiences and selected content to meet listeners' needs.

Preachers today are torn apart, not by horses pulling in two directions, but by conflicting forces within the role of ministry. They have a demanding message to share with a people who resist external demands on their time and their lives. They have a message of moral absolutes to preach to people who believe everyone has the right to do his own thing as long as it doesn't infringe on the rights of someone else. They have a message of eternal truth to preach to people who are consumed by temporal matters. In short, the concerns and demands of our hearers are often in direct conflict with a preacher's own personal sense of call, mission and urgency.

How do we move our people from where they are to where God wants them to be? How can we involve them in our sermons and in Christian growth?

The full-orbed inductive process seems a promising answer.

This format offers a way to combine quest and conquest in our sermons—both search and salvation. It can enable us to respect our hearers and our Heavenly Father, too. It promises to unite our compassion and our confidence in the same sermon. It starts where the people are, but it leads to God's truth.

The World Book says in its entry under "Inductive Method": "By combining induction and deduction science unifies theory and practice." Isn't that the goal of every preacher, every sermon? When, and only when, we can unify the "theory" of God's eternal truth with the "practice" of our people's daily lives, we fulfill our high calling as preachers. And when that happens we can know for certain our listeners will be involved.

10 In the Study

I still vividly recall attending a large ministerial gathering as a young
student pastor. During a break between sessions I took a trip to a
crowded men's room where I happened to overhear a conversation
between a nationally known preacher and another man. The noted
preacher was boasting about selling all his books because he had
enough sermons to last him the rest of his ministry (he was in his
forties at the time).

A bit disillusioned by the revelation, but possessed with the ideal-
ism and brassiness of youth, I couldn't help reacting. As I finished
drying my hands I looked up and said, just loud enough for everyone
in the restroom to hear, "It sounds to me like someone's already dead
at the top." Then I turned and walked out.

Nearly forty years have passed, so I hope I've mellowed a bit. But
many of the attitudes I've seen and heard expressed about sermon
preparation since that time still disturb me.

I knew a young pastor early in my ministry who told me he stayed
up all night every Saturday night. Sometimes he'd sleep on the couch
for an hour about dawn. He lamented his habit of last-night preparation. He confessed it was a plague on his family life. "But I just have
to have that pressure. I can't get my sermons prepared any other
way."

Recently, after a preaching workshop, a pastor came up to me and
shared his continuous struggle to find time for sermon preparation.
He'd just moved to a new parish with a broad variety of outreach and
community programs he was expected to supervise. The administra-
tive tasks kept him so busy he just couldn't prepare his sermons as he
felt he should. When he expressed his frustration to a couple of
ministerial colleagues in his denomination, they shrugged him off.

One of them actually told him, "Preparing isn't any problem. Just turn off your TV at 10 on Saturday night and spend the hour before you go to bed outlining your sermon. That's what I do."

Unfortunately that kind of attitude is far too prevalent. In fact, one large evangelical publisher put out a book a few years ago with the rather clever title, *Saturday Night Specials*. The book was a compilation of more than 200 sermon ideas on a broad variety of texts and topics—outlines that could supposedly be fleshed out into effective sermons the night before they were to be preached.

And then there was the pastor of a big city church, a preacher known throughout his mainline denomination as a reformer, a prophetic voice to the church and a rabid evangelical. Driving to church with his wife on Sunday mornings he would often say, "I think I'll preach on forgiveness (or grace, sin, regeneration or whatever) this morning, dear. Could you find me a text?" His wife would thumb through the Scriptures there in the car and he'd have his text by the time they pulled into the church parking lot.

Preparation. How crucial is it to our preaching?

One recent survey revealed that those pastors who spend twenty hours or more on their Sunday sermons preach to hundreds more every week than those who spend five hours or less in preparation. You could argue about which is cause and which is effect, but the correlation between study time and congregation size ought to say something to all of us.

One famous preacher gained skill in the pulpit by spending an hour of preparation for every hundred words he wrote in his sermon. Another who worked sixty hours on each sermon preached for fifty-two years in one thriving church. Yet, too much preparation time creates other problems within the preacher's family as well as with the congregation. Jonathan Edwards so often cloistered himself in his study his people complained about never seeing him. Despite his effective preaching, he was asked to leave Northampton Church after nearly a quarter-century of ministry—only twenty-three of the more than two hundred male members voted to retain him.

Two centuries have passed since then. But the conflict remains. Effective preaching requires extensive preparation. But other demands—family, personal and pastoral—eat away at our study time.

The conflict is often reflected when a layman says, "Our minister is a fine pastor, but he's not much of a preacher." Or the other side of the coin, "His sermons are great every Sunday; we just wish he was more available during the week." Many times I've heard people analyze their ministers in two parts—as a pastor and as a preacher. Just as often I've talked to ministers who try to cope with what seems like impossible expectations of their people by deciding to concentrate their energies on one half of the job or the other. They say, "I see my role as a preacher, so I leave the pastoral work to others on my staff." Or, "I'm a pastor first of all. I find that when I do that well, the people don't need or expect as much in my preaching."

Specialization is one of the biggest trends of our age. And in churches with a multiple staff it may sometimes be the answer to the preaching/pastoring time problem. But what happens when you feel forced to make a choice? Which is more important? My experience and 2,000 years of church history tell me a congregation needs both.

So how do we balance the demands of the pulpit and the parish? In our rocket-paced world with people-problems so complicated and tragic we despair over our own inadequacy to help. How do we find the time and energy to pastor *and* preach to our people?

I suspect this is a conflict we'll never escape. There are no easy answers.

But we could perhaps relieve a little of the pressure if we'd attempt to alter our attitudes toward the two halves of our job as ministers. What if we looked at our pastoral duties not as an interference with our sermon preparation time but as an essential part of that preparation?

Why are so many pastors able to help people in crisis all week and seem so helpless in the pulpit? How can they be so resourceful and alive Monday through Saturday and be so dead on Sunday mornings?

Part of the problem is this artificial dichotomy we've created in our jobs between our pastoral and preaching duties. What if we could make every pastoral duty—every counseling session, every pastoral call, every hospital visit, every parishioner contact—an integral part of our sermon preparation?

We can do it. In fact, if we want to preach inductively and involve people in our preaching we have to do it.

We've said earlier in this book that one of the basics of the inductive approach is to start the sermon where the people are. But how do we know where that is?

Craddock mentions one key to staying in tune with life when he says: "The battle can be waged with some success simply by staying alive. This means that the preacher does not allow himself to become only a dealer in those commodities that allow others to live; he himself lives. He does not just announce the hymns, he sings; he does not just lead in prayer, he prays. If the imagery of his sermons is to be real, he must see life as real—not as an illustration under Point Two."

In addition to utilizing and referring to our own life and our own experiences in preparing and preaching to our people, an equally necessary means of keeping in tune with real life is to learn from and use the life experience of the people we serve. Pastoral contact can be the mother lode from which we mine invaluable resources for involving our people in our sermons.

But how do we get from the raw material of life experience to the finished product of a full-orbed inductive sermon? This is the question we'll try to answer as the remainder of this chapter details the progressive stages of inductive sermon preparation.

Before we start, I want to acknowledge that most of what is said about preparation here centers on the first side, the inductive portion, of the combined sermon structure presented in Chapter Eight. Preparation of the deductive phase of a sermon—the biblical exposition, exegesis and hermeneutics—has been analyzed and amplified in a thousand books on preaching. So the necessary focus here is on the preparation of the inductive process which will get the people involved in the sermon prior to the deductive portion of the full-orbed endeavor.

Exposure—Stage One of Inductive Sermon Preparation
Contact with people will not only present us with raw material for illustrating and spicing up our sermons, but our pastoral interaction with the daily life experience of our people will often help reveal the problems we need to be preaching about. It's the emotions we see our people battling, the crises we try to help them through that should be the starting point for getting our listeners involved in our messages on Sunday morning.

Every contact, every member of our congregation offers a potential contribution to our preaching. Certainly we know some members of our churches who don't have a care in the world, but those are the ones we don't know very well, aren't they? When we really get to know people we discover they all have some hurt, some need, some problem.

Our pastoral duties take on a totally new dimension when we view them as the means of getting to the needs of our people, as research for upcoming sermons. They then become not obstacles to our preaching task but opportunities to learn and prepare for our sermons.

Let's consider an imaginary week of pastoral contacts. (We'll build on these examples throughout this chapter as we discuss the various steps of inductive sermon preparation.)

Early in the week I call on an elderly couple—long-time members of the church. The woman fell recently and has been confined to bed. I want to pray with them and express the concern of our congregation. But in the course of my visit I learn this couple isn't as concerned about health (she's recovering well) as they are about the cost of their everyday necessities. Living as they are on a fixed income, inflation is eating away at their meager savings at what seems like a terrifying rate.

After a Wednesday night church board meeting I hear two members discussing the soaring costs of college education. One of them says, "I always wanted my daughter to attend a Christian school. But it looks as if all we can afford next fall is the state university."

On Thursday I see my neighbor in his yard and stop to talk. He tells me he's hoping the county school system doesn't write off the special education program he teaches in when the Board of Education meets next month.

In the afternoon I visit young parents at the hospital where their premature baby daughter has been kept for three weeks now. The father is torn between his new love for his baby and the overwhelming hospital bill, already over $40,000. The couple has no insurance.

That evening I call on another young couple with three kids who've visited our church the last couple Sundays. They're new in town. They act a little embarrassed by their crowded two-bedroom apartment. As we talk they bemoan the housing market crisis and admit real discouragement about ever having a place of their own.

Friday I deliver three bags of groceries paid for by the church's benevolent fund to a young mother with year-old twins whose father deserted them all last month.

Saturday my own wife returns from a trip to the grocery store distressed that her bill totalled more than $100 and the only meat she bought was one package of hamburger.

By the end of the week, the combined experiences of my ministerial duties have exposed to me a recurring concern in my community and congregation: anxiety over financial pressures. My exposure to life through my pastoral duties has helped me identify a need, an area where I feel people are searching for help.

Once I have a potential need identified, I try to measure the size of the problem. Based on what I read, what I see in the media, what I continue to observe around me, I ask, *Is this serious enough or universal enough to warrant a sermon in response?* When I decide that it is, I ask another question: *Is this something God wants me to preach about?* After careful and prayerful consideration I answer yes. And then I begin planning to preach to this pressing need in the immediate future.

At this stage I'm not yet sure of everything I need to say, or of everything God has to say in his Word on this subject. The people need encouragement, but I know I'll have to be careful not to be too simplistic. I will want to remind them of God's concern and ability to help, but I won't want to condemn or make light of the very real and understandable emotions of fear and frustration in the midst of an economic crunch. I know the sermon will present a big challenge for me.

Before moving on to the next stage of sermon preparation, I need to make clear that I'm not saying the spark idea for every sermon will or should come from our exposure to our peoples' experience. Sometimes a sermon will spring from a thought we've read in our own devotions or from a truth we discover in an in-depth study of the Scriptures. The exposure stage of preparation involves both exposure to contemporary life and exposure to God's Word; it's another case where we ought to remember the *both and* principle mentioned earlier. I've emphasized the potential we can find in our exposure to contemporary life because this has too often been ignored in the homiletics texts and the preaching classes of our seminaries. If we desire God's guidance for our preaching, we need to be as sensitive to his voice when we go about our pastoral duties as we are when we close our study door.

Gathering—Stage Two of Inductive Sermon Preparation
Once my exposure has convinced me of a need and I have a tentative direction, I'm ready to start thinking about what will go into the sermon.

Since the inductive part of preaching begins with experience and (as we've seen in Chapters Seven and Eight) examples precede any argument, an inductive sermon requires more illustrative material than a deductive approach. When I emphasize this point in class or in preaching workshops, I see concern register on my students' faces. Invariably one of the first questions asked at preachers' workshops is, "Where do I get all these illustrations?"

Where do the narrative stories, the parables, case studies, analogies, the dialogue, the personal experiences and the other inductive ingredients come from? Where do we get the building blocks to construct the inductive structure we discussed in preceding chapters?

Wouldn't it be great if every pastor's study came equipped with a divinely programmed computer that could spit out a ream of raw sermon material on any topic punched into it? Too farfetched? I don't think so. The human mind still does things IBM only dreams about. Every pastor has a memory bank chock-full of potential sermon material. Unique, relevant, fresh material. The trick is tapping the supply. How is this to be done?

Personal brainstorming. We need to learn this skill. Maybe we've shied away from it because it sounds a bit too Freudian for us, but free association can unlock a wealth of material from the storehouse of our minds. (In sixty years the human brain commits 200 billion bits to visual and other memory.) If you've never tried this, here's one way to get started: Take a large sheet of blank paper and write the subject or need at the top—let's say our sermon on financial pressure and anxiety and God's provision. Then let your mind go and jot down everything you think of that's even remotely related to the topic: anecdotes, quotes, experiences, topics, facts, questions. Don't censor or select yet—just write.

Maybe you want to start with the pastoral experiences of the past week. But don't stop there. Think about your personal life, your own experience, history, biography, literature, relationships you've known and seen, your family, your travels, your church. You'll go specifically to the Scripture later, but if passages, verses or Bible characters spring to mind now, write them down. When you've brainstormed until the storm has passed, you may want to choose something you've written and start another sheet of free association.

To give an idea of where this can take you, I brainstormed one evening on our subject of financial pressure and anxiety and God's provision. One of the first things that popped into my mind was the verse, "My God shall supply all your needs according to his riches in glory." I started there. I thought about the personal pronoun "my" and it released an avalanche of vivid personal experiences and feelings.

> My dog, my place at the table, my dad going blind, my bed, my fifty-cent bike, my teacher, my first suit, my house on fire, my girl, my brother, my swimming hole, my doctor, my pastor, my conversion, my church, my call, my wedding, my wife, my job, my joy, my baby, my boy, my sons, my family, my vacation, my mother's death, my burden, my book, my friend, my sermons—my entire life passes in review.

I remember that Luther insisted genuine religion consists in the pronouns.

I consider the idea "permanent possessions" and it underscores in my thinking the relational, spiritual, cultural, mental blessings which never fail when fiscal and physical assets fade. My inventory of assets keeps the focus on real values.

Bible input includes the psalmist's observation, "I was young and now am old, but I haven't seen the righteous forsaken or his seed begging bread"; Psalm 23; Malachi's promise of the heavenly windows opened; Jesus—"Seek ye first . . . and all these things. . . ," feeding the multitudes, paying taxes, "What would it profit to gain the whole world"; the rich fool; Abraham and Lot; Achan's greed; Judas' silver; the Son of Man with no place to lay his head. And more Bible examples mixed in with other ideas.

Examples from life include: Great Depression belt-tightening. My father had income of twenty-six cents for four months with a family of six. Needy seminary students—one with a son who said, "Boy, Dad, the money's comin' in faster'n we're even prayin' for it." Another student facing a financial crisis found a $2,000 check in his seminary mailbox. A story an orange-grower told me about a Florida hurricane which lifted at the last minute. Al Hafed and Acres of Diamonds. Plus examples and names of many men and women who thought they could write the beginning, middle and end of the Book of Job.

I went to bed for the night after writing this surging flood of graphic examples, satisfied I had plenty of ideas to float a sermon on God's provision. Before daylight the next morning I awakened with a persistent procession of more examples from both life and the Bible clamoring to get into the sermon. Examples from history and literature came later for me.

I'm amazed at the newness, the vividness, variety, the graphic detail and emotions this simple exercise of recall has triggered. In more than forty years of ministry, I've only used a couple of these two dozen life examples that came to me as a result of my brainstorming on this topic.

Recently one of my sons shared a brainstorming technique with me—a variation and perhaps an improvement on the listing procedure I've always used. Instead of putting the topic at the top of the page, you place it in the middle in a small circle. When you think of a related idea you draw a spokelike line out from the center, write the idea and circle it. The second idea may spark two or three related thoughts; if so, you draw more spokes out from the second circle and include the newest thoughts. Then you go back to the main idea and brainstorm again from there. By the time you are done your paper may look like this:

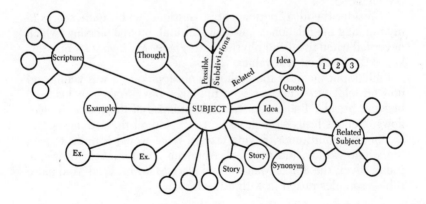

You may even want to center some of your secondary ideas on separate sheets and brainstorm from them.

As with the brainstorm lists, you want to jot down everything that comes to mind. But there are at least two advantages to this newer technique. First, the visual layout helps your thinking to go in a variety of directions. And second, related ideas can be easily grouped together as you go, no matter what order you think of them. Organization into a more linear outline can easily be done later.

Most of the things I write down in my personal brainstorming sessions will never leave my study. Maybe only a tenth or less will find its way into the sermon.

I know I'll have to be careful not just to indulge myself in a boring trip down my own memory lane. I'll eventually have to sift down to those examples, experiences, illustrations and ingredients that my listeners will best understand and relate to. But that selection process comes later in preparation. At this stage I want quantity as well as quality.

Even those thoughts and anecdotes that eventually end up in the study wastebasket serve a purpose, because intensive brainstorming does more than provide usable material. For example, as a seminary professor I've been isolated from some aspects of the job market for more than twenty years. I've had permanent employment, tenure and apparent security. But brainstorming this topic has sparked thought processes and increased sensitivities needed to preach a sermon that will offer more than Pollyanna-type pronouncements to a congregation which may include members suffering the agony of unemployment. Brainstorming primes the pumps of our hearts, minds and spirits.

Surveying the Scripture. Gathering doesn't stop with our little paper and pencil exercise of free association. Next we need to look again to the Word.

In Chapters Seven and Eight we talked about using scriptural material as part of the inductive side of the full-orbed preaching process. This is the point in the preparation process where we look for that scriptural material—biblical anecdotes, characters and analogies. We should probably start with those that came to mind during the brainstorming process. We may sometimes want to do some expositional or exegetical study at this stage, but most of that will take place at other stages. Here we're most concerned about pulling together a body of useful biblical material. So we might well conduct a topical study and search for additional Bible input relevant to our topic. We may even want to make a list of related words and see where a concordance will take us.

I realize this last suggestion is abhorrent to many homileticians, but a topical concordance is a most useful tool in preparation. Certainly it is no substitute for sound exegesis. However, if we're careful about not taking passages out of context, there is no reason to fear taking a need or a problem to the Scripture to try to discover what God has to say to us

This is perhaps a good point for a brief side trip to say that the preparation suggestions spelled out thus far in this chapter may require a little adaptation if you are preaching your way through a book of the Bible or if you're preparing a series of sermons on a passage of Scripture such as the Lord's Prayer.

That's because the easiest way to be truly inductive in our preaching is to start with a need of our people and take that need to the Scripture for God's help and response. The inductive structures we've talked about just naturally start with the particulars, the problems and the questions that lead to the biblical conclusions and their application.

It's more difficult to preach with an inductive spirit of mutual exploration when the whole congregation knows your sermon is going to take up with the chapter or verse where you left off last week. But it can be done.

The simplest way to do this would begin with your careful study of the passage. Then you need to ask yourself, "What problem do my people face, what need do they have, what issue do they wrestle with, what question do they ask that this passage deals with?" You need to rely greatly on God's guidance for insight here, as well as when you ask a second question: "What is the truth God has in this passage to help my people with their problem, need, issue or question?" The answer to this second question can become the conclusion, the corporate concept you want the people to reach with you at the end of the inductive part of the full-orbed sermon. This is the truth you build on and apply in the deductive side of the sermon. The answer to the first question—the problem, need, issue or question your people face—helps set the direction of your quest that will lead you and them through the inductive process of the sermon to the truth.

Once you've asked these questions about a passage, you're ready to think through the exposures you've had and gather material for the sermon in much the same way we've already suggested. Even the surveying of the Scriptures is a good process; though you may already know your text, you will get a broader biblical picture and perhaps find additional inductive support material to increase the Bible content of the sermon.

I'm convinced it's possible to preach a full-orbed inductive sermon on any passage, any Bible truth or teaching, any biblical doctrine you'd want or need to preach on. What's required are inductive ingredients and an inductive structure with delayed assertions and examples preceding all arguments and declarations.

Scanning the Field. Once we've done our brainstorming and searched the Scripture for potential material to include in our sermon, there's one more step at the gathering stage of preparation. Here's where we take our preparation beyond our own experience and thinking. We survey both the past and present in quest of related material. What's been done and said? What is now being done and said about the subject we're preaching on?

Karl Barth, the homiletical fundamentalist, used to say he prepared his sermons with a Bible on one knee and a newspaper on the other. That's a model we need to remember as we prepare. A newspaper should be a necessity for us, but it's not enough. Scanning the field could well mean spending half a day at the public library checking periodical guides and card catalogues. Or it could require digging through our pastoral library to see what other preachers have preached, what Christian writers have written

There's an information explosion going on right now in a field computer people refer to as artificial intelligence. Electronic data banks may soon offer incredible potential for sermon illustrations. Today, for a charge of $2.75-$15 per hour (depending on the time of day), Source Telecomputing Corp. of McLean, Virginia will tie into the UPI newswire and sort news items via key words. There will be many more such services in the near future.

I recently heard a homiletics expert say to a group of ministers, "You can't preach effectively today without watching TV." When you realize that the television is on about fifty hours a week in the average home, you have to think he may be right. It has become such a huge part of American life that we can no longer afford to ignore what it is saying to our people as we prepare our counter-messages for Sunday morning.

But not all the field scanning should be through the mass media. Barth also made a regular practice of preaching in local jails to remind himself of the real needs of people. Perhaps we need to visit the unemployment office or chat with a loan officer at our bank in preparation for our sermon on financial pressures. Firsthand experience or personal interviews could add real depth and interest to sermons on many topics. We need only think of the creative opportunities.

Another means of broadening the input for our sermons would be to make a habit of talking to some of our congregation ahead of time about their experiences. I heard of one minister who tried every week to incorporate one example, anecdote or illustration suggested to him by a member of his congregation and to give that member credit.

Think about the added involvement we'd get in our sermon each week if we said, "Jim Peterson told me about moving to this community ten years ago without a job, not knowing what he was going to do. . . ." Or, "Just this week Mrs. Adams told me about a man she knew in this community whose wife left him with three small children. He doesn't know how he's going to care for the kids because he can't afford day care. . . ."

In the regular course of our pastoral contact we could mention to people the subject of upcoming sermons and ask for examples from their experience. We wouldn't have to use every suggestion or go into great length in the pulpit. What potential for examples and illustrations! Our people would love it. We'd have guaranteed involvement.

The gathering stage is crucial to the preparation of an effective sermon. It takes creativity and effort. It takes prayer; we need to ask God to open our eyes and our minds to the strongest, most relevant material. And it takes time. For some topics we may want to be working and planning an hour or two at a time for months. But the triple approach—brainstorming, searching the Scripture and scanning the field should give us a wealth of material for any sermon topic. The hard part should be deciding what great material to leave out.

Focusing—Stage Three of Inductive Sermon Preparation
I recently heard the story about the young son of a minister who entered the pastor's study one day to find his father furiously writing at his desk. "What are you doing, Daddy?" he asked.

His father hardly looked up to reply, "I'm trying to finish my sermon before supper."

"How do you know what to say in your sermon?" the kindergartener asked, walking to his father's side.

"God tells me," the minister said, still not stopping his writing.

The boy stared at the paper in front of his dad for only a moment before he asked, "Then why did you cross some of it out?"

This is the stage of sermon preparation where we should start crossing things out. This is the point where we sift through the conglomeration of ideas, illustrations, Scripture and everything else we've gathered and begin narrowing and refining our focus, searching for a unifying theme or a thread that winds its way through the tangled skein.

Even if we start our preparation with a predetermined text and truth to share with our people, this is the point where we decide just how we are going to inductively arrive at that truth as a corporate conclusion and how we're going to state that truth when we get to it.

In short, this is the point where we finally answer the question: What do I really have to say in this sermon?

There's no simple step-by-step guide to finding the key, the central truth, the corporate concept which should be the heart of any inductive sermon. Our own reasoning and sensitivity play a big role as we review the gathered ingredients and look for the most relevant material, the most helpful approach, the most valuable message for our people.

Sometimes it's helpful to talk through a sermon subject with someone else—a spouse, a friend, a colleague. And, not to negate the importance of God's guidance at other stages of preparation, this is perhaps the point at which we need to be most prayerful and open to God's inspiration and leading.

I often find it helpful to think of focusing as a progressive, narrowing process. For example, in the gathering of material on the subject of financial pressure and anxiety one of the Scriptures I seemed most drawn to was Psalm 23. I'd meditated on it and jotted down a number of concepts. My list looked like this:

The Lord	Trust	Provision	Discipline—"rod"
Shepherd	Tribulation	Evil	Support—"staff"
Satisfaction	Suffering	Companionship	Peace
Supply	Dependency	Contentment	Protection
Needs, desires	Comfort	Boldness	Confidence
Struggles	Deliverance	Success	Eternity
Personal—"my"	Abiding	Righteousness	Fear
Security	Abundance	Guidance	Following him

Obviously one sermon can't possibly focus on all these concepts; so I have to narrow the sermon down some more. I could combine a couple of the concepts—that of "Lord" and "shepherd." But what do I want and need to say about "The Lord is my shepherd" that will tie into the need of financial pressure and anxiety?

Sometimes the narrowing process doesn't end at a usable point, and you need to go back to the big mass of material again. Other times, as I do here, you narrow the focus, expand it a little again and find a new sharper focus.

When I got to the idea of "The Lord is my shepherd" I tried to think of ways that could fit into our sermon topic on financial concerns. And in true ministerial fashion I broadened my thinking a little with an alliterative list of concepts. I thought of God's person, his provision, his protection, his peace, his presence. The word *plenty* came to mind, as did permanent, practical, personal and participating.

As I looked at this newly refined list, the idea of provision seemed to be the most promising. I felt sure a sermon on God's provision could be a valuable response to the need I wanted to meet. Some of the other concepts would work, but this one just seemed a little more to the point, more specific.

But even after we find the key idea for our sermon, we can bring it into still sharper focus. Since an inductive sermon doesn't begin with an assertion or conclusion, but as a search, a mutual quest of preacher and congregation, the refining, focusing process is helped when we take the main thrust of our message, the key, the primary idea, the corporate concept we want to get across to our people, and form a key question that is answered by our key idea. It's a little like the long-time TV game show *Jeopardy*, where the contestants were given only the answers and had to come up with the pertinent questions to go with them.

Our goal is to pose a question our people will want answered, a question that asks something they would really like to know. For example, we could refine our sermon on the key idea of God's provision with this key question: Does God provide today? Sometimes the key question can be sharpened by adding a bit of bite—a touch of cynicism that acknowledges the doubt some listeners may hold: Does God *really* provide today?

Every inductive sermon needs to begin with an over-arching key question. This helps establish the common ground from which preacher and people proceed. That question may actually be posed in the sermon itself, or it could just be implied. Either way, a key question helps focus the sermon by giving it direction, by framing the entire sermon into a quest for the answer.

Once we've focused a sermon enough to find the key question, we need to rethink and sharpen our basic answer to the question. Do we have a reasonable, believable answer? Do we actually come to a corporate conclusion that can lead to deductive application? Is there some aspect of the question we aren't prepared to answer, where we may arouse doubts or where we don't have enough information or evidence? We may need to reword the question or do more directed study of Scripture, a little more thinking about our answer. Again at this stage we might do well to share our key question and corporate conclusion with someone who will try to suggest additions or potential weaknesses. Often our sermons could be improved if they were refined by just one more person's perspective. We can get so close to our material we often don't hear what we're saying. Yet a simple reaction from someone else may reveal a gaping hole or pinpoint a strength we need to emphasize.

In addition to discovering where God wants us to take our people in a sermon, another important goal of the focusing stage of preparation is to find where our people are in order to start the sermon from there. Henry Ward Beecher very early in his ministry discovered this need, which he called "taking aim." Two and a half years after he began a mediocre ministry in Indiana he became discouraged by the meager results of his work. So he studied the methods used by the apostles in the Book of Acts and decided to follow their example of adapting their message to their specific hearers. He then marshalled about forty universals held by his people and proceeded in his next sermon to use all his personal concern, all his logical and emotional appeal to build on those givens: "We all know . . ." "We all know this . . ." "We all know that . . ."

Describing the results of that historic message, Beecher said, ". . . there were seventeen men awakened under that sermon. I never felt so triumphant in my life. I cried all the way home. And I said to myself, 'Now I know how to preach. I have learned to take aim.' " That was the beginning of a transformed ministry that made Beecher one of the most effective, influential preachers of his day.

Focusing is the point in preparation where we spot the questions our people are asking and we select the answers we're going to try to convey. Time spent on focus can extend the range and increase the impact of our sermons. It sometimes makes the difference between a shotgun loaded with birdshot and a big-game rifle.

This is the time we take aim.

Constructing—Stage Four of Inductive Sermon Preparation
Once we've found our focus and direction we're ready to start constructing a sermon from the building blocks we've collected at the gathering stage. So here, as in the focusing stage, we need to dig back through all the material.

The initial task in construction is actually sorting. We choose those most pertinent experiences, the most germane memories, the most accurate examples (biblical and contemporary) to fit the focus of the sermon. We're looking now for illustrative material that both asks the key question and leads the people to our conclusion.

We may not use every example we sort out at this point. And we may find before we complete construction of the sermon that we need to go back to the gathering stage for a little more brainstorming to fill in the gaps. But once we've selected what we feel are the most representative and realistic examples, we're ready to start building the actual outline of the sermon.

Since Chapters Seven and Eight dealt at length with the structure of inductive sermons, we need only summarize the rest of the constructing stage of preparation here. This is the time where we decide how we're going to state and present our case, what inductive material to include and where we're going with the shape, movement and flow of the sermon.

We emphasized in our chapters on structure that the goal of the inductive portion of a sermon is to bring all our people along until they arrive at the same scriptural conclusion we do. For our sample financial-concern sermon, that conclusion could be: *Yes, God really does provide for us today.*

Making certain the people get where we want them to be, that they reach our corporate concept, that they believe and accept that conclusion and are ready then for us to go on to declare, elaborate on, reaffirm and apply that message deductively—this is the result of the sensitive selection and arrangement of what we want to say and how we want to say it.

That's what happens in the constructing stage of preparation.

Reviewing—Stage Five of Inductive Sermon Preparation
Even after the inductive part of the sermon is constructed, there's one last stage in the inductive preparation process: review. This is the stage where we look at what we plan to say and measure it against a series of checklists (see Appendix 2) for:

Inductive attitudes
Inductive process
Inductive ingredients
Inductive illustrations
Inductive order
Inductive movement

Here's when we need to honestly ask ourselves questions such as these:

Does the sermon start where the people are—with their needs, problems, issues and questions?
Does it come on too strong, too fast?
Does it ask a question they are asking?
Does it arouse interest by appealing to senses, feelings, emotions?
Does it include a variety of inductive elements to involve people?
Does it have a focus?
Is it realistic? Life-related? Scriptural?
Does the structure logically lead to the corporate conclusion?
Does the corporate conclusion answer the key question?
Does it prepare the way for any deduction to follow?

If we can answer yes to all these questions, the inductive part of our sermon is ready to be preached. If not, we'll need to do a little more work until we can.

In a way this chapter on preparation has been broken into five artificial divisions or stages. For while all five stages are necessary for an effective inductive sermon, they can't be perfectly divided or even perfectly ordered as stages 1, 2, 3, 4, and 5. We can't program our very human minds to stay completely on track. We're really gathering in the exposure stage. We're focusing and perhaps even constructing some of what we want to say even as we're gathering. And we should be asking ourselves the review questions throughout the entire preparation process.

Preparation for the deductive part of the sermon could be considered as a sixth stage. But we've omitted it here for two reasons. First, as we said at the beginning of the chapter you can find truckloads of books on how to prepare a deductive sermon. Second, preparation for the inductive and deductive parts of the sermon greatly overlap. Final compilation of the deductive portion may not be a totally separate stage at all. Much of the material used in the second "half" of a full-orbed sermon could come from the research and work done in preparing the inductive side. Illustrative material not used in the first part could be plugged into the second. Sometimes the very points declared on the deductive side will merely be a restatement or a reemphasizing of those made by induction in the first part of the sermon.

Any and all exegetical study done in the inductive preparation stages will prepare for and strengthen any additional study done specifically for the deductive side of the sermon.

So what has been presented here in this chapter is not meant as restrictive, step-by-step directions, but as a general guide to preparing for a full-orbed inductive approach.

Preparation. How crucial is it to our preaching?

Let me answer that with the story of a minister who wanted to be so sensitive to God's leading in his preaching that he made a habit of only preparing the first half of every sermon. That way, he reasoned, he'd allow God to show him where to go and what to say during the second half.

One day he was sharing this strategy with one of the laymen in his congregation. The man listened to the preacher, thought for a moment, and then said, "I guess I ought to congratulate you then, pastor. Your half of the sermon is invariably better than God's."

God can certainly inspire us at any stage of the sermon process, and we need to be open to his leading at all times. But most of us would be better off to rely on his guidance as much in the study as we do in the pulpit.

11 Behind the Pulpit

For more than twenty years now I've been a regular at voluntary seminary chapel services. And I've tried to use the opportunity as an objective laboratory to study preaching. It's often a fascinating and revealing study.

I remember the day when missionary statesman E. Stanley Jones came to preach. Young seminarians crowded into the pews and surged to the balcony to hear him. His voice wavered and cracked with age. His physical stature seemed slight and unimposing. Yet, for the full length of his sermon he held his listeners in rapt attention.

A quick survey of those sitting in front of me showed that visible bodily motion slowed to approximately ten movements per minute per hundred people. All fidgeting and seemingly all breathing stopped at one dramatic moment in the course of a story he told to punctuate a point. His quiet intensity made him a slow-burning human torch illuminating the passageways surrounding the hidden treasure, the richness and power of his message on the meaning of the Christian life. His personal involvement, his passion to reveal that message and his desire to be plain, personal and helpful showed through and held the hundreds of enthralled listeners in his palm.

Later the same week a retired minister spoke in the same chapel setting. I clocked his tired, plodding pace at sixty-six words per minute. His failure to involve the audience was very evident in furtive glances toward the door, shifting shoulders, shuffling feet, stretching, sliding, tilting and a myriad of other movements as listeners tried to yawn with closed mouths. I estimated more than two hundred movements per minute per hundred people.

After sitting through roughly two thousand chapel sermons and listening to another twenty thousand sermons or talks delivered by my students over the years of my seminary teaching, I've come to the conclusion that success in winning listener involvement is often independent of subject matter, setting or the speaker's credentials. A speaker may epitomize all the positive things we've talked about in this book—a servant spirit, an understanding and care for his audience, even an inductive sermon structure—and still fail to actually involve his listeners in the message.

A preacher can carefully and conscientiously prepare a sermon as suggested in Chapter Nine. His attitude, his content and his structure can reflect his genuine desire to involve the listener, and yet he still may fail in his goal if the presentation doesn't complement the rest of his effort.

Presentation can make a difference as great as the difference in the chapel response to E. Stanley Jones and the poor preacher who followed him. Delivery can amplify the effectiveness of everything else we've talked about, or it can negate much of it.

Directness

Directness is the first of three major aspects of presentation that hold great implications for us if we want to involve people in our preaching. Like so many of the things we've talked about in this book, directness of preaching must have its roots in the attitude of the preacher. To be direct, a preacher must want to be practically helpful, sharing as a friendly witness rather than an antagonistic advocate. In this way the message becomes a testimonial rather than a defensively declared dogma.

Visual directness has come to new significance in our video age. It's taken on added importance for preachers because the people in our congregations are programmed by TV and movies to relate to the warmth and personality expressed in the faces and eyes of professional actors. Many of them, out of sheer habit, will judge both our character and the content of our messages on the basis of eye contact.

History tells us Bourdaloue, the famous French court preacher, scarcely ever lifted his eyes from the manuscript page. At other times he preached entire sermons with his eyes shut to keep the congregation from distracting him. Charles Wesley in older life sometimes preached with closed eyes too.

Unfortunately not all such examples are relegated to the history books. I once watched a minister conducting a revival preach for ten minutes in the middle of his sermon without so much as a flitting glance at the congregation. Afterwards he explained, "Sometimes people bother me when I preach; so I just shut my eyes and go on with the sermon." What a contrast to Augustine who sometimes changed his sermon in midstream when his watchful eyes told him audience response indicated a need for a different approach.

However, visual indirectness is much more common than shutting out the people by shutting the eyes. I've seen some preachers give the impression they were reading their sermon off the ceiling of the sanctuary. Others seem to stargaze into the regions beyond, or carefully fix their eyes on empty spaces in the pews between parishioners. Even more common are speakers who crop off the heads of their listeners by staring six inches above them.

I've heard some people insist Scripture should be read without looking up—that the Word seems more sacred without human eye contact. But evidence doesn't support that thesis. Why encourage the congregation to shift attention away from the reading by failing to establish eye contact?

Visual contact is much more than a picky little homiletics rule or just another concept for Basic Speech 101 profs to drum into shy college freshmen. It does as much as words, if not more, to convey concern, cooperation, communication and courage. Compassion must flow through visual lines. We can't show genuine caring or expect to involve our people in our preaching if we don't acknowledge their presence. And we can't do that if we don't look at them.

But visual directness is only part of the problem. Vocal directness should be another concern.

Many ministers subject their listeners to strange, otherworldly tones—a sort of a singsong mutation of speech and music that has plagued the pulpit since chanting became the fad in the Middle Ages. Some preachers who wouldn't dare chant strike the flag to half-mast and preach almost *sotto voce*—without voice in a sanctified stage whisper. Still others deliver their doctrine through the nose in a practiced nasal twang.

All such artificial incantations interfere with the goal of involvement by making our message seem remote, impersonal and strained. Today, when the polished naturalness of media stars often seems more real than reality itself, any stained-glass tones echoing through our sanctuaries may be read as pompous, irrelevant and perhaps even a tad weird. At best, our holy whining will be thought unnatural; at worst, some listeners may look upon us with suspicion, wondering if we aren't trying to deceptively stretch the shadow of a limited personality.

What's the remedy for ministerial monotone and other symptoms of vocal indirectness? Many good speech texts discuss the basics of voice and tone. But I tell young ministerial students that another cure is to prepare sermons *for people*, not *about subjects*. After the sermon is completely prepared, rethink it with the congregation in mind. Then when you step to the pulpit, speak to the people as individuals you need to befriend, not as a group you want to impress. If you begin as straightforwardly as you would converse about something exciting you, your tone will be direct and the message will make its own impression.

Physical posture also plays a role in directness. If we're going to involve everyone, we can't face, gesture toward or preach to only one half of the church, whether our favorite point of focus is front or back, right or left. Such habits are easy to fall into as I've seen time and time again in watching preachers cast and recast their words over one favorite segment of the sanctuary.

Directness of posture demands that words and bodily language agree. A nose elevated an inch too high can speak volumes—even during a wonderful sermon on humility. The seemingly unmistakable words "I love you" lose their warmth and credibility if delivered with a clenched fist or a scowl.

One of the most amusing sights in my years of seminary teaching was a student preacher leaning over his manuscript, reading with great intensity while his hands were going through feverish gesticulations above and behind his bent-over head. This incredibly awkward result was totally unimpressive; his words and actions seemed totally unrelated, with neither being aimed at those of us in the audience.

But directness isn't just affected by what we do when we speak. It's often a product of what we say. Attempts at diplomatic verbiage often lose their punch in the process. Saying "One would ultimately desire . . ." just doesn't communicate as well as the more straightforward "I hope . . ." "Someone may question the feasibility . . ." doesn't come across as strongly as "You may ask . . ."

The secret to directness of vocabulary is really no secret at all; it's as basic as choosing simple, direct and common words. But there are a couple of major perils preachers need to avoid.

The first problem area is that of easy intellectualism. "McLuhanisms" offer a poignant example of this danger. We can in our preaching replicate or ramify the redundant, remediative ratiocinations of the renowned writer whose books on communication referred to ideas such as "reconceptualization," "retinal experience" and "digital experience" instead of just saying "remember," "see," and "feel." We can lose meaning and listeners in the course of our polysyllabic pronouncements.

The second area of danger is one John Wesley warned against— professional jargon in the body of divinity. We need to beware of Christian cliches, slogans and terminology. Much of what is said in American evangelical pulpits is so laced with traditional "Christianese" that the average man or woman off the street would have as much trouble sorting out our meanings as you and I would have understanding the scientific papers read at a convention of nuclear physicists.

If we're going to be direct with our message we must be simple, vivid and clear. We preach an urgent message for our day. Urgency clamors for clarity, and clarity shines as the primary quality of directness.

Long before we step to our pulpits we should pray for a passion to make our message plain. And then we might check and adjust our word choice with the following guidelines for directness.

(1) Use precisely the "right" word. Say "It was oval," not "It was sort of round."

(2) Use specific, not generic words. Say "pinto pony"—not just "horse." Say "shack," "mansion," "lean-to," not just "building."

(3) Use descriptive words. Say "The wind whined and clawed at the corner of the house," not "The wind blew hard."

(4) Use action verbs. Say "He tore out," "breezed out," "strolled out"—not "went out."

(5) Use short, forceful Anglo-Saxon words. Say "He died"—not "He passed away"; "next to"—not "contiguous."

(6) Use words found in your listeners' speaking vocabulary. Say "mixed group," not "heterogeneous assembly." Say "swollen," not "distended"; "I like you" and not "I hold you in high esteem."

(7) Use imitative words that imitate natural sounds. Say "soothe," "lull," "smooth," "bang."

(8) Use words with significant contemporary meaning. Say "home" not "residence," "meal" not "repast."

(9) Avoid cliches, pastoral patter, trade talk and stale fancy phrases.

If we would carefully and consistently weigh our words against these measures, our sermons would pack an extra wallop of relevance. Our directness would be greatly enhanced.

There's one more simple path to increased directness in our preaching, and that's the use of direct address. Some recent writers about preaching have warned against ministers overusing "you" and "I." But I've come to agree with H. H. Farmer, the British writer on preaching, who says it's impossible to preach in the New Testament sense without coming to the "you" of direct personal application.

We've already seen in Chapter Six how Jesus depended on direct address, questions and dialogue with his audience. "You" or "your" is either stated or implied 221 times in the Sermon on the Mount. A further study of New Testament epistles shows recurring concentrations of "you" in direct address. The writers of the epistles consistently used the direct-address technique to establish common ground in the early portions of their letters and to apply their message in concluding verses.

Direct address is one of the most common characteristics of biblical sermons. And yet it's so often overlooked as a means of achieving involvement in contemporary preaching.

Oral Style

A second major aspect of presentation, oral style, is one almost ignored in most books on preaching. And yet many of my students express more excitement and gratification for our study of oral style than nearly any other aspect of my courses in preaching.

Studies show the average person speaks 95 percent or more of all his or her communication and writes only 5 percent or less. And yet throughout all our years of education we are trained almost exclusively for communication through writing rather than for the preponderant vocal composition our daily life demands. There's a definite difference between the everyday language of living and the copious copy of so many college composition courses. But too few preachers seem to understand that difference or to apply the principles of oral style to their tasks of communicating the Good News to their people.

A sermon needs to be more than a vocalized religious theme, expostulated before a comfortably seated congregation. In a sermon, as in any spoken communication, meanings are communicated through language, voice and action. And every sermon, because it is delivered orally, can be strengthened with an infusion of natural style.

Both written and spoken communication demand clarity, energy and interest; those are the big three goals of either communication mode. But an additional goal of writing is permanence. The quest of speech, on the other hand, is immediate perception and a ready response.

Writing and reading are usually solitary activities, but by their very nature speaking and listening are social. Written language represents *outcome* of thinking while the language of speaking represents *thinking-going-on*. The spoken word exists only in the moment of utterance, but written language is congealed, set. Speaking is addressed to a particular audience, at a particular time, on a particular occasion, but writing is addressed to unseen and sometimes unknown readers. The speaker-listener relationship is usually immediate and close, the writer-reader contact distant in time and space. The listener's response is simultaneous, the reader's response seldom communicated to the author.

So despite some overlap, some similarity, the differences between the two kinds of communication are many. And those differences demand very different styles for most effective communication.

We've all spent years studying written style in every Comp, English and Lit. course we ever took. So there's not much point in rehashing that here. But what are the distinguishing characteristics of oral style?

Oral or spoken style must be instantly intelligible. Oral style has more vividness. Oral style has more sensuous words rather than abstract, more specific words rather than general. It has more variety—with both long and short sentences. Oral style for preaching has more suspense and climax, more connectives to punctuate sentences and hold phrases and clauses together. It has more repetition and restatement, more energy and movement. It has more objective elements of vividness such as direct discourse, analogy, allusions, figures of speech, more personal pronouns, more vigorous verbs, more reliance upon strong nouns. Oral style uses more illustrations, more comparison and contrast, more figurative language, more questions, more personal elements of address. It is more informal, more personal, more direct, more conversational. It's climactic in order.

Oral style has more eagerness and straightforwardness. It utilizes many principal clauses, few relative clauses. Spoken style has more pronounced rhythm and smoothness, more active voice—less passive. It has more present tense than past or future.

Anglo-Saxon terms, which make up the vivid, vital and unvarnished language of childhood and youth, lend strength and force to an oral style. The Latinized forms we accumulate in the course of formal education often burden speech, while "less intellectual," "less sophisticated" language communicates more easily, more vigorously, more completely to listeners today.

In one experiment conducted with two thousand students, approximately 10 percent more information was imparted when speeches incorporated a number of oral style elements. The added potency of oral over nonoral style held true throughout this test whether listeners heard one or the other of two speakers involved and whether they heard a live speaker or a tape recording.

Oral style offers the strongest chance for our preaching to attain the triple goals of style we mentioned—clarity, energy and interest. No one element of oral style can guarantee these results in our preaching. But a combination of elements can make a terrific difference in the effectiveness of our preaching.

A good way to understand this would be to consider the following charts. The first chart breaks style down into its three goals and lists the major factors that impact on each goal—clarity, energy and interest.

Style

Clarity:	Energy:	Interest:
ideas	concrete words	sensory images
words	specific words	figures
sentences	graphic words	variety
examples	sentence balance	conflict/suspense
sequence	repetition	rhythm
transitions	direct discourse	vitality
directness	personal pronouns	vividness
	verbs	comparison/contrast

This second chart shows the differences between oral and written style by citing the comparative use of these subfactors that make up the essence of style.

Oral Style

more illustrations	more rhythm
more suspense	more questions
more personal pronouns	more energy
more straightforwardness	more eagerness
more comparison/contrast	more movement
more direct discourse	more personal references
more Anglo-Saxon terms	fewer Latin terms
more vividness	more smoothness
more climax	more direct
more active voice	less passive voice
more repetition	more variety
more contractions	more connectives
more verbs	more simplicity
	climactic order

We've talked throughout this book about the importance of experience as one of the elements of an inductive approach; we've explained how it's the basis on which we build inductive involvement. Experience is also a goal of our preaching; we want our people not only to experience the gospel we preach, but to experience the inductive process with us as we preach. So it follows that the speaker who can vividly reconstruct experience can best communicate to people. The task of a preacher, therefore, especially an inductive preacher, is to clarify and intensify experience—to make it graphic. And one of the strongest tools for the task is oral style.

Look again at the last chart. Consider a sampling of the factors listed and how they might be incorporated into your next sermon.

Comparison. The clarity and intensity of an experience can be increased by comparing it with another experience. There may be a likeness of attribute—"bright as a new penny"; likeness of a trait or behavior—"fierce as a wounded grizzly"; or likeness of function—"the puddle winked like an eye every time a raindrop hit it."

Concreteness. An experience can be made more graphic by concreteness if the experience is narrated and described with abundant concrete details. There are levels of concreteness in verbs as well as nouns. For instance, the verb *to go* can be prance, slink, bounce, lumber, etc. The noun *vegetation* can be much more concrete and specific—bush, evergreen, underbrush, grapevine, etc.

The background and experience of listeners will determine the degree of concreteness the speaker uses. For example, a cow is a cow and a wrench is a wrench to most listeners, but speaking to farmers a cow may be far more concrete—Angus, black, skinny, six-year-old, fresh, lame, diseased, sway-backed, etc. Or when speaking to plumbers a wrench may be a pipe wrench, Stillson, 24-inch, bent, rusty, loose, worn, old, discarded, etc.

Clarity and intensity of an experience are further increased when narrated and described in familiar words and terms. Note the words with only one syllable in the Sermon on the Mount. While shortest words are not always the most potent, it is good sense to use words so clear in the minds of listeners they demand no translating. In our English language, Anglo-Saxon words usually best meet these requirements.

Should you doubt the sufficiency of short words, consider the findings of one analyst of literature. In his text *Creative Writing for Advanced College Classes,* George C. Williams reports that 70-78 percent of the words used by many authors are of one syllable. He lists Somerset Maugham, Sinclair Lewis, Robert Louis Stevenson, Charles Dickens and others. If writers of this stature can confine themselves to simplicity, we shouldn't fear to censor some of our polysyllabic verbiage from our sermons each week. What we may lose in intellectual sophistication we'll more than make up in meaning and impact.

The graphic nature of an experience can also be intensified when that experience is narrated and described in multi-sensory words. For example, verbs such as "gush," "sob" and "chop" each arouse strong sensations of sight, sound and movement. Adjectives such as "pitchy," "snowy," "leaden," "raw," "fiery" conjure up at least two sensations each. "Pitchy" suggests the feeling of stickiness and the color black; the word "fiery" creates the visual image of flames and the tactile sensation of heat, etc. By appealing to an orchestration of senses, such words involve listeners in a combination of ways.

For an example of a contemporary oral style sermon that attempts to incorporate comparisons, concreteness, simple and multi-sensory words (as well as many of the other subfactors on the oral style chart), turn to Appendix 1 and the sermon "Does Jesus Weep Through Us?" For a biblical example of sermons which incorporate numerous subfactors of oral style, we can look to Jesus.

First, let's reconsider the Sermon on the Mount. We've already mentioned Jesus' use of direct discourse (221 times "you" or "your") and questions (nineteen) in this eighteen-minute sermon and his simple, one-syllable words. But Jesus also uses 404 verbs for energy in this 2,320-word message. He includes 320 pronouns. He cites twenty clear contrasts and many more comparisons and illustrations. He makes extensive use of connective words: "that" (fifty-one times); "for" (twenty-four times); "therefore" (thirteen times); "but" (eight times); "into" (fifty-nine times); "no," "not," "neither," "nor" (seventy times). Repetition is another of his obvious techniques: "heaven" (eighteen times); "father" (seventeen times); "but I say" (fourteen times); "kingdom" (eight times); "you have heard" (six times).

Jesus' oral style is evident throughout the Gospel records. Mark's account of the soil parable shows:

106 words
6 sentences
18 words per sentence
25 verbs
20 nouns
21 adverbs
16 conjunctions
12 pronouns
3 prepositions
4 adjectives.

The parable of the soils can be condensed to twelve simple words—six nouns and six verbs:

sower sowed, seed fell,
birds devoured, sun scorched,
thorns choked, soil yielded.

A comparison of thirty parables, fifteen in Matthew and fifteen in Luke, shows that Matthew's accounts have a little more verbal thrust. But both records show sentences averaging about eighteen and a half words in length; two and a half nouns per sentence (13.5 percent); three and a half or four verbs per sentence (19.2 and 21.4 percent). That means about one in five of Jesus' words is a verb. His adjectives average less than one per sentence or about 5 percent of his total words in his parables. In Luke, his parable of the selfish neighbor employs a surprising forty-two pronouns in nine verses.

Jesus is a consistent model of oral style in preaching. And I strongly recommend that my students study his techniques to better understand the elements of oral style.

There's another exercise I use in my classes which has proved very effective in helping students grasp the basics and experience the poignancy of an oral style. After we discuss the factors that make up an oral style, I ask them to write one of their most vivid personal experiences or memories. Their task is to make that experience as graphic as possible, using the list of subfactors of an oral style. The ultimate goal is to convey that experience in a manner and in words which will enable others to see, hear and feel that same experience in their minds.

I'd suggest that any preacher who wants to understand oral style try this exercise. It's usually as fun as it is enlightening. And once you experiment with a personal experience you might look back at one or two of your recent sermons to revise sentences and substitute words that might better help your listeners see, hear and feel what you preached about.

If your experience is like mine and that of thousands of my students, you'll discover a new power and forcefulness to your presentation when you adopt more of an oral style. You'll find this a simple, yet valuable way of increasing the involvement of your people in your preaching.

Delivery

The third and last major aspect of presentation that impacts on the potential involvement of our listeners is the delivery of the sermon itself. Directness and oral style are a part of this to be sure, but delivery is more than that. It's the process by which the result of our presentation—all our planning, thinking, studying and praying—is actually communicated to our congregations. When everything else is said and done, our delivery is *how* it's said and done.

The importance of delivery in the effectiveness of preaching can hardly be overemphasized. This is what our people see. They never actually observe the hours of preparation in the study. For them, what is said and done in that few minutes we're behind the pulpit *is* the sermon. And its success or failure can hinge on delivery.

Manuscript reading and extemporaneous preaching are the two most common means of delivery. But variations of the two cover the total spectrum of preaching. On one hand, a carefully prepared manuscript may be so well rehearsed that it's delivered totally from memory. At the other extreme, an extemporaneous sermon may be so slightly prepared it becomes virtually an impromptu talk.

There's not much point in explaining what is meant by manuscript reading; the term is self-explanatory. However, confusion seems to abound about extemporaneous delivery.

Even in the Lyman Beecher Lectures on Preaching given annually at Yale, some lecturers depreciate extempore speech as an ill-prepared spur of the moment attempt. These critics confuse extemporaneous and impromptu speaking. The two should not be the same.

The truth is, effective extemporaneous preaching demands a step of preparation beyond manuscript preaching. It requires that a minister become so well prepared, so familiar with his material that he is able to convey his earnest message to his people without having to read it word for word.

Many objective studies have tested listener reactions to reading from a manuscript versus speaking extemporaneously with no more than notes for reference. Early tests revealed listeners retain approximately 36 percent more of the content when the message is delivered via extemporaneous speech. Additional tests have found audience reactions more sympathetic and more attentive when speakers use extemporaneous delivery rather than manuscript reading.

I wouldn't go so far as to say a preacher can't deliver an effective sermon or can't involve his listeners by using a manuscript reading presentation. For eighteen years I've sat under the weekly ministry of Dr. David Seamands, who is consistently, week after week, year after year, an exceptionally effective, insightful and challenging preacher. He is so well prepared, his presentation so natural that sometimes few of his listeners ever realize he's delivering his message virtually word for word as it's written in his manuscript.

So manuscript preaching can be done and done well. But for every preacher I've seen who can pull it off, I've witnessed a hundred so chained to their manuscripts that a large portion of their listeners resort to daydreaming or dozing in an attempt to escape the drudgery of their preacher's prose.

But it's not just the listeners who have expressed opinions on the method of delivery. George A. Buttrick, British-born Presbyterian pastor, author, preaching professor and lecturer from Harvard, Yale, Union, Vanderbilt, Garrett and Southern Baptist Seminaries, contended, "In most churches a manuscript even dramatically read would be a barrier between preacher and people." Henry Ward Beecher, who preached to standing-room-only crowds for nearly forty years at Plymouth Church in Brooklyn, once said, "A written sermon is apt to reach out like a gloved hand; an unwritten sermon reaches out the warm and glowing palm, bare to the touch."

No less a preacher than John Calvin, though scholarly in all his tastes, was a determined champion of extemporaneous preaching. In fact, he even went so far as to declare the Spirit of God could *only* pour forth in extempore speech. The image some non-Calvinists have of Calvin—cold, dull, lost in his manuscript, pedantic—is not at all accurate. He always spoke extemporaneously, entirely without manuscript. Many of his sermons were delivered without even specific preparation—impromptu. And some of them reflect it. But before we judge him too harshly for that, we must realize his continuous general study often had to suffice as his preparation during the years when he preached almost daily.

Could it be merely coincidence that the greatest revivals and church growth have usually occurred in periods of history when extemporaneous preaching was a vital aspect of the religious scene? For centuries in England and on the continent, Christian worship has been marked by the reading of manuscripts rather than the preaching of sermons. Yet the great evangelical awakening grew out of the vigorous, extemporaneous styles of men like the Wesleys, Whitefield, Fletcher, Coke, Nelson and others like them. Just how much credit for the Great Awakening and the subsequent growth of the Baptists, Methodists and Presbyterians belongs to extemporaneous preaching that was so different from the usual high church fare? Could there be similar reasons in our day for the decline of mainline denominations and the recent remarkable growth of fundamentalist and Pentecostal groups? Those are interesting questions and difficult to answer.

But one church historian, more than a hundred years closer to the Great Awakening than we are, may have offered a clue when he wrote this about the early Methodist preachers:

"They preached fervently and directly. They cast aside that dull, cold, heavy, lifeless mode of delivery which had long made sermons a very proverb for dullness. They proclaimed the words of faith with faith, and the story of life with life" (John C. Ryle, *The Christian Leaders of the Last Century*, London: T. Nelson and Sons, 1869).

Despite the testimony of testing and of history, some ministers cling to the manuscript habit with the argument that a written sermon will have lasting value. Yet the enduring qualities of sermon manuscripts are of little or no consequence to most congregations or preachers. Who reads printed sermons of past centuries or even recent decades? Only seminary classes in preaching. A few preachers read sermon magazines. But who else? Almost no one *reads* sermons; but millions *hear* them every week.

Since sermons are always heard and almost never read, it seems only logical that we should devote more concern about how we *say* what we want to say than how we *write* what we want to say. If we're concerned about the permanence of a particular sermon, we might do well to follow the advice of Augustine who suggested writing out sermons only after they were preached. Or we could very easily utilize an option unavailable to Augustine and simply transcribe a tape of the sermon.

But such concern for the enduring value of a manuscript isn't the only reason many neglect an extemporaneous approach. The primary factor is more often a combination of unfamiliarity and perhaps a little insecurity about extempore speaking. It may take a leap of faith for a minister to face a congregation without the habitual manuscript or copious notes. But Broadus urged such a shift by advising, "Plunge in, trembling knees and all." Spurgeon encouraged young preachers to develop freedom of delivery at all cost and then to use it regularly, always remembering that the skill can be lost, just as it can be learned.

It's possible to change. Many ministers switch over with no real deliberation as they gain confidence and experience in the pulpit. Others, after long years of careful manuscript writing, have consciously weaned themselves to an outline and finally to preaching without any notes at all.

The mere mention of the words "no notes" is enough to send some preachers into a bout of knee-knocking that could be heard from choir loft to narthex. But the longer quotations, the more intricate statistics and the greater details made possible by notes often have little or no relationship to a sermon's effectiveness. Rounded statistics, indelible short quotes and details sketched by memory serve the same purpose while offering none of the disadvantages of reading elaborate figures and long, dry quotations.

But whether you use notes or not, an extemporaneous style of delivery is your best choice for conveying life and faith through your preaching.

In fact, if our listeners had to choose between a manuscript reader who adhered to the rhetorical intricacies of Kenneth Burke's speech analysis and the preacher who followed the sometimes superficial commonplaces of Dale Carnegie's crass pragmatism in *A Quick and Easy Way to Learn to Speak in Public*, we'd have a landslide vote. For there is much more than shallow superficiality in Carnegie's advice to: "speak about something that (1) You've earned the right to talk about through study and experience; (2) You are excited about; and (3) You are eager to tell your listeners about."

Carnegie's suggestions are simple. He says: make brief notes of the interesting things you want to mention; don't write out your talks; never memorize a talk word for word; fill your talk with illustrations and examples; know forty times as much about your subject as you can use; rehearse your talk by conversing with friends; instead of worrying about your delivery, get busy with the causes that produce it ("If your attitude is right—your talk will be"); and don't imitate others—be yourself.

I'm certain these very basic rules have inspired much careless and chaffy chatter. But I also know I've heard thousands of sermons that could have been easily and greatly improved if the preachers would have observed even two or three of these basics.

To be sure, extemporaneous preaching is not without its dangers. Spurgeon, who strongly advocated the practice, also warned those who would attempt extemporizing, "Beware of letting your tongue outrun your brain. Guard against a feeble fluency, a garrulous prosiness, a facility of saying nothing. My brethren, it is a hideous gift to possess, to be able to say nothing at extreme length. . . . Elongated nonsense . . . (is) the scandal and shame of extemporizing. Even when the sentiments of no value are beautifully expressed and neatly worded, what is the use of them? Out of nothing comes nothing. Extemporary speech without study is a cloud without rain, a well without water, a fatal gift, injurious equally to its possessor and his flock."

That pretty well summarizes the dangers. Too many extemporaneous sermons evidence no depth, no urgency, no focus. But those pitfalls can easily be avoided by adequate preparation. So they aren't reason enough to discount a whole method of delivery—especially when that method has so many advantages to recommend it.

A major value in extempore preaching is its naturalness. It better conveys the character and attitude of the preacher which we've discussed earlier. It's more convincing because it conveys the earnestness of the preacher. And if we're going to involve our listeners in our preaching, they have to see we're urgent. We can be more concerned about misspeaking ourselves than about a seeming coldness of heart. We must care about grammar and sentence structure, but not at the expense of earnestness.

An extemporaneous delivery allows room for the preacher's emotion and personal involvement. And it's much easier to get others involved in our sermons if they can see we are.

Extempore preaching is idea-centered rather than word-centered. The goal is not precise rhetoric polished to shine brightly, but ideas tempered to burn deeply. Its flexibility allows a preacher to adapt and adjust a sermon to the response of the audience even as he preaches. And there's the added benefit that an extemporaneous sermon is easier to revise for another occasion.

Another advantage of extempore delivery, the biggest reason I've spent so much time on the subject here in this book, is that it is ideally suited to the requirements of inductive preaching. An inductive approach doesn't demand a tight, word for word logic; the concern is for a reasonable flow rather than the careful order of major and minor premises. Narrative, human instances and inductive movement are easier to remember and thus easily presented extemporaneously.

Any inductive approach to communication can be greatly complemented by extemporaneous delivery because this delivery style creates a feeling of a present and ongoing process. Extemporaneous preaching is thinking in the presence of the audience which evidences a preacher's involvement with his people and at the same time encourages their involvement with him in the thinking process of his inductive sermon.

I've heard too many sermons seemingly born out of a choice the preachers imagined they had to make—a choice between presenting a great sermon and achieving great results. There should be no such choice. No preacher will ever preach a great sermon unless he aims at achieving great results.

We should never aim to be eloquent. We should rather aim to communicate. We must preach not for effect, but for effectiveness. To be effective we must involve our listeners. And as we've said before, involvement is the strength of induction.

A presentation that combines the elements of directness, oral style and extemporaneous delivery only makes our goal of involvement that much easier to attain.

12   *End to our Means*

Twelve thousand young people from many states converge for a May weekend of contemporary Christian music. The grassy hillside amphitheatre stretches outward and upward from an improvised, high-voltage stage to farm fences a thousand feet away. Blankets and ground tarps mark the temporary claims of hundreds of assorted groups huddled together to relish the music along with their hot dogs and picnic meals.

The fringes of the crowd frazzle a bit after each number by the Christian recording artists. Footballs and frisbees periodically fill the air. There's an easy freedom, a constant ebb and flow in the large crowd.

One of the bands finishes its set and the reverberations die slowly away. Then a big booming voice on mike proclaims, "And now one of America's leading youth speakers. Here he is. Give him a big hand . . ."

The speaker steps to the microphone, takes out his pocket New Testament and says, "Let me read a few verses from the Bible."

Instantaneously the ebb and flow movement of the crowd becomes a tidal wave as a thousand young people stand and surge for the edges of the throng. Three times the speaker speaks this day. Three times he begins by reading the Scripture. And for the sake of a Protestant formality 3,000 potential listeners respond by fleeing his opening words.

Yet this speaker knows young people. Every time he speaks he holds 10,000 of them in place for the twenty-minute duration of his talk. His message focuses on experience, life and living. He seizes his listeners' attention with case studies and human instances. He narrates. The content and the structure of his messages are models of induction; he postpones his assertions until his audience is with him.

He's done his homework; he's obviously prepared. Standing on the stage fashioned from the trailer of a flatbed truck, he's amazingly direct—with his eyes, his posture, his words, his total delivery. He does everything an inductive preacher can do.

And he gets results. Each time he speaks, he closes with an invitation that brings a stream of kids down out of the crowd to talk with counselors in a building behind the stage. Three messages, three invitations, and hundreds of young people make their personal response to Christ.

I watch with fascination as the events of this day unfold. In one day, one speaker, even one sermon, I see two extremes. It's a preacher's nightmare come true; a thousand would-be listeners stand and exit before he gets his sermon launched. And yet hundreds of young people come forward to make Christian commitments. I recall the example here because this single experience showed me the range of response speakers can expect—both what we dread and what we long and pray for.

Involvement. Throughout this book we've said involvement is the response we strive for, the goal of our preaching, a Holy Grail of our calling. We talked about some inductive means to that end, but we haven't dissected the term itself.

Obviously, if after a sermon hundreds of people come forward to make Christian commitments, you probably have their involvement. But if a thousand people stand and walk out when you begin a sermon, you certainly don't have theirs. So what then is this response we call involvement? How can we have it and not have it in the same sermon? How do we get it?

Audience response is the least predictable variable in our preaching. The audience is the only one of Aristotle's three parts of the communication process which can't be directly controlled by the speaker. And so it is that the audience's response poses the greatest potential frustration in our preaching.

Perhaps this frustration, this impotence to demand a predetermined response is a major reason most books on preaching have little or nothing to say about the people in our pews. Instead, homiletics texts and even more popular preaching books concentrate almost exclusively on the sermon and the preaching process itself.

By ignoring the audience factor, homiletics training often implies that contemporary sermons should come in a package labeled "one size fits all." And yet very few spokesmen on preaching would recommend the same sermon be preached the same way to a golden-agers' banquet and a junior-high retreat. Common sense clearly indicates the need to tailor our sermons to fit our listeners, or we will quickly lose those listeners.

And as Aristotle acknowledged 2,000 years ago, you can't have communication without an audience to hear and respond. If we don't start giving them more consideration in our preaching and in our training of preachers, the frustration will only increase as any hope for achieving our goal of involvement slips quickly and quietly out the back doors of our sanctuaries.

There will always be an element of frustration in our preaching because the response will always be the audience's choice. Not even the Holy Spirit will strong-arm our listeners into submission. And yet there is increased hope for involvement if we give more careful consideration to our listeners and to what motivates their response.

Motivational psychology is one of the most complicated and controversial fields of psychological study. But a summary of most of its current theory suggests that human beings have to go through several steps or stages in the motivational process before they can respond or act in a certain manner. If we expect listeners to respond to our preaching, our sermons must account for and encourage each of these steps.

Step 1: Attention—awareness is gained, something is perceived, words are distinguished, conscious hearing takes place.

Step 2: Evaluation—each bit of information is appraised as good or bad, potentially harmful or beneficial.

Step 3: Recognition—desire will be aroused, action tendencies will surface, motives become apparent.

Step 4: Decision—action is chosen after the positives and negatives are weighed.

Inductive preaching can readily tie in to the various stages of the motivational process. For example, starting with the experience or needs of the audience increases the chances for winning attention in Step 1. Positive experience, good memories and imagination of future satisfaction can be applied inductively to Step 2. Then an inductive sermon reaches a point of discovery, of revelation (Step 3), and finally a choice is offered in Step 4.

If we expect to motivate listeners to respond to our preaching, our sermons must encourage them to progress through all four motivational stages. And we can guide them and sometimes gently prod them through the process to response, if we understand and utilize a combination of four different types of appeal.

We touched on the first appeal briefly in Chapter Two—*the ethical appeal of the speaker himself* as a person of intelligence, Christian character, service and goodwill. An empathy or affinity to the preacher helps construct a triangular relationship binding the speaker and his message to the audience. For when the people embrace the preacher, they more willingly embrace the message and the chance of a positive response rises dramatically.

There's no need to reiterate Chapter Two's discussion on the importance of the speaker, Aristotle's first element of the communication process. But it should be clear from the intervening discussion that one of the strengths of the inductive approach to preaching is the potential it offers for mutual identification between preacher and people. It's on this foundation of preacher/people identification that the other appeals are built. Without its firm support, they can carry very little weight.

The second appeal at our disposal is the *rational* appeal. We can lead our listeners toward the response we want by means of reasonable, logical appeals reinforced by sensible and interesting supporting materials. Much of this book—especially the discussions of inductive logic, inductive movement and the various structures of inductive sermons—has concentrated on the implications of inductive preaching and the rational appeal.

While I would never claim that the inductive approach offers the only hope for our sermons to exert a strong rational appeal, the common-sense logic of induction is closer to the everyday experience of our audience than is deductive reasoning. Plus, as has been stated earlier, inductive logic raises fewer defenses.

As one of my students shared after a classroom discussion on inductive preaching, "A sermon like that won me to the Lord. For years I was so argumentative. I'd argue with any preacher and win every time—at least in my own mind. Then I heard this radio preacher who was different. He got me going with him at the start of his sermon. Since I didn't have to argue, I began to agree with him. And he hooked me with my own common sense."

Another student standing with us added, "A cynical history prof sitting in your congregation can start picking a sermon to pieces, paragraph by paragraph, if you start with a proposition in typical homiletical style. But by starting where he is, at 'ground zero' you might say, he doesn't have anything to argue with at the start of the sermon."

Of course there's no guarantee a hostile listener will not argue with the conclusion reached at the end of an inductive sermon. But the longer we can keep the audience thinking with us, accepting the reasonableness of our accumulating proofs, the higher the hopes for a positive response to our sermons.

The third motivational tool available to every preacher is the *emo-*

tional appeal. Its frequent misuse in the past has drawn considerable criticism, created unfortunate misunderstandings, and greatly curtailed its use and potential impact in contemporary preaching.

When many modern preachers think about sermons with emotional appeal, they conjure up images of leather-lunged tent-meeting evangelists bellowing their fire and brimstone threats. Or they think of great orators of the past who laced their sermons with tear-jerking tales carefully calculated to manipulate listeners by tugging at heartstrings or by playing on manufactured guilt.

However, emotional appeals needn't be artificial, excessive or manipulative. Sensitive, conscientious preachers can effectively utilize emotional appeals that are sincere, responsible and appropriate for our modern, sophisticated audiences. For there's much more to emotional appeals than histrionics, volume and purple prose.

Inductive preaching, by its very nature, should appeal to the emotions of our listeners because it starts with the lives of our hearers—their needs, their values and their experience. Emotion is such a large part of life that including many of the inductive life-related elements we've already discussed will just naturally arouse emotion. If we realize this potential, allow for it, even plan on it, the emotional appeal of our preaching can result in greater impact and response.

For example, our senses arouse emotion. When people see, hear, taste, smell and touch, they respond emotionally. Henry Ward Beecher provided a classic illustration of this when he toured Great Britain before the Civil War to gain support for the Cotton Blockade. On one occasion he preached for an hour and a half in vain, trying to be heard above the jeers and catcalls of the southern-sympathizing crowd. A few days later he was to speak in one of the textile centers that promised an even more hostile audience because the British mills relied on slave system cotton. Beecher walked onto the platform dragging heavy chains which he dropped with a clatter as he shouted, "These chains have held human hands." And he preached that day without interruption because the sight and the sound of those iron bonds touched the emotions of his listeners.

Obviously there are limitations to the use of "show and tell" techniques in our preaching. But creativity could provide many effective object-lessons and visual aids appropriate in our pulpits. We can verbally draw on our listeners' senses with sensory words and illustrations.

Emotions don't depend solely on the physical senses. Memory and emotion are so intertwined that by sparking the memories of our listeners we often arouse emotions as well. Imagination, too, often is tied to our emotions; if we get people dreaming and imagining, inner feelings rise to the surface. Moods open other emotional doors; so setting and maintaining an appropriate mood in a sermon enhances the response.

Perhaps the most common and most effective emotion-arousing tool for any preacher is the life-related story, anecdote or illustration. The importance of this was reemphasized by Dr. Evyn M. Adams in his Ph. D. work at Drew University when he explored Kierkegaard's view of communication and its application to Christian preaching in Japan. Adams became the founding director of Methodist radio broadcasting on Hokkaido. He says, "Every six months we brought in pedestrians from the sidewalks to evaluate our broadcasts. We discovered some surprising concepts for communicating the gospel:

(1) People love *stories;*
(2) They love stories about *people;*
(3) They love people-stories with *pathos;*
(4) *Feeling* is the key to persuasion.

"When we began to incorporate these concepts in our radio broadcasts, good things began to happen. When we inserted more personal warmth and feeling into our programs, letters began filling our mailboxes.

"Pathos is the key to persuasion—even for unemotional oriental people. The charts on our broadcasts prove even those who seem to live with least obvious emotion respond to the feeling appeal."

Kierkegaard's view of communication as a dialectical-pathetic process includes two accents: the dialectical, intellectual column where theory, logic and reason reign supreme, and the pathetic, feeling intuitive column where emotions have their say and sway. Sermons on doctrine and theological instruction often fit into the dialectical area. And there's certainly nothing wrong with an intellectual thrust in sermons. But often in our erudite way we magnify the cognitive and cerebral and minimize the realm of feeling, the intuitive, the relational, the emotional in our preaching.

We forget that people feel as well as think. Yet people live much of their lives within the parameters of Kierkegaard's other arena—of feelings and relationships. Even the great thinkers live much of life on the feeling level. Those who only think they think live most of their lives in the area of feelings. We know human instances and feelings communicate. We don't need to go to Japan for evidence. Look at the written word. *Reader's Digest* weaves into each issue vivid human instances with deep human feelings that reach an estimated readership of 100 million. *Guideposts* squeezes the emotional juices out of its cases and examples for multitudes each month in a style some cynics dismiss as sentimental normanvincentpealism. These magazines communicate.

Like it or not, daytime television drama communicates as well. Why else do researchers find that a majority of viewers say they watch soap operas to find answers to the problems in their own lives?

The secret to emotional appeals in our sermons isn't simply to reenact drama in real life or to present a Sunday soap from the pulpit; we could go too far. But we seldom go far enough. The experience and emotion of daily life lie entirely outside the scope of too many sermons. When that happens, when the head stands at center stage and the heart doesn't even make a cameo appearance, our sermons aren't going to get the kind of response we hope for. It takes a combination of all these traditional types of appeals—ethical, emotional and rational—blended throughout a sermon for most effective persuasion.

In addition to these three historic appeals which have been identified, if not always applied, since Aristotle, the ongoing contemporary research in cognitive science suggests another motivational factor. And while this fourth factor may often overlap the rational and emotional appeals already discussed, recent discoveries in psychobiology raise so many interesting questions pertinent to preaching that it warrants mention here as a fresh, valuable consideration in motivating our listeners. Let's call it *the whole-brain appeal*.

In the audience portion of Chapter Two, our discussion of how people learn briefly introduced recent suggestions by psychobiologists that the human mind delegates different processes to the two hemispheres of the brain. To generalize the conclusions of recent research, it seems that most analytical, theoretical, sequential and diagnostic functions are assigned to the left hemisphere of the brain. The right side of the brain plays a primary role in imaginative, inventive, visuo-spatial, intuitive, holistic and nonverbal functions.

Traditional homiletics for centuries has emphasized a left-brained pattern of verbal, analytical, sequential appeals. And it has downplayed appeals that would involve right-brain functions such as memory, imagination, emotions, relationships, divergent thinking, imagery, integration of personal experience.

The Bible, in contrast, utilizes many right-brain appeals. The nonverbal, the metaphoric, the timeless, the prophetic, the exploratory—all shine out in Scripture. The inductive ingredients and the inductive process so prominently evidenced in God's Word (as discussed in Chapters Five and Six) are themselves right-brain appeals.

So if we want to involve the whole mind of our listeners, if we want a better chance to motivate them to a positive response with our preaching, we need to check our sermons for all four of the appeals we've mentioned. Before we deliver any sermon we would do well to ask ourselves:

Does my Christian character support what I'm saying?

Will the sermon touch people at the feeling level?

Can the message hold up rationally?

Does the sermon allow whole-brain involvement by including both right- and left-brain appeals?

If we can say yes to all four questions, our preaching will see results.

For several pages now we've discussed a speaker's means of influencing the audience's response. But what is the response we want? We've used the term "involvement" throughout the book. But to what end? For what purpose?

Lest I be accused of leaving God out of persuasion, let me recognize that neither preachers nor sermons change people. Transformation is God's specialty. Yet he honors us with a role in his work.

Our goal needs to be God's goal, the gospel's goal. And that goal is change. Whether it translates as commitment, recommitment, or Christian growth, the response we want from our listeners is change.

We want to see beliefs changed; that takes an appeal to the head and to reason. We want to see feelings changed; that takes an appeal to the heart and the emotions. And when those two things happen, relationships and lives change and God is at work.

Inductive preaching can be a valuable tool in that work.

Conclusion

One of my students, a retired army colonel, came up to talk to me after one of my seminary senior preaching classes. "Last Sunday," Don reported, "a thirty-five-year-old man came to Christ when I preached an inductive sermon in my student charge. The man said he'd never heard a preacher who respected him as a person before. I guess he was saying I was the only inductive preacher he'd ever heard.

"I spent twenty-two years in the military after I became a Christian," he added. "So I moved around a lot. I've never been in a church in all these years where people didn't need an inductive approach.

"I'll tell you, I'm really sold on this idea of induction," Don said. "The inductive approach has greatly helped my preaching. I've done an about-face in my thinking about the meaning of authoritative preaching. When I preach inductively, even the most secular people in my congregation listen and respond to my messages. And the saints like it too."

For more than twenty years now my lifework has been to help young ministers improve their preaching. That experience and the continuous response of students and former students have provided much of the impetus for this book. Numerous former students have returned from pastorates around the country to report the results of preaching what they've practiced in class. "Inductive preaching really does work." "My people's response sags incredibly any Sunday I fail to be inductive." "Inductive sermons have been my lifesaver in my new parish." "Everything you said about induction is true in my ministry."

I wouldn't want to declare inductive sermons the instant panacea for all the problems in preaching today. But a lifetime of experience and study has convinced me that inductive preaching holds incredible, untapped potential for twentieth-century preachers. I continue to teach it and preach it because it stands up to three important tests of its validity and value.

The biblical test. Is inductive preaching truly biblical? The answer is unequivocally "yes" on two counts. First, as emphasized in Chapters Five and Six, it's biblical in the sense that it follows the model of Jesus' preaching, most preaching documented in the Bible, and the style of the Bible itself as God's inductive communication with humankind.

And second, as I hope Chapters Seven and Eight made clear, the message of an inductive sermon can be and ought to be as scriptural as any other sermon, however classified. I want to reemphasize here that the truth we declare, the meat of our message, is always God's Word. The fact that an inductive sermon may reach that truth at the end, rather than asserting it at the beginning, makes the truth no less central or foundational to the sermon.

Perhaps some readers will struggle with the claims of this preceding paragraph. The manuscript of this book was read and critiqued by some staunch proponents of expository preaching who wondered how any approach to preaching that didn't call for verse-by-verse exposition could be adequately biblical.

These critics of induction probably will be surprised that I can agree with John R. W. Stott's assertion in *Between Two Worlds* (Grand Rapids: Eerdmans, 1982): "All true Christian preaching is expository preaching." Stott goes on to say: "If by an 'expository' sermon is meant a verse-by-verse explanation of a lengthy passage of Scripture . . . this would be a misuse of the word. Properly speaking, 'exposition' has a much broader meaning. It refers to the content of the sermon (biblical truth) rather than its style (a running commentary). To expound Scripture is to bring out of the text what is there and expose it to view. But the text in question could be a verse or a sentence or even a single word. It could equally be a paragraph, a chapter or a whole book. Whether it is long or short, our responsibility as expositors is to open it up in such a way that it speaks its message clearly, plainly, accurately, relevantly, without addition, subtraction or falsification."

This too should be the goal of inductive preaching. So it is that inductive preaching can be expository—expository preaching that respects the hearer and the Word.

The historical test. A great deal of the thinking, organization and inspiration of this book grew out of a lengthy personal study of the ninety-six preachers and the 411 sermons included in the thirteen-volume work, *Twenty Centuries of Great Preaching* (compiled by William M. Pinson, Jr. and Clyde E. Fant, Jr., Waco, Texas: Word Books, 1971). Careful examination of sermon examples by the most effective preachers from Jesus, Paul and Augustine to Helmut Thielicke, Martin Luther King and Billy Graham shows an impressive reliance on inductive ingredients, attitudes and structure. (See Appendix 3 for brief summaries of each of the ninety-six preachers and their inductive orientation.) Virtually all those judged worthy of mention as outstanding preachers portray some or several inductive strengths.

Through the ages the most effective Christian missionaries have taught, preached and lived out the inductive process by beginning where their people were and then leading them to God's truth. Effective evangelists have leaned heavily on examples, references to experience, case studies, human interest, imagination and other inductive ingredients. A more recently developed field of Christian service, youth ministry, often models the inductive approach. It's been my experience and observation that effective youth workers depend heavily on induction; in order to survive in their ministry they have learned to delay assertions, carefully achieve authority, earn credibility, and only then hit home with the gospel message young people need.

So it is that 2,000 years of Christian ministry seems to support the validity of induction. Christian history teaches us much about the inductive process. And inductive preaching passes the historical test.

The test of contemporary experience. We've already talked about the electronic, computerized, televised age we live in and the nonverbal, nonlinear logic trends of our day and how the inductive approach lends itself to the human habits of our technological age. But some other thoughts about induction and the contemporary scene bear consideration.

When do most dropouts from Sunday school and church occur? Isn't it at the age when we shift away from stories, drama and other inductive approaches in Christian education and expect junior-high and senior-high teens to begin more intensive indoctrination, catechism and the like?

With a growing realization that few of our parishioners know the difference between an alpha and a sigma, and even fewer care, recent seminary training is moving toward more practical theology, supervised ministry, counseling, crisis ministry and relational skills. There's an increasing concern that ministers need to be able to take the foundational information mastered in theology, Bible and ancient language classes and apply it to the everyday lives and problems of the average man, woman and child in our congregations.

However, this growing sensitivity to the combined emotional, psychological and spiritual needs of the individual has yet to impact the formal teaching of preaching itself. Whereas traditional homiletics ignores and often contradicts the shift to more personal ministry, inductive preaching could dovetail beautifully with other interpersonal emphases to unify all areas of ministry into a cohesive whole.

Churches and church membership are changing today. The forces of secularism are seen and felt in our pews. Church members in our day are more like nonchurch members than at any time in the history of our faith. And since most of us preach to committed and noncommitted listeners simultaneously, we need a strategy that can speak equally well to both.

Induction can be that strategy because it asserts and assumes nothing at the outset. Instead, it strives for respect, for agreement, for commonality, for credibility before it declares the truth everyone needs.

Student pastors and professor colleagues who serve local churches have reported something that greatly intrigues and encourages me. They tell me that when they preach a sermon with inductive movement and accent, they arouse response and comments from a group of parishioners who are usually silent. The usual encouragers at the door after the service are accompanied by an additional clientele of new complimenters and well-wishers.

Could it be that inductive preaching can increase the impact and response of preaching in our day? The test of contemporary experience would answer a resounding "Yes."

In closing it may be well to restate a point I've already tried to make many times, many ways in this book. It's the heart and soul of what I believe and teach about preaching: a sermon can be factually correct, homiletically sound, biblically accurate, doctrinally orthodox and still achieve nothing because it fails to involve the listeners. Involvement is the key. And listener involvement is the strength of the inductive process in preaching.

The Bible, the models of great preachers throughout history, and contemporary experience all combine to point to the great potential of inductive preaching. So I wouldn't claim induction is something new and revolutionary. Yet I'm convinced it could revolutionize your preaching.

You needn't accept my opinions or the claims of this book. Simply try inductive preaching. Then judge for yourself.

Would you like innovative applications and further help in applying these inductive concepts for biblical preaching? For individual and classroom use, you may order a Creative Guidebook for Inductive Preaching: Helping People Listen. *This guide contains charts, exercises, inductive experiments, bibliography and hands-on projects that will appeal to the imaginative right side of the brain. It's available for $3.95 (plus $1 postage and handling). Write:*

Inductive Preaching Guidebook
Asbury Theological Seminary
Wilmore, KY 40390

Appendix 1
Inductive Preaching—Two Examples

To better illustrate the idea of inductive sermons, two of the author's own messages are included here.

"Deliver Us?"
This first inductive sermon example grew out of a long personal study of the Lord's Prayer. The author preached the sermon in the Wilmore United Methodist Church in Wilmore, Kentucky to a congregation that included many seminary and college students.

The sermon's inductive whirlpool movement follows a question-answer format. The text of the sermon and accompanying notes highlighting its inductive characteristics will follow this brief outline and diagram of the sermon.

Outline: "Deliver Us?"
Unstated, but implied key question: Is this portion of the Lord's Prayer really relevant to us today?
 I. Anybody need deliverance?
    Facts, anecdotes, reminders of real life.
    Tentative conclusion: The need is all around us.
 II. Anybody being delivered in our day?
    Numerous anecdotes of contemporary experience.
    Tentative conclusion: Many are being delivered.
 III. Anybody been delivered in the past?
    Examples from history and Scripture.
    Tentative conclusion: God has delivered many people in many different ways.
 IV. Anybody want to be delivered now?
    Contemporary, personal and scriptural proof of the deductive as-

sertion that we all need to pray "deliver us," that God will honor this petition, and the listeners need only ask. Conclusion: the prayer is not only relevant but essential.

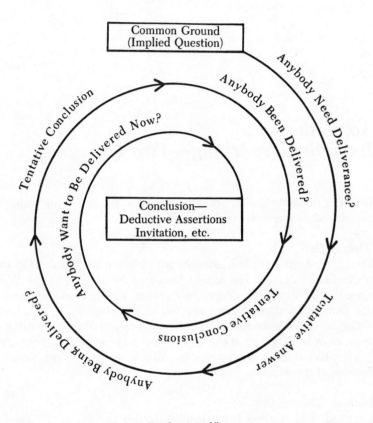

"Deliver Us?"

Sermon Text: "Deliver Us?"

"Our Father which art in heaven, hallowed be thy name. Thy kingdom come. Thy will be done in earth, as it is in heaven. Give us this day our daily bread. And forgive us our trespasses, as we forgive those who trespass against us. Lead us not into temptation. But deliver us. . ."

Deliver us. . .

Deliver us?

The implied question here at the outset: Is this portion of the Lord's Prayer still relevant? helps establish a common ground of questioning.

Anybody need to be delivered today? Here? Have you and I outgrown this prayer? Have you and I outlived this seventh petition of our Lord's Prayer? Is it outmoded? Obsolete?

Every Sunday we say, "Deliver us." Sometimes we seem to say, "Deliver us, but now now." "Deliver us—but not totally." "Deliver us, but not too much." "Deliver us, but not too specifically." "Deliver us, but later." "In my own way."

We pray, "Deliver us from sickness; deliver us from suffering; deliver us from fear; deliver us from poverty." Oh, yes, Deliver us from poverty! Deliver us from unpopularity. Deliver us from hardships. Deliver us from struggle. Deliver us from discipline.

Is there anyone here who can't look up and see need? Is there anyone here who can't look around and see human weakness? Is there anyone here who can't see and sigh and say "Deliver us"?

Oh, not that you added up all your burdens. Not that you saw all your needs. Not that you summarized all your sighs and struggles. Not that you gathered up all your groans when you said, "Deliver us."

But let's think together about this seventh petition in our Lord's Prayer. "Deliver us."

We know the other petitions, don't we? Give us. We're not apt to forget that—Gimme! Gimme! Gimme! Give us. Forgive us. Lead us. But "Deliver us"?

Anything you need to be delivered from? Anything you want to be delivered from? Any new levels you want to be delivered to?

More than 400 times the Bible uses this word "deliver." Liberation theology—rising out of the Third World, the have-nots—in recent years has put its major focus on the Exodus, a deliverance. They say everybody needs to be delivered from today's political and economic bondage.

Anybody in our land need to be delivered? Ask in the breaking and broken homes. Ask in broken and breaking hearts. Ask breaking and broken bodies at the hospital. Anybody need to be delivered?

Ask the broken and breaking lives in jails. Ask in the bars where the broken and breaking dreams lie all about the floor. Ask on the job. Ask in the marketplace.

1. First question builds on common ground.

References to common (weekly) experiences.

Questions rather than assertions.

Allusions to personal emotions and felt needs.

Aligns speaker with audience/cooperative effort.

References to life experience.

Appeal to experience of listeners: ask, ask, ask.

Ask in schools. Ask America's twelve to fifteen million alcoholics.

Anybody need to be delivered? Ask the frantic, frustrated families of these millions cursed by alcohol. Ask on the highways. The people in the North load up their burdens and go south in their trailers. The people in the South load their trailers with their cares and burdens to travel north. Three weeks later they all go back home, carrying their burdens with them.

Any need to be delivered? Ask the quarter of a million who attempted suicide last year. Ask these 250,000 people who tried to be delivered at their own hand. Any need for deliverance, anybody need to be delivered?

Ask one who has been so overwhelmed by personal problems and the cares of life and family pressures that he cannot speak audible words. He can only look into the face of God and say, "Oh, God. Oh, God. Oh, God." Ask him, "Is there any need for deliverance?"

Look around and see the love of money, which the Bible says is the root of all evil. Look around and see the secular slant on life. Look around and see the holiday binge, the pleasure-mad society. People are imprisoned in all these. Then ask, Is there any need for deliverance today? Any need at all? Look around and you'll see the need is universal. *Tentative conclusion: answering question I on the basis of evidence laid out.*

The second great question: Is anybody being delivered today? Is it only Gideon? And Daniel? And Joseph? Is it only those in Bible times who know about deliverance? *II. Question II asked and reiterated.*

Why is the word used more than 400 times in the Bible? Is deliverance a key concept in Christian history? Is deliverance a key concept today? Anybody being delivered today?

Some of you have seen along the interstate north of Georgetown what I've seen for the last three or four years. Every time I've driven by, I see in fading paint on a large storage trailer: Deliverance Revival. Isn't every revival a deliverance revival? *Contemporary examples.*

A few weeks ago I got some mail inviting me to a Deliverance Seminar. For eighty dollars I could be taught how to deliver people from demons. It didn't say seventy-five dollars went to the Lord and five dollars went to the preacher. It didn't say what the eighty bucks went for.

But there's been a kind of exorcist craze—a focus of attention on demons and possession by demons. The Church too often has left this accent on deliverance to the crackpots. Some have told me they've gone to exorcism parties where they've tried to cast out the demon of sleep, and the demon of left-handedness, and the demon of comfort, and the demon of laziness. Some claim, "The devil made me do it."

Some people see a demon under every bush—sometimes when there isn't even a bush! They remind me of the man with the anti-elephant whistle. He got a bright red whistle and he said, "This is my anti-elephant whistle. Guaranteed to prevent trampling by elephants." His friend said, "How much did you pay for it?" "Five dollars," he said. "It's a great anti-elephant whistle." And he gave a toot to demonstrate. "Why, there's not an elephant within 500 miles of here," his friend said. "Sure," said the man with the whistle. "See how well it works?"

Some people see deliverance only in terms of the exotic, the spectacular. But is anybody being delivered today?

In a June chapel service for which I was responsible, I asked four young people to share. These youth—both male and female—shared how they'd been delivered, gloriously delivered—from drink and dope and sex and suicide. Delivered from that meaningless and vicious cycle and circle. And there are many other deliverances.

Scores could witness here today. We hear (and we ought to) about sports figures who have found spiritual deliverance—Tommy John, Steve Bartkowski, Terry Cummings. We hear about Chuck Colson, and we ought to. We hear (and we ought to) about singers and actors and other celebrities who have found deliverance.

But some you have not heard about. S.W. was driving home from college along Interstate 75. As he started around a big semi with a trailer, he suddenly thought, "What would I do if my car caught on fire?" He was going along about fifty-five miles an hour in his

More contemporary examples.

little sports car, just overtaking this monster of death. His rear bumper just passed the front bumper of this huge leviathan of the road when suddenly his whole cockpit was filled with orange flame.

What did he do? He wheeled to the right, just grazing the front bumper of the tractor trailer, pulled onto the grass, turned off the ignition, opened the door and rolled out onto the ground. Delivered—in the same way he'd been thinking ten seconds before.

A.G. was scuba diving in the Gulf of Mexico. He was having a great time spearing red snappers down by an old shipwreck. Suddenly a gray shadow flicked by him and brushed him. He looked up, saw the sharp tail and knew it was a shark. He looked, but no place to hide.

Then another gray shadow flicked and brushed him. He started his flippers going and headed for the surface. When they hauled him out frantically on the deck, he'd been brushed by five sharks. He almost died of the bends on the deck. But he'd been delivered— five times on the way up.

C.M. was delivered. It was a leisurely Sunday afternoon in Georgia. Walking through the woods a group of boys found an abandoned house, a gallon of gasoline and an abandoned well. They fiddled around and poured the gallon of gas down the well. They ignited a piece of newspaper and dropped it fluttering into the hole. They waited. Nothing happened. They waited some more. Nothing happened.

C.M. leaned over to see what was going to happen just as it reached the "whoof" stage. And the Silica sand of that Georgia well came exploding up, driven through his eyeballs. He was blinded. For a month he couldn't see the light of day. This summer he finished seminary and you'd never know he had ever been blind at all. Because he's been delivered. He's been delivered by the God of all grace.

J.C. was in an auto accident. He'd just finished high school. It was a great lark. After the accident they brought him into the hospital. The examining physician said, "He's DOA," dead on arrival. They put him out on a gurney before they took his body down to the morgue.

A Jewish physician on his day off came to the hospital—by accident, you say? No. He came to the hospital and walking by said, "Who's that on the gurney out here?" They said, "It's J.C.—high school graduate of last week."

He went over and stooped down. "Bring the crew," he shouted. "Red alert—there's life here," he said as he swung into action. "Impossible," they said. "He'll never be more than a vegetable if he could survive."

They sent out a prayer call to all the Jewish synagogues, to all the Catholic churches, to all the United Methodist churches in that New Jersey town and people began to pray. The cynics said, "He'll never be more than a vegetable."

A few years ago he came to seminary and just to prove he wasn't a vegetable, he applied to medical school. He was cutting it in medical school when he felt the call of God sending him back to seminary, where he finished. He's out in ministry now. He's been delivered.

Another with the same initials, J.C., some of you heard a week ago. You heard him bellow like a bull in a cornfield—this man who in his early years was so weakened by TB the doctors said he'd never be able to preach again. Holes in his lungs big enough you could run your fist through them because of his TB. He's still being delivered.

Sixty years later and some of you saw him lift 300 pounds above his head. He's being delivered by the Lord. The day before he reached ninety he water skiied twenty-three miles—on one ski. He's still being delivered.

One here this morning, at the age of two, crawled through the gate of the barnyard and was riding around on the tail of a mean buckskin horse when his mother found him. The mean buckskin horse had his ears laid back and was ready to kick the slats out of anything that moved. Every week or so he kicked the planks off his stall. Nobody could quite understand why he didn't kick the brains out of the man who stands before you this morning.

Delivered. One here this morning was delivered when he saw the cow jump over the moon. It was bad enough for a boy to have to walk one way when he went to bring in the cows. Back on the rear forty he'd trained the cows when he was six or seven. When they were walking by the creek bank he would jump on and ride them back to the barn. He'd play cowboy that way.

One day he was coming by the high bank, and the cow turned and bolted down it. He slid right over the cow's head since there was no saddle horn to hold him on that old bovine. He looked up and saw that cow jump over him and the moon far up in the sky. More than once I've remembered those flailing hooves and the cow that seemed to be jumping over the moon. Delivered.

And all of us here have been delivered—from car accidents. A preacher in Cadillac, Michigan told me he was driving along, thinking about whatever preachers think about—something or nothing. He was driving along and he crossed a railroad track. He heard a noise behind him and he looked back. There on the front of a train engine went his rear bumper. He'd been delivered and didn't know it. *Contemporary examples continued.*

Or bike accidents. Or falls. Or what have you. Or storms. Tornadoes. Delivered.

When one of the infrequent storms went ripping through southeastern Michigan, it went through posh Grosse Isle. It leveled a huge house and picked up a baby. A boat had slipped its moorings and was out in the middle of a 200-acre lake. This flying baby was gently set down in that loose boat in the midst of the storm. Detroit papers called it "the miracle baby."

There's a sense in which every one of us has been delivered. In a sense every one of us is a miracle baby.

D. was driving a runaway truck racing down a Pennsylvania mountain. He prayed, "Lord, if you deliver me I'll go. I don't think seminary would be so much worse than this." He prayed, and God delivered him. He's finished now and out in full-time ministry.

R. was in an Indiana jail and he said, "Lord, if you'll just get me out—if you'll just deliver me . . ." And the Lord did deliver him.

B.J. was a native of this county. He and his family went for a picnic along Jessamine Creek back when it wasn't off limits to go to Chrisman Cave. They discovered they hadn't taken any salt along. And what's watermelon without salt for some people? Or a muskmelon without salt?

So they said "B.J., you climb up the cliff, run to the

car and bring us some salt for the melon." I'm sure his mother said, "Be careful." Surely his father said, "Hurry!"

He climbed up the cliff beyond the entrance to Chrisman Cave. When he got up near the top, there was a huge flat rock. It was as big as a room. He crawled up on that rock and started to scramble across it. He was up on ground level now and just as he started across, that huge rock shifted and began to slide—back toward the gorge from which he'd just crawled. He leaped backward, cried out and looked up. He could see a whole truckload of rocks coming. He cried out—and did God deliver him by repealing the law of gravity? Did God send those rocks back up where they came from? No. God had made preparation to deliver him in another way. Seepage from the rocks had softened the ground on the ledge below him. God didn't repeal the law of gravity and send those rocks to the stars. God delivered him in a more natural, a more normal fashion.

That huge flat rock kept on coming. It pressed him right down into that water-softened earth, and he spent the next nine months of his life in the hospital. But God delivered him. I never see him walk our streets without remembering that here is one God has delivered.

Some of you have read a book by a Miami, Florida lawyer. He was caught up in cocaine peddling and a lot of other things. He had a six-figure income every year. Thumbing his nose at life and society, he ignored everything decent. Money rolled in, but the authorities finally nailed him and sent him to prison for fifty years. And was he delivered? Yes. In two years he was out, telling people what God had done for him—how God had delivered.

And you've known people who've been delivered. Anybody being delivered today?

Some people from their religiosity. Some people from their emptiness. Some people from their love of money. Some people from the cares of life. Some from their business jungle.

Deliver us. Deliver us from everything? Deliver us from everything immediately?

Did you ever see someone help a cocoon become a butterfly by helping it out so it didn't have to be deliv- *Examples from nature.*

ered by the usual slow process? And what happens?
The butterfly never makes it.

Did you ever know of anybody trying to help a little
chick become free without the struggle of being delivered from the tomb of the eggshell? What happens? If
it's going to hatch and become a healthy chicken, it
must struggle in its deliverance. It must struggle by
itself. It must struggle through the course of nature.

Did you ever see an infant trying to crawl? You don't
pick it up and say, "Oh, I'll deliver you from all of this."

Did you ever see an infant learning to walk? You
don't say, "Oh no, don't try to walk. Wait till you're five
years of age and you can run." No.

You see a child trying to tie a shoe. Do you say, "Oh,
don't go through the struggle"? See a child trying to
ride a bike. Do you say, "Oh, don't try that. You'll skin
your knees. Wait until you're older"?

Did you ever see a student with lessons in math,
Hebrew or Greek—well, at least Greek—who prays for
deliverance and wants an easy course—who wants deliverance from the regulations, the thrusting and the
struggle? You don't make butterflies by easing them—
delivering them from all struggle. You don't make
chicks by cracking their shell and letting them out
without any struggle.

Is this life a testing ground, a proving ground? Do we *Questions*
need to be delivered from everything? From all dirt *rather than*
without sweeping? From all debt without discipline? *assertions.*
From all doubt without doubting our doubts? From all
danger without learning? From all desperation without
seeing the facts of life? Delivered from all disappointments without learning what life is all about?

Do you know anybody who is delivered from
death—that is, for a thousand years? Any need for discipline? For digging? For learning what you need to
hang onto, and what you need to let go of?

Do you know anybody being delivered today? How *Tentative*
much? How much need? How much deliverance do *conclusion.*
you want? How much burden do you have? How much *Answer to*
bondage? Are you being delivered today? Many are. *question II.*

Anybody been delivered in the past? We could look *III. Third*
here for a long time, but we'll hurry this along. *question.*

Freedom walks a long history. The Renaissance and *Allusions to*
the Reformation. The revolutions. Colonialisms. *history.*

Dozens of nations. Thousands freed from social and racial slavery. The Jews. Corrie ten Boom.
But what about the millions who were not delivered? Not delivered from Hitler?
Some of you think May and June of 1940 is ancient history. For some of us it is contemporary history. At Dunkirk hundreds of thousands of British soldiers were trapped on the beaches just across the channel from Great Britain. *Historical examples.*
Churchill said it would be a miracle if 90,000 could be delivered. Then came what he called "the Mosquito Armada"—861 vessels, from lifeboats to battleships. 243 were sunk in the process. They were being bombed by day and by night. Were 90,000 delivered so there was a miracle? No. A hundred thousand, then 200,000 and then 300,000 were delivered, and then 338,000—delivered. Delivered from Dunkirk.

If Hitler had known that in the vast resources of Great Britain there was only one repair axle for the railroads, he wouldn't have waited to invade Britain. But they were delivered from this.

When the Spanish Armada had amassed the greatest fleet in history, a storm blew them off into the North Sea. Delivered.

Yes, we could look at history. Bondage and slavery remain for some people today. Yes.

A hundred and twenty-five years ago an underground railroad was dedicated to delivering people. Blacks from the South moved toward Canada and deliverance. Southern statistics say 100,000 were delivered with a value of $30 million as slaves. Northern figures were more modest. They said maybe 500 a year were delivered. The U.S. census for those years shows about 500 a year were being delivered, but there were more than 1,500 agents on the Underground Railroad—in Ohio alone—all dedicated to delivering people. So we've been exposed to some of this.

History walks a long trail. A long road's filled with people who've been delivered in one way or another.

Delivered from child labor and sweatshops. From poverty. From the caste system. Some places in Kentucky the tenant farming is not far from a caste system. The minimum wage—do you know any man who can raise his family on the minimum wage?

We look at the American Revolution and we say that's great. But all other revolution is bad.

The Church has not always been in the middle of the freedom marches. But Jesus was always in the midst in his day.

Liberating freedom—freeing people—liberating those in bondage. "Where the Spirit of the Lord is, there is liberty." You find this accent in both the Old and New Testaments.

You take a jet trip through history and what do you see? When you look at the past, anybody been delivered? What kind of deliverance? From all diseases? Oh, we rejoice when we hear of cancer miracles today. We could wish there were a million more, but is everybody delivered from all diseases? All these diseases? *Appeal to imagination.*

No, there's an unknown quantity here when the Bible says, "According to your faith be it unto you." But we're in a mortal, marred world.

Any delivered from death? Sure. But it's appointed unto humanity once to die, the Scripture says.

It's so easy for us to look for exceptions. But the mortality rate for all faith healers is 100 percent. The mortality rate for Christians is one to one. No one in these days is escaping for longer than a hundred and ten years or so maximum.

From Aimee Semple McPherson to Kathryn Kuhlman, we are mortal. I'm not lampooning. When we pray for deliverance we need to see some of the limitations. We're in a mortal, marred world.

Are we delivered from all discouragement? From all distress? From all darkness so no shadow falls, no rain falls in our lives? From all desire so we have instant Nirvana? No desire? No discipline? No doubts—delivered from all doubts? How are you going to learn to doubt your doubts? From all development? *More questions rather than assertions.*

One of the requirements regarding the Land of Promise was, it was to be a gradual deliverance so the land wouldn't be overrun with obstacles and barriers and enemies. And so it is with character.

Does God build character instantly? He delivers in some areas instantly, but does he deliver us from all demands? All disappointments? From all oppression or opposition?

Some people give you the impression the devil is going to be on your side. No. He's going to be a constant opponent. But we have the victory because God delivers us. We have the victory through Jesus Christ our Lord.

Some would make more of demons than the Bible does, but he has promised us a way of escape. He brings victory so we can be more than conquerors.

How has God delivered? How does he deliver in the past? From fears? From cares? From worries? Physically? Spiritually? From emotional bondage and servitude? Socially and financially? From political and ecclesiastical bondage? From moral evil?

In varied circumstances with varied methods. The Bible is a record of personal deliverances.

John was incarcerated on the Isle of Patmos, exiled, but he was a free spirit. He was in the Spirit on the Lord's day. Peter was in prison, but he was delivered by an angel. Paul and Silas were delivered by an earthquake. Lazarus, in death, was delivered by a word from Jesus. The paralyzed man and his four friends—Jesus saw their faith and delivered the man.

Multiple biblical references as examples.

From diseases and ailments of all kinds—"you shall be delivered," Jesus said, "by your faith." Blind Bartimaeus by a cry. Out of the Egyptian bondage, the Bible says, "the Lord heard your cry." And the Lord led them out by a pillar—a cloud by day and fire by night. The three Hebrew children in the fiery furnace were delivered by the fourth man in the furnace. Daniel in the lions' den—delivered how? The king prayed for him and fasted all night.

In the Babylonian captivity the Hebrew people hung up their guitars; but despite their discouragement, God delivered them. Hezekiah was delivered by a fig poultice—for fifteen years he was delivered. Naaman was delivered by seven dips in the Jordan River. Jonah was delivered by a great fish God had prepared. God also prepared a gourd, an east wind and a worm. Jonah was delivered.

In the day of Esther the whole nation was delivered by one wise woman. You remember in Elisha's day, Sennacharib and the Assyrian hosts came and the people were delivered by an angel. And 185,000 corpses littered the ground the next morning. And remember the famine when the four lepers went out. The enemy heard a noise and scattered pots and pans and C-rations all the way to the Jordan River and beyond. God's people were delivered.

Remember when Elisha was surrounded? Gehazi said, "Oh, we're cut off—surrounded." The prophet prayed, "O Lord, open his eyes." And he saw the mountain filled with chariots.

Remember the time of the judges. Ordinary men became extraordinary men because the Spirit of God came upon them, and they were delivered.

Noah, delivered by a boat he built with his own bare hands. Yes, God has delivered in the past in many fashions.

Answer to Question III.

Through this Lord's Prayer? Yes. By the turning of events? By insights? By discovery? By our resolve not to fail those who trust us? Yes. By work? And by worship? By the work of God.

Experience past and present says, "There is deliverance." Christ is the answer. He is the complete promise and assurance. He has taught us to pray, "Deliver us."

"Deliver us." And what are the principles? Perhaps we ought to have a whole series of sermons on the principles of being delivered.

There is responsibility. You can't write it off by saying, "The devil made me do it."

There is reality. God is not always spectacular. God is not always instant. God is not always complete. God does not always work permanently. You and I live in a mortal world. And God's given us our reason. He's given us our heads. He's also given us the means of grace. He says, "Resist the devil and he will flee from you." He has given us prayer. He has given us trust and faith. He's given us Romans 8:28 and says, "In all things God works."

Assertions, tentative conclusions based on preceding evidence.

Deliverance belongs to the Lord. He is able to deliver you.

But the greatest question of all is not, "Is there any need?" The greatest question of all is not, "Is there deliverance today?", or "Have there been deliverances in the past?"

The greatest question is, "Does anybody want to be delivered now?"

God's accent is always on deliverance. God wants a free people. Let my people go, is God's refrain.

Does God want to answer this prayer? Does he want to grant this Lord's Prayer Jesus taught us, to deliver us from evil? Loose him and let him go! He is saying what Jesus said as he took the girl by the hand and lifted her up. Awake, you sleepers, and arise from the dead, and Christ shall give you light and life and liberty.

God's in the deliverance business. He sent Immanuel to deliver us. God with us to deliver us.

Jesus says in Luke 4 his great task is to deliver the captives. This is God's desire and pattern in your life and mine. Deliver us.

What is the conclusion? There is universal need for us to pray, "Deliver us."

In a moment I'd like to ask you all a question. How many of you could raise your hands and say, "I've been delivered"? Let's see the hands of those who can say, "In one fashion or another I've been delivered." Look at all those hands. Of course God delivers.

Some think about being delivered by the new birth. Some by the means of grace. Some by the Holy Spirit in times of new commitment.

Now I'd like to ask you an even more important question. Some of you have been delivered more than once—in spectacular fashion—in some great ways, and God is still in the process of delivering you and giving you deliverance.

Hundreds of you lift your hands to say God delivers. He delivers you. Your lives bear witness. You've been delivered. But does anyone want to be delivered now?

All kinds of bondage. All kinds of need. History shows a long record of deliverance. God is able to deliver.

That's the accent of both Testaments. Paraphrased, Psalm 34 says, "I sought the Lord, and he answered me and delivered me from all my fears. This poor man cried, and the Lord heard and delivered him out of all his troubles. The angel of the Lord encamps around those who fear him and delivers them. When the righteous cry for help, the Lord hears and delivers them

IV. Fourth question.

Here's the basic conclusion of the sermon based on preceding evidence.

Now the application and implication come. From here to the sermon's end is more deductive.

Assertions previously proved are reemphasized.

out of all their troubles. The Lord is near to the broken-hearted and saves the crushed in spirit. Many are the afflictions of the righteous, but the Lord delivers out of them all. Yes, deliverance belongs unto the Lord."

The Lord is able to wrap up your circumstances. God is able to wrap up your life. God is able to wrap up your need. God is able to encircle you and wrap up you, and deliver you. Underneath are the everlasting arms. Deliverance belongs unto the Lord.

More assertions based on preceding evidence.

Whoever calls on the name of the Lord shall be saved—shall be delivered. Whom the Son sets free is free indeed. Where the Spirit of the Lord is, there is liberty.

Four hundred times and more in the Bible there is deliverance. A million times in life—there is deliverance. God delivers.

Paul asks in Romans chapter seven, when he talks about that inner turmoil of carnality and anguish of spirit, "Who shall deliver us from the body of this death?" Then he comes back with the answer, "I thank God through our Lord Jesus Christ." This is God's pattern for life to deliver us—to deliver you and to deliver me.

He delivers today. From evil. Now. He delivers tomorrow from mortality.

During the closing hymn there will be opportunity to come and pray here at the altar if you feel the need for God's deliverance today.

Deliver us. . .

Deliver us from evil. For thine is the kingdom. And the power. The power to deliver. And thine is the glory forever and ever. Amen.

In summary: The basic four-question outline, 138 questions in the text, and the many life-related and biblical examples lead inductively throughout this sermon. Straightforward, direct sentences average eight to ten words each.

(Closing Hymn)

Come, almighty to deliver,
Let us all thy life receive;
Suddenly return and never
Never more thy temples leave.

Finish, then, thy new creation;
Pure and spotless let us be.
Let us see thy great salvation
Perfectly restored in thee.
—Charles Wesley

Does Jesus Weep Through Us?
The following inductive sermon is a slightly adapted version of a message delivered by the author in a regular chapel session at Asbury Theological Seminary, Wilmore, Kentucky. It is selected for inclusion here because it's a clear example of a complex-inductive sermon structure. Not only is the overall outline inductive, but each of its major segments develops by additional inductive means. Drawing on the structural analogy used in chapters Seven—Nine, this sermon contains whirlpools within the whirlpool.

Included below is a text of the sermon with margin notes pointing out inductive elements. The outline and diagrams should add to the reader's understanding of induction as it's used in this sermon.

Outline: Does Jesus Weep Through Us?
Stated key question: How can our world see a clearer picture of Jesus as both Son of God and Son of Man?
I. Let's look at our world.
Enumeration of facts, figures, quotes, life-related anecdotes and allusions to common experience.
Tentative conclusion: Our changing world is full of lonely, hurting people.
II. Let's look at our Lord in our world.
Introduction, multiple questions, then a basic question-answer inductive format throughout this section.
Tentative conclusion: Our Lord loved in word, in attitude, in action.
III. Let's look at our task for our Lord in our world.
Anecdote, analogy, question, then answer.
Conclusion: Thesis of sermon stated. Basic assertion declared. Implications and applications made. Challenge given. Sermon ended.

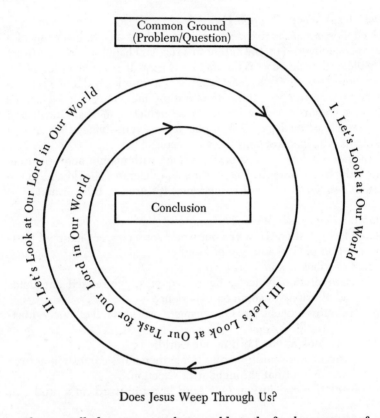

Does Jesus Weep Through Us?

The overall three-step outline could easily fit the pattern of an inductive-exploration type sermon; the minister leads his listeners as they walk around the problem/question posed at the very beginning. Even the word choice of the basic outline suggests exploration: Let's look; let's look; let's look. After examining the world, the Lord in the world, and our task for the Lord in our world, the answer is discovered.

But each of the three steps is also inductive in itself. Part I follows the inductive whirlpool pattern of enumeration—arranging facts, figures, and examples one after another until a picture is painted of what the world is like.

Part II starts off with some initial introductory comments, lists a lot of questions, then follows an inductive question-answer, question-answer, question-answer format until it presents a picture of Christ in the world.

Part III begins by asking a question, presents an anecdote that serves as an analogy and thus leads to the answer and the basic conclusion of the entire sermon.

In addition to the single whirlpool diagram above, this sermon might also be diagrammed like this:

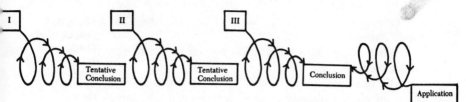

Does Jesus Weep Through Us?
In theologically conservative circles we have stressed Jesus, the Son of God; but have we neglected Jesus, the Son of Man? How can our world see a clearer picture of Jesus as both Son of God *and* Son of Man?

Let us look at our world.

As young people we may shout, "Hurray! We're in the Pepsi generation!" But is life in our world more than a big fizz—more than carbonated bubbles?

This is the space age.

An eighty-year-old woman wrote a letter to space pioneer Dr. Wernher von Braun: "Why must we go to the moon?" she asked. "Why don't we stay on earth and watch television as the good Lord intended?"

Our world is changing. An electronic device scarcely known forty years ago is now accepted as part of original creation.

This is our world:

5,000 years from sailboat to steamboat.
100 years from steamboat to airplane.
40 years from air age to atomic age.
12 years from atomic age to space age.
Now the computer age develops simultaneously with the space age.

Since 1960, according to the Space Computer Center in Alabama, we have been doubling our fund of facts every two years. Now, every six months we compile as much new information as the entire world possessed before.

From the time of Christ until 1760, world knowledge doubled once. From 1760 to 1880 it doubled again. In 1914 it had doubled the third time. Now the raw mass of human knowledge doubles twice a year. Think of it.

Very brief introduction poses the question/ problem to be explored.

I. Phase One of the exploration starts here. Commercial/ life-related.

Anecdote/ humor.

Facts building to lead to point.

Use of "we" and "our" helps establish commonality, sets stage for sermon as a joint quest.

Today microcosm and macrocosm are twin frontiers for exploration. Our world is getting smaller and larger at the same time.

Ours is a world of daily change. Finite change. Cosmic change.

Stories and facts have led this far.

What other characteristics do we see in our space-age, computer-age world?

We see declining optimism, rising pessimism. We see an almost obsessive quest for success, pleasure, power, satisfaction and security. (Some say as we enter the eighties we're in the grip of a security psychosis.) Perhaps we can see our world best in some brief examples:

Assertions here. But these assertions would be acceptable, palatable to listeners.

Oh, see the people! the people! the people!

Come with me to the living room of an average American home. Husband and wife look at each other, then she blurts out desperately: "It would be hell to go on living like this."

Life-related examples.

In another living room the young wife says, "I have a wonderful family, a fine husband with a good job, two fine children, home paid for—if only life had some meaning."

Come to a hospital—a children's ward. A little child throws his chubby arms around your legs and pleads: "Will you wock me? Will you wock me?" You pick up the youngster and begin to rock as he cuddles and snuggles up close to you. The doctor comes in and says: "We don't understand this child. We've X-rayed every way but inside out and can't find a thing—but so insecure and so lonely." Will you wock me?

Use of "you" increases listener involvement, puts listener's imagination to work.

Come to the rest homes where the aged and the destitute clasp and hold your hand, stroking it softly with their bony fingers. "No one cares any more," they say.

Even use of "come" calls for involvement.

Come to the sick beds. A cancer patient looks up into your face and asks: "How sick do you have to be to die?"

Come to the cocktail parties where everyone is talking, no one listening. Come to the bars where lonely men sit and weep in their beer.

Come to city and county jails where I've seen puddles of tears splash on the cold concrete floor as men talk of home, family, business, yesterday, loneliness and sin.

Come to the hobo jungles by the railroad tracks—see these homeless men huddled around a fire. They put canned heat into an old sock and squeeze out the alcohol to drink. I've actually seen this inside the city limits of one of the world's cultural centers.

Spaced-out junkies, addle-brained alcoholics, burned-out, mixed-up, throwaway people. We've all seen them.

Come to the sidewalks of the great cities—everyone looking, no one seeing. What a mad rush as men look for the rainbow. The throngs search the sea of faces for a friendly glance—but no one sees. No one cares. Turn the corner and here is skid row. These men have been teachers, lawyers, business and professional men—fathers, husbands, brothers, sons of respectable families. Around the block are the streetwalkers—pretty faces, hollow, empty, haunting, soulless eyes with personality and identity gone. Come to the abortion clinics with their plastic bags filled with unwanted babies. Come to some counties of our nation where more than half of all births are out of wedlock.

Come to our great stadiums and huge sports arenas any weekend where men throng for thrills. They sit as the people did around the cross of Jesus—"and sitting down they watched him there." When the excitement is over, they surge out through the gates to eat and drink. Hours later they must go back to the house they used to call "home." *Reference to common experience.*

Come to millions of bedrooms in America and around the world where every morning the first words are: "Good morning, heartache—here we go again."

Come to our own county just last week to a hovel within 200 feet of a medical center. See the empty bottles, the rags, the hungry children, and a baby with seven maggots in its navel!

Come in our own county on a summer afternoon since high school graduation four months ago. See a young genius, high in his class, but from a broken lonely home—no security, no sense of worth, no sense of purpose—a desperately lonely boy with no one to love him, no one to care. Because he fears his girlfriend might be leaning toward his best boyfriend, he shoots and kills himself to end his teenaged loneliness. What a tragedy! *Local experiences.*

Come to orphanages, county and state homes for youth. See the unwanted children sitting, waiting to be rejected again.

Can't you see and hear the throngs of people—old people, middle-aged men and women, young parents, college youth, teenagers, boys and girls? *Is it nothing to all ye who pass by?* Does anybody care? "I looked and no man cared for my soul!"

See the lonely crowd.

Our world has changed. But has it?

The Flintstones in a cave, the Smiths in a suburb, Buck Rogers on the moon. We're all lonely.

Microcosm. Macrocosm. Sometimes the space "in here," in the heart, seems as vast as the space "out there," in the heavens. It seems the more high tech we get, the more high touch we need.

Does the Bible speak to this constant human need—this loneliness? Do the Scriptures speak a universal language to lonely, suffering, sinful people?

To answer that, let us look at our Lord in our world.

Here at the seminary we begin with Jesus the Son of God—and we should. He is the Son of God—we need to teach it—we need to preach it. He is the Son of God! We all believe this.

But this is only half the truth. Jesus is also the Son of Man. Over eighty times in the Gospel record he is called Son of Man. This is his favorite name for himself—Son of Man.

Because some have overemphasized his humanity, we tend to swing to the other extreme. We accent his deity as Son of God. We tend to neglect his humanity as Son of Man.

Some ancient manuscripts were written in silver ink on purple vellum. When the scribe came to the name of Jesus he used gold ink. But he is both Son of God and Son of Man. He is both divine and human.

We may have accepted him as Son of God—our Savior. We may refuse him as Son of Man—our example.

Our purpose today is not to explore or to sponsor any of the schools or views of the kenosis, the divine emptying of the Son of God who became the Son of Man. Our purpose is to look at Jesus—to see Jesus as our example—the Son of Man.

Enumeration in Phase One has built to this conclusion: our changing world is full of lonely, hurting people.

II. Phase Two: the exploration begins. Common ground with this audience. These assertions are accepted by this audience.

Is he our pattern of self-giving in Christian compassion? Isn't he our example of sensitivity to sin and suffering? Is he our example of serving in a physical, personal way? Isn't he our example of saving individuals and lives as well as souls? Is he Son of Man when he shows his humanity is both ideal and real? He is deity stooping down—he is humanity standing on tiptoe. Above all else he is sensitive—he is as sensitive as a raw nerve exposed.

Our Lord is the Son of Man and he loves people. He is Christian compassion in person. Knowing, feeling, acting—he is Christian love.

Love is no mere theory with him. Love is no fancy phrase.

Can we see our Lord's love in his words? Never man spake like him—gentle, comforting, personal. Hear him:

"Come unto me all ye that labor and are heavy laden." "I will give you rest." "Neither do I condemn you—go and sin no more." "Fear not, little flock, it is the Father's good pleasure to give you the Kingdom." "Let not your hearts be troubled." "I go to prepare a place for you that where I am, ye may be also." "I am the resurrection and the life." "I am the Good Shepherd; the Good Shepherd giveth His life for the sheep." "I am the Door, I am the Vine, I am the Bread, I am the Water of Life." "I am the Way, the Truth, the Life." "I have prayed for you." "I have loved you."

He speaks the language of the human heart. He shows love in his words.

Can we see his love in his attitudes? He forgives sinners. He has compassion on hungry multitudes. He welcomes little children. He is gentle with women, boys and girls. He accepts outcasts. He seeks out segregated Samaritans and stays in their village. He makes them heroes of his stories. He is kind, unselfish, thoughtful. He honors and respects the individual. He champions the cause of the oppressed. He is patient with his disciples. He is friend of the publicans and sinners. Even his rebukes arise from deep love.

Can we see his love in his actions? Loving in word and in attitude are not enough for the Son of Man. He says, "Not everyone who cries, Lord, Lord, will enter in—but he who *does!*" Love must get into our *action*—

Use of questions.

Inductive question/ answer format. Scripture used not as assertion here, but as evidence.

Question/ answer.

Question/ answer.

it did with our Lord. The text for his first sermon was from Isaiah:

"The Spirit of the Lord has anointed me to do six things: Preach to the poor; heal the brokenhearted; preach deliverance to the captives; recovery of sight to the blind; set at liberty the bruised; preach the acceptable year of the Lord."

But did not our Lord do much more than preach? He became poor. He died of a broken heart—his grain of wheat had fallen to the ground to die long before he came to Calvary! He delivered captives. He gave sight to the blind. He set at liberty the bruised, broken, and bleeding.

Our Lord "went about doing good." Let's look at this sentence, "He went about doing good." "He"—this was direct service. "He went about"—he made opportunity; he sought a place to serve. Crowds came to the compassionate Son of Man. He was not content—"He went into all Galilee, healing all." "He went about doing"—see the personal effort and exertion here. This is no passive, lazy, flooding of sentiment; no mere well-wishing.

No! John Henry Newman couldn't be speaking of the Son of Man when he wrote: "But he who lets his feeling run/ In soft luxurious flow,/ Shrinks where hard service must be done/ And faints at every woe."

No! Our Lord is the Son of Man who shows his love in his actions:

Do you see him? He weeps at the grave of Lazarus. He weeps over the city of Jerusalem. He eats with publicans and sinners. He feeds the hungry multitudes. He touches lepers—the untouchables! He touches the blind with their running, festering eyes. He raises the dead.

The deaf hear, dumb speak, lame leap, halt run, blind see, thirsty drink, hungry eat. His love gets into his actions.

He lived and died in love—his life was a constant stream of love. Our Lord in our world was loving and compassionate.

The lonely lepers and blind beggars ran homeward crying in amazement at his tender compassion: "He touched me!" "He touched me!" "He touched me." "He loves me." "He loves me." "He loves me."

Tentative conclusion. Summary of evidence examined in Phase Two.

Our Lord loved in word, in attitude, in action.

We have seen our world, and our Lord in our world.

Now, third and finally, let's look at our task for our Lord in our world.

What is our task?

There's a story told about the early days of broadcasting. A king is sending an important message around the globe in a worldwide broadcast. An electrical cord begins to smoke; it smolders, then bursts into flames. The broadcast engineer has no replacement cord, so he seizes the bare wire connections on each side of the short. The surging, throbbing current flows through his own body. And the king's message goes around the world.

That man became a channel for his king's message.

What is our task?

Jesus wept!

He *was* the Son of Man. He *is* the same—yesterday, today and forever. But how does Jesus weep today? He must weep through our eyes.

Then this is our task. We too must be channels. Living sacrifices through which our King's loving compassion can flow.

In a practical, personal, nontheological way, Christ must become flesh in us.

Simply stated, today's thesis is this: If our world is going to see a clearer picture of our Lord, Spirit-filled Christians are going to have to give their personalities to be channels for Christ's tears, his compassion and love to men.

This is not easy! It is much easier to yield the soul to God—but the world sees personality. Men see our spirit, our attitude. They see our compassion. They feel our concern. They sense our human warmth, our friendliness, our personal interest, our Christian love. It is much easier to call him Lord and flee into cliches and theology (as good and as important as theology is).

It is easier to take refuge in a religious experience of the past. And sometimes we are so polemical, so defensive, we never get personal or friendly with people. Or we may not even try to learn their names or get acquainted.

Jim Vaus says: "Too often we're willing to preach, but we're not willing to get involved." He says, "When

III. Phase Three begins. Question/not assertion. Anecdote serves as an analogy.

Question.

Comparison/ analogy.

Basic conclusion: The sermon's primary assertion is reached.

Life-related implications and applications are stated. From here on, the sermon moves deductively toward the challenging question at the very end.

we really love, our message will be heard—even in the streets of New York City!"

If we are to be followers of Jesus, the Son of Man, we will come to a higher commitment of our personality, our friendliness, our human interest, our kindness, our sympathy, our empathy as Christians with a shepherd heart.

We are to offer our bodies, our spirits, our all—as walking sacrifices of love every day—a love offering to God, a human sacrifice to people—a channel of God's love to men about us. This is not easy. For many this is the most difficult part of the Christian life. Some have taken Jesus as the Savior of their souls but have never taken him as the example of their lives. Some seem to have surrendered their souls for the *crisis* of sanctification but have never surrendered their personalities for the later *process* of sanctification.

In a way there must be incarnation in each of us. The world must see Jesus and his love in us. God wants to love the world through us. He wants to "shed his love abroad in our hearts by the Holy Spirit who is given unto us." But we need more than love for *souls*—we need to love *people*. We may talk of our love for souls and be indifferent to individuals. We may draw near with the mouth and honor with the lips, but still have a heart far removed.

You've heard of the man who deeply loved the human race—but he despised people!

What is our task?

"Jesus wept. Then said the Jews, Behold how he loved him" (John 11:35, 36).

"Jesus wept. So the Jews said, See how he loved him" (RSV).

Modern man is lonely. Today men long for the human touch of Christian compassion . . . for human concern. They yearn to find someone who loves them; someone who cares.

Can you see the people, like the Hindu tapping his way through life—tapping on trees and rocks, seeking for God? "Are you there? Are you there?" See the South American Indians shouting into dark mountain caves and canyons, "Are you there? God, are you there?"

Can you see the men of our generation search the face of every man they meet? "Do you care? Do you care? Do I matter? Do I count? Do you really love me?" The world searches the face, the words, the attitudes, the actions of every Christian—pleading, yearning, asking, "Are you looking for me? Or are you just searching for souls? Are you trying to save your soul and build your evangelist's reputation on me—or do I count? Do you love me? Or do you just love my soul?"

What is our task? "Bear one another's burdens and so fulfill the law of Christ." "This is faith that works by love."

This is our task!

"Jesus wept. And the Jews said, See how he loved him." Today too the lonely people of our world stand by fresh graves. They have broken hearts, blasted hopes, empty lives, unfulfilled dreams. See their wretched homes, frustrated plans, tangled relationships. They have perverted appetites, inner cravings, slavish sins.

What happens? Do they feel our compassion? Do they see our tears? Do they say of *us*, "See how he loved"? Jesus wept. He was the Son of Man. And the Jews said, "Behold, see how he loved him." Friend, does Jesus weep through you today?

Appendix 2
Checklist of Inductive Characteristics

How do you decide if a sermon you are preparing or a sermon you hear is inductive? Here's a checklist of characteristics to be found in inductive sermons.

Accents human experience and learning from experience.

Accepts hearers with respect "as are" and where they are; acceptance differs from approval.

Accommodates, adjusts to hearers' needs and limited faith, not just to preacher's status.

After reaching agreement and cooperative conclusion the sermon may push for action.

Analogy created via parable, experience, human instances and figures of speech.

Arranged to proceed from particulars, examples, instances to reach cooperative conclusion.

Assertions are delayed until vital, interesting evidence leads to a convincing conclusion.

Assumes positive sharing posture—not defensive negative stance.

Audience analyzed to determine their hostilities, needs, reservations and hang-ups.

Authority is achieved, earned, not assumed; authority holds low profile at first.

Avoids threat, rigidity, abstract generalizations and premature conclusions.

Based on deep-seated human habit of induction—learning from experience.

Begins where the people are—not where the preacher is.

Begins with *attitude* of acceptance, charity, respect toward hearers.

Begins with common sense instead of theoretical abstract logic.

Begins with life and experience, not just rational exercise.

Begins with parable, facts, experience, case, human instance, interest, examples.

Bible used as example before it is cited as the ultimate authority.

Coincides with Protestant heritage—every man his own priest with opportunity, responsibility.

Combines well with deductive *after* reaching compelling, cooperative conclusion.

Compares and contrasts before jumping to conclusions.

Conclusions come at the end; tentative, partial conclusions follow the evidence.

Concrete common sense instead of theoretical abstract logic—especially early.

Conflict, polemics, defense and negative stance are all out of place in induction.

Directness includes: direct discourse, "you," "we," "our," "us."

Doctrines often must be felt to be true before they can be understood to be true.

Evidence precedes verdict, problem prior to solution, questions before answers.

Examples from life form a basis for learning, involving, concluding.

Experience, examples and evidence come before assertions, thesis or conclusions.

Experience serves as early proof, basis for learning and life.

Feeling and involvement follow naturally from shared experience.

Feeling and reality should be underscored rather than words or ideas alone.

Harnesses deep-seated human habit of induction; rides crest of current cultural trend.

Hearer agreement and involvement precedes all exhortation or proclamation.

Hearers identify and become involved with shared experience and cooperative conclusions.

Human instances aim at interest and involvement.

Human interest precedes instruction, indoctrination or exhortation.

Ideal for uninformed, unconvinced, uninitiated, uncommitted, indifferent or hostile hearers.

Illustrates rather than coerces or forces: illustrations are innately interesting.

Illustrations *precede* propositions; facts precede force, persuasion or fervor.

Intellect and will alone cannot receive the whole truth—feelings are vital too.

Intensity and urgency *follow* initial induction and come after tentative conclusions.

Interest and involvement are seen as higher goals than mere indoctrination.

Investigates before it instructs; solves problems before giving answers.

Jesus related to experience of his hearers via narrative and parable.

Key question establishes common ground—may be stated or only implied.

Key questions set the agenda—not previous conclusions of the preacher.

Leads in cooperative quest rather than pushes to conclusion.

Leaves options, choice and responsibility to the hearer.

Lends itself to variety, interest, involvement, cooperation and commitment.

Moves from known to unknown, from analogy to reality, from facts to faith, life to God.

Narrative element precedes exhortation (postpones or perhaps even precludes hortatory).

Nonadversary method appeals to many today.

Open attitude and stance bring hearers to consider options.

Organized to give vital and interesting evidence leading to cooperative conclusion.

Past is viewed as experience—not as tradition or basis for authority only.

Personal involvement of the preacher is vital for involving hearers.

Picture thinking creates imagery, parables, interest, involvement.

Psychologically sound—begins where hearers are and guides via sense and experience.

Reasonable common sense has more appeal than authority and abstract logic.

Reasons from particular facts, experiences, instances in cumulative manner.

Relates to hearers and their needs, seeks to share rather than shove.

Sermon leads up to conclusion, rather than running down from proposition to the end.

Specific instances cited before drawing any generalizations or making any assertions.

Today's accent more on *see*, *feel* and *do* than on traditional *hear* and *think* only.

Appendix 3
Ninety-six Inductive Preachers from 20 Centuries

Though my belief in the ideas behind inductive preaching is rooted in years of study and professional experience, my "Eureka cry" came during a sabbatical project reading the 411 sermons in *Twenty Centuries of Great Preaching* (compiled by William M. Pinson, Jr. and Clyde E. Fant, Waco, Tex.: Word Books, 1971). Suddenly I realized that all ninety-six of the notable speakers included in this thirteen-volume work used some inductive ingredients and showed signs of inductive process. The common thread through their greatness was not some secret aspect of exposition or oratory. It was induction.

This discovery provided much of the inspiration and impetus for the further study and thought which has led to this book. So I want to share with the readers a brief summary of the inductive discoveries from the work of these model preachers. These findings serve both as background and support for what I have attempted to say.

You'll note as you read that these ninety-six preachers[1] are listed chronologically (for the most part). And the length of my summaries is more dependent on the number of inductive ingredients I found than the measure of importance or orthodoxy of the speaker. Early Christian preachers as a rule employ more elements of the inductive approach than some later speakers. But then we have more ready examples of the most recent preachers.

Volume 1. Christ's Sermon on the Mount bursts forth first with the

---

[1]Sixteen of these ninety-six preachers are also included among the thirty-seven James Cox cites in *The Twentieth Century Pulpit*. These sixteen most famous duplicated preachers average using more than twenty questions per sermon. Interestingly, the other twenty-one preachers featured by Cox alone average only about half as many (eleven) questions. Only two of his twenty-one generally lesser-known men use more than twenty questions. While not conclusive, these facts hint at a growing insight—the greatest preachers tend to be more inductive—almost without exception.

freshness of life itself in Volume 1 of the thirteen-volume work, *Twenty Centuries of Great Preaching*. Traditionally the Beatitudes have been viewed as crystallized rules for entering the Kingdom, but their cumulative inductive impact leaps at us if we see them as astute observations of Jesus. Actually the words "Life shows" or "See how" can precede each beatitude to emphasize his keen insights and show how this sermon relates to learning from inductive experiences of life.

"Life shows how happy are those who know they are spiritually poor," or "See how lucky those are who mourn," etc. These are only two of the more than a hundred times Jesus refers to experience in this short walk-around, discovery-type sermon. Comparisons and contrasts, questions and illustrations, imagery and figures of speech abound. Strict logical sequence seems to be sacrificed for human interest and involvement of hearers in this sermon, designed as a nonadversary exploration of true human happiness. Personal involvement and response come to climax with the strong choice demanded by the two trees, two ways, two gates, two foundations in the conclusion of this cumulative inductive message, which explores multiple aspects of the happy person's life.

The sermon at Pentecost, a five-minute message by Peter, is without any questions, but does begin with the inductive problem-solving routine. The assembled crowd comes from scattered parts of the world, but they're unified by faith and practice. Therefore, his three extensive quotes and his repeated references to David serve to unify them even more. He refers to experience, to David, to Joel, and then to Jesus because his hearers can accept the authorities he cites.

Stephen's defense illustrates inductive use of historical narrative to defer the speaker's assertions. He seeks to placate by narrating, by quoting their accepted authorities, by referring to Old Testament situations until he blasts them with his scorching accusations. Thus he postpones his death by the length of his inductive talk.

Paul's inductive sermon on Mars Hill cites experience, relates to Greek religious practices, quotes their poets and seeks to win their acceptance, agreement and approval. I've heard some shortsighted contemporary criticism miss the stated results of this classic sermon: "Some men joined him and believed; among them was Dionysius, a member of the Areopagus, a woman named Damaris, and some others."

Paul's sermon before King Agrippa shows his sensitivity to social amenities, the narrative use of biography and testimonial witness in nonadversary fashion.

An anonymous sermon on Isaiah 54:1 is cited by Pinson and Fant as the oldest surviving sermon manuscript. It employs fourteen questions in twenty-two paragraphs with a great amount of pronoun directness. For example, in the 247 words of the first paragraph the author uses thirty-five pronouns—we, our, us, he, him, his—to achieve involvement. The preacher makes repeated references to experience and spends paragraph 19 depreciating himself so he won't seem to be preaching from an adversary position when he makes his concluding appeal.

Origen, the zealous and almost fanatical Christian student, has become notorious for his use of allegory. But he establishes the form of the sermon as a discourse on a specific biblical text and is the first to stress the importance of careful exegesis of the sermon text. Until Origen, in the middle of the third century, preaching is primarily informal, inductive-type testimony, and nearly every Christian considers himself a preacher of the gospel willing to share his unstudied, loose and unstructured witness. Origen's homily, a simple study of Scripture given in a continuous narrative based on one particular Bible passage, shows repeated comparisons and analogies and uses nine questions along with references to common experience.

Chrysostom with the golden mouth is plagued by applause and pickpockets during his sermons. His compassion and concern focus on the most common and perplexing problems Christians face. Courage is his hallmark as he attacks the burning issues of the day. He often inserts lengthy comparisons with Old Testament figures as he relates to the common experiences of his hearers. His descriptive ability is illustrated on nearly every page with similes and comparisons. He uses narrative, imagination, many questions and strong appeals to emotion as he relates to the people, seeking their involvement and response.

Augustine speaks to the abiding, relevant, explosive questions of life. He is more concerned about getting hearers involved than impressing them with his learning. His countless illustrations from daily experience heighten the enduring interest of his sermons. In his Lord's Prayer sermon he uses 157 comparisons and seventy questions.

Bernard of Clairvaux preaches about married bliss for eighteen years—in regular sermons based on the first two chapters of Solomon's Song and directed exclusively to monks and other men. But his sermons are acclaimed by noble and commoner alike as he relates elsewhere to all the issues of his day. Allegory marks his extemporaneous preaching. In his fifteen-minute sermon "On David and Goliath" he uses forty-two comparisons, five questions and twenty-eight Bible quotes. Bernard's sermon on his brother Gerard employs thirty-eight questions, with references to experience, memory and deep emotion.

Francis of Assisi in his fanatic commitment to poverty tries desperately to involve the common people in the living out of religious commitment. He insists, "We must act rather than teach, and our acting and teaching must go together. Unless you preach everywhere you go, there is no use to go anywhere to preach." He speaks from the fullness of his experience, with great respect for the people and great concern for the poor.

Thomas Aquinas, called the Great Dumb Ox of Sicily, joins the Dominican preaching order. He often dictates to as many as three or four secretaries at once in his learned defenses against heresy. His brief homilies seem dull and meager, but he actually has to pause in his discourses to let the congregation weep. Despite his closed eyes or heavenward gaze during his sermons, his free and direct delivery elicits deep involvement and almost total response of the people. His extant outlines appear to be just that—mere bony skeletons of his effective sermons with much obvious reference to experience.

John Tauler, with his deep mystical leanings, is warmly appealing, personal, fanciful and excessively emotional in his preaching. He is more practical and his sermons more related to life than other mystics. His sermons, although addressed to nuns, draw their imagery from hunting, war, seafaring, farming, trade and natural history. He is fascinated with the implications of human experience, but excessive allegory mars his ministry. His simple homilies show many comparisons and frequent references to experience.

John Wycliffe, "The Morningstar of the Reformation," like Luther a well-educated Catholic priest and a superb preacher, still lives in his sermons. His Latin sermons are scholastic, his English sermons popular in style and content. Complex arguments in polemical tone mar the simple beginnings of many sermons, along with his preoccupation with the past, allegory and other common blemishes of the Scholastic period. More than 300 of his brief sermon outlines survive, but they generally lack the directness implied by the twenty questions found in his thirty-five-minute sermon, "The Body of Christ." He exalts preaching and inaugurates tinerant sermons in the common language of the people, but some of the specific inductive elements of earlier inductive preaching have largely faded by the time of the Reformation.

Savonarola, orator, reformer and martyr, persists in practicing after his early failures until he develops strong pulpit skills. He is more negative than positive in preaching, but his sermons reveal some strong inductive elements. His sermon, "The Ascension of Christ" is introduced by a treatise on how we know only through the senses (inductively). He says we know from our eyes—colors; ears—sounds; nose—scents; tongue—flavors; and from our touch we know heat, cold, hard and soft. The idea of "know" repeated forty-five times accents induction. He enunciates a basic concept of induction when he says, "Your experience will tell you."

Volume 2. Martin Luther's teaching and preaching follow the subsequently traditional European deductive sequence. In his two-hour sermon, "The Third Sunday After Trinity" he seems defensive with his seventy-two references to twenty-six different adversaries. This didactic essay refers to thirty-seven Bible verses, gives his deductive thesis in the first paragraph and decries learning from experience. He does use nineteen questions, and a slight glimmer of induction appears when he personifies Peter and narrates an extended Petrine example in the first person.

Zwingli evokes strong response from the common people when he preaches his lively evangelical and relevant sermons without manuscript. He puts aside the standard commentaries and goes directly to Scripture as he preaches his way through various books of the Bible with continuous biblical exposition, adjusting to the practical needs of the people. He claims to pattern his sermons after the example of Jesus' preaching, adjusted to the needs of a changing day.

John Calvin often speaks movingly about his religious experiences, but the central concept of his faith is the sovereignty of God. His extemporaneous sermons show concern for all aspects of human relations with much energy expended on social issues, although he is an autocrat with an autocrat's personality. His sermons are without humor and imagination, but his simple, brief and direct words are suited to the common hearers of his daily preaching. He uses examples from the farm, wine-making, cooking and city life with vigorous expression, analogies, proverbs and realistic dialogue. In Calvin's forty-five-minute sermon, "Behavior in the Church" he uses thirty-four questions and "we," "our" or "us" 294 times, "know" twenty-eight times (besides sixteen synonyms). Forty-three questions appear in his "Final Advent" sermon.

John Knox, an ordained priest and affiliated with Protestants, is captured, placed on a French warship, chained as a galley slave and forced to pull oars, but returns to preach in Scotland. His sermon on the first temptation of Christ mixes narration and interpretation, uses twelve questions, and is adverbial in structure with questions and many Bible examples in clusters. His sermon on kingly power cites over fifty references to Bible persons or places and uses twenty-three direct questions.

Richard Baxter, self-educated, without university training, writes 170 volumes, and is first to use an oral, talking style in his preaching. He uses a natural, conversational manner of delivery in the plainest words. He strives for plainness and achieves eloquent preaching "as a dying man to dying men," but forever changing, flexible in his thinking. After he fights a former friend to the grave he realizes, "In a learning way men are ready to receive the truth, but in a disputing way, they come armed against it with prejudice and animosity." This concept influences his preaching with some inductive insight. His sermon, "Making Light of Christ" uses seventy-four questions, and his sermon on repentance with seventy subdivisions uses the direct "you" 438 times, with fifty-four questions in the last pages.

Bossuet brings his eloquence and love for Scripture to bear in ministering to a French court where the bedroom is central in the king's new Versailles palace. He is a practical man with ethos and strong Bible content. Few of his sermons are put on paper before delivery; he uses direct questions to lead the people into involvement.

John Bunyan spends his life within five miles of where he was born, but his writing and preaching extend his fame. He continues preaching from prison as he pleads for freedom of religion. His sermons are lively and picturesque with simple, vigorous language and masterful dialogue in the vocabulary of the common people. His carefully outlined sermon, "The Heavenly Footman" shows thirty-eight subdivisions and twenty-six questions (ten on its final page). "The Barren Fig Tree" uses twenty-nine questions and refers to "this professor" twelve times and "barren professor" nine times.

Louis Bourdaloue serves thirty-four years as leading court preacher to Louis XIV with his bony, overworked sermons, but still he is honest and shares ethical relevance. He uses imaginary discourse and skillful rhetorical questions in clusters.

Fenelon, another court preacher, shows great social awareness, but with few sermonic notes remaining since he doesn't usually write out his sermons. His directness, reference to experience and dialogue lead hearers to become involved.

Massillon, courageous court preacher, is sensitive to great social issues, the insensitivity of nobles and the suffering of the poor. He appeals to imagination, description, the compassion of God. He employs strong Bible content and many Bible examples. His 117 questions in one sermon and eighty-eight in another indicate the inductive involvement this courageous, uncompromising preacher sought even in a king's corrupt court. Hundreds of figures, sometimes more than forty appearing on a page in his sermon, "Charity," are accompanied by as many as forty-six direct references ("you") per page.

Volume 3. John Wesley, fifteenth of nineteen children (his mother was the twenty-fifth child of her father), preaches more than 42,000 sermons and writes more than 200 books in his lively style. In his sermon, "On the Omnipresence of God" eight of his first ten sentences are questions to foster involvement. "True Christianity Defended" shows seventy-seven questions and several references to experience. "Human Life a Dream" is a sermon of 4,000 words (about thirty minutes), but employs ten questions on page 2, eleven on page 3, sixteen on page 4 and eighteen on page 5, with repeated citings of common experience.

Jonathan Edwards, frail, sickly, with thin, weak voice and dim eyes, reads passively and without gesture from a manuscript only four inches square held close to his eyes when he delivers "Sinners in the Hands of an Angry God," the most famous sermon of this era. A youth holds a lantern over his shoulder while hearers cry out for mercy and cling to trees and lamp posts to keep from falling into perdition. This masterpiece of imagery turns from picture to picture, and descriptions follow one another in direct, personal application—"you," "this congregation" and "today." The sermon is nearly an hour long with seven pages of direct application using "you," examples, figures and the directness of questions and pronouns. His sermon "Christian Love," with forty-six subdivisions, employs twenty-one questions for involvement and direct appeal in the final two pages.

George Whitefield often preaches in the fields to 25,000 at a time. He preaches once to nearly 100,000 persons and after the one and a half hour sermon has 10,000 converts. He refers much to personal experience and employs humor (different from Wesley) in his lively, emotional and energetic preaching. He uses "I," "me" or "my" 254 times in "All Men's Place" after stating his inductive view of learning from experience in the introduction. He incorporates twenty-four examples including biblical and personal memory. "The Burning Bush" begins inductively, referring to our own experience. Humor and examples are prominent. Forty-one questions in "Repentance and Conversion" seek to involve hearers with much directness, illustrating common experience.

Timothy Dwight, extemporaneous, evangelistic grandson of Jonathan Edwards, speaks rapidly in dignified manner without gestures. He uses questions, contrast and limited reference to experience.

Lyman Beecher appeals to imagination, uses more illustrations than others, cites experience for involving hearers. In "The Native Character of Man" he asks fifty-two questions, and in "The Remedy for Dueling" among eighty-seven questions he releases a series of nineteen in a row.

Thomas Chalmers, a popular genius and advocate of the poor, deals with real problems of the real people. His sermons are descriptive, imaginative, colorful and clear despite some 400-word sentences. Oral style helps clarity too. His sermon, "Immortality" uses twenty-two questions, and twenty-four appear in "Fury Not in God," where he speaks of "your common sense and common experience." In "The Expulsive Power of a New Affection," he shows strong, repeated appeals to experience and places six of the sermon's nine questions on the last page.

Charles G. Finney, ardent evangelist and zealous social reformer, speaks in simple language, illustrating from common experience and delivering the sermon extemporaneously in conversational tone. He is repetitive, argumentative. His lawyerlike questions, intricate subdivisions and repeated references to experience mark his sermons. "God's Love for a Sinning World" shows fifty-seven questions and his sermon on "Excuses" with forty-three subdivisions bombards listeners with an incredible 160 questions.

Volume 4. John Henry Newman reads his sermon manuscripts without gesture, but with quiet, restrained impact, using incredible numbers of references to Bible characters. In Saul's biography he gives 135 proper nouns from the Bible, asks seventeen questions and arranges the entire sermon inductively.

Horace Bushnell, author of *Christian Nurture,* employs questions and much human experience as examples in his sermons.

Thomas Guthrie studies the prophets and Jesus to become one of the most inductive of Christian preachers in these twenty centuries. He uses many and varied illustrations, aims at "proving, painting and persuading" with much colorful description. Perhaps as inductive as his nineteenth century demanded, he focuses on descriptive examples and many questions. "True Religion" follows inductive format in its effusive verbiage, but asks twenty-two questions. "The Christian's Life" asks forty-nine questions and uses fifty examples besides many comparisons, similes, metaphors and contrasts. He describes imaginatively in his frequent biblical examples: "The tumbling sea, the rolling boat, the howling wind, the sheets of spray could not wake him. . . ." And, "A hand out of the darkness dealt his enemies a blow which sent them staggering prostrate to the ground." "Man's Great Duty," an inductive sermon, has thirty-five examples, and "The Inheritance," with twenty-nine questions, reveals some eighty-four examples on first reading, besides pictures and figures.

Theodore Parker makes steady appeal to the head, plans sermons four years in advance and uses huge clusters of examples, sometimes ten or fifteen per page. In his "Crime" sermon he calls the people to "remember" seventeen times, uses fourteen questions and multitudes of examples.

John Jasper, twenty-fourth child of a slave family, is much in demand as a funeral preacher. His sermons are a series of pictures from beginning to end, full of biblical illustrations and quotations with many citings of imaginative experience.

Robert Murray McCheyne, using simple descriptive outlines, writes out his sermons, but preaches them without notes. His "Dry Bones" sermon asks twenty-five questions, "Do What You Can" thirty questions with eighteen of them in sequence; "Christ The Way" asks twenty-four questions.

Henry Ward Beecher goes to the twenty-one-member church in Brooklyn and adds nearly 4,600 more during his ministry there. He learns the value of aim in his so-called "homiletical lawlessness," harnesses his creative imagination in uniting his thoughts on a theme. His sermons are long—"The Fruits of the Spirit," nearly an hour in length, asks thirty-four questions and makes repeated references to experience. "The Holy Scriptures" clusters twenty-three of its fifty questions in a group, but its attraction lies largely in the expansive man and his delivery rather than in his words or sermon format.

F. W. Robertson, in his intensive ministry to the poor, preaches extemporaneous sermons, writing them out on Sunday night after he had preached them. He urges establishing positive truth instead of seeking negatively to demolish error, depreciates using propositions, teaches suggestively rather than dogmatically, and preaches variations on two-part themes. Despite giving his two-pronged thesis in his opening sentence, his comparison and contrast bring a clarity that captures public appeal. His sermon "Inspiration" clusters ten of the eighteen questions in the introduction, but he makes little use of other inductive elements.

Alexander Maclaren devotes two hours daily to reading Scripture in original languages, but unlike many expositors with their dry discourses, he accents the personal element with a strong note of urgency. As master of illustration, he fills sermons with analogies, stories and human experience, but he preaches largely to Christians and assumes little need for the inductive approach. Some of his sermons ask no questions at all.

John A. Broadus uses narrative, vivid description as well as examples from experience. His sermon "Be Careful for Nothing" begins in experience and stitches the entire message to daily life, asks twenty questions and uses vivid imagination in spots.

Henry Liddon preaches long, loud, dogmatic and analytical sermons with very limited use of inductive elements. Biographical narrative in his sermon on Gehazi defers assertions until he draws three lessons from ancient history at the end.

R. W. Dale mixes evangelism and ethics in his usual manuscript preaching. He quotes Coleridge on learning from life: "Experience is too often like the stern lights of a ship; it illuminates only the path over which we have traveled, and it gives no enlightenment of guidance for conduct in the future."

William Booth preaches 60,000 sermons in his rugged, direct and simple style during his sixty-year street ministry among the poor, the alcoholics, prostitutes and other have-nots of society. Flying bricks, eggs and spoiled fruit teach him much about the audience response, how to capture attention, and how to mute some of the violent reactions. Some sermons begin with questions, but he is always aggressive, dominating and passionately concerned with persons. In his earthy, dramatic talks he makes no effort to instruct or edify—only to interrupt, to intersect their mad race to destruction.

Joseph Parker skillfully employs questions—sometimes as topic sentences—for holding his hearers in his varied, versatile and vivid sermons.

T. DeWitt Talmadge is no propositional preacher. Flamboyant and oratorical, he never even uses a pulpit. But his regular congregations exceed 5,000, and twenty million persons read his sermons each week as published in 3,000 world newspapers. His sermons lean heavily upon illustration, life-situation and application with little time for exposition, word studies or background materials. He uses historic present tense in his imaginative, dramatic and descriptive narrative sermons, with cascading examples leading listeners via emotional involvement to response and commitment. For example, the sermon "The Ministry of Tears" goes swiftly from one moving example to another, asking thirty-four questions and drawing hearers on into the mainstream of the message via biblical and contemporary illustrations. The inductive movement carries the congregation along to the conclusion. "Question of Questions" asks fifty-four times in this imaginative, descriptive mixture of biblical and life experiences.

Volume 6. Charles Haddon Spurgeon at twenty-two is the most popular preacher of his day, preaching to 10,000 each week. He focuses attention on the people rather than upon the sermon. He writes manuscripts only after he has preached a sermon; so he develops an excellent oral style, directness and impact. Narrative, references to experience and many questions characterize his dramatic preaching.

Phillips Brooks, prince of preachers, views his people as individuals in need of ministry rather than a congregation assembled for his preaching. This intense love for the pastoral phase of ministry gives warmth and impact to his sermons. "The Eternal Humanity" asks more than fifty-five questions, and his preaching shows use of imagination and experience to involve hearers.

Washington Gladden is a pioneer in Christian social concerns. His religious convictions grow out of his experience as he preaches his biblical narrative sermons in ministering to the needs of his people. He is imaginative in describing his illustrations from daily life, the Bible, biography and nature.

Alexander Whyte, gifted with vivid imagination, preaches dramatic, abundantly illustrated, biblical sermons without perceptible organization as he draws from biography, autobiography and common experience. His biographies of Bible characters show many aspects of inductive preaching.

Dwight L. Moody, apostle of love, rejects fear as a primary motive in his evangelistic preaching. Personal experience, narrative and strong emotion augment his simple Bible messages. His sermons show little organization and rely mostly on examples in an inductive, cumulative approach to preaching. His references to experience exceed his questions.

Evangelist Sam Jones meanders through his messages with many questions, illustrations and frequent references to experience. "Eternal Punishment" cites forty-two questions and engrosses listeners in much direct conversation.

F. B. Meyer, extemporaneous devotional and expository preacher, is primarily deductive except in his "excellent biographical sermons." His references to experience, description and imagination with some rhetorical questions help hearers get involved.

Volume 7. John Watson (Ian Maclaren) employs thirty-two questions (twelve on the last page) in the sermon "The Mercy of Future Punishment" and twenty-two (seventeen on page 2) in "Public Spirit," with many references to experience.

Charles E. Jefferson is influenced by Phillips Brooks to leave law for the ministry, where he continues to imitate the famous preacher with style and relevance in impressionistic sermons flowing along like a river. He speaks in picture language with short, simple, powerful sentences sweeping listeners along in a floodtide of illustration. "The Importance of Little Things" cites experience, asks twenty-eight questions (thirteen on the final page), and describes with feeling. "The Man of Bethesda" uses twenty-two questions, vivid description in extensive Bible examples and relevant application.

Gipsy Smith becomes a gifted speaker with warm, personal touch and strong emotional appeal. His humor and pathos move the people by sermons buttressed with personal experience. His sermon "Strength and Beauty" employs twelve of its twenty-eight questions on the first page, and he leads to involvement and evangelistic response by citing experience and examples.

Walter Rauschenbusch, an evangelical with strong social concerns, preaches vivid, compassionate sermons with a variety of illustrative material. Most of his short sermons show few inductive strengths, but "The Kingship of Christ" uses seventeen questions.

Charles R. Brown preaches with conversational style, using abundant brief illustrations. In "The Helpless Christ" he asks twenty-eight questions (sixteen on one page) as he deals with the problem of suffering. "What Jonah Did" uses narrative followed by four divisions of the sermon application in his most inductive endeavor.

Billy Sunday's anti-intellectual tirades gush out at a 300 words-per-minute hypnotic rate. "Gethsemane" employs fifteen questions, several examples, references to experience and direct discourses with hearers. "Motherhood" with its twenty questions uses the biblical account of Moses' mother along with many examples and citings from experience. In "Second Coming" there are twenty-five questions; in "Dancing, Drinking, Card-Playing," thirty-one queries and a constant flow of experiences and examples. But other elements of induction are largely unused since he approaches preaching from a strong authoritarian stance without apparent respect for hearers.

Rufus Jones, Quaker mystic, uses only five questions in four sermons. Yet he speaks from experience to experience in his popular impromptu college talks. His sermons are short, full of humor and vivid illustrations.

Volume 8. G. Campbell Morgan preaches his first sermon at thirteen, is preaching regularly at fifteen, but at twenty-five is rejected by the Methodist Church because his trial sermon shows "no promise." This noted biblical expositor probes background and word studies, but in a fresh and interesting style. Sometimes he uses problem-solution, progression, "ladder" and one-point or "jewel" arrangement; but generally he gives more running commentary. Contrast and conflict mark the sermon as he follows Jacob and Esau in "The Kingdom Shall Be the Lord's," using eleven questions.

John Henry Jowett shows great compassion for the personal problems of people, directing his sermons toward human hurt. Sometimes he begins with a series of questions in a life-situation approach. He always works from manuscript, feeling great dependence upon it, yet with conversational tone.

S. Parkes Cadman pioneers the talk-back format of preaching in his courageous, positive messages. Sometimes his pollysyllabic verbiage makes for high-level complexity. His sermon "Vanity of Vanities" with thirteen questions shows far less induction than the Bible book providing the text, but he does make some references to experience.

George W. Truett, a great Baptist evangelist, has been called one of the most exciting preachers to hear and one of the most disappointing to read. As a master of lively oral style, he preaches without manuscript. His life-situation and evangelistic sermons especially use skillful illustrations and experiences, along with many emotional appeals. His concern for involving hearers and winning their favorable response is shown by his variety, frequent questions and abundance of illustrations. He gives evidence of the evangelist's inductive approach to involving hearers and leading them to full response.

Frank W. Boreham's preaching is suggestive, persuasive, and conversational. He leads hearers to answer their own questions. He depends greatly on illustrations, and many of his graphic examples are biographical and contribute to his inductive tone. His abundant examples include frequent reference to experience.

Arthur J. Gossip blends personal experience with a literary style to bring a vivid impact upon vital and universal human feelings in his classic "But When Life Tumbles In, What Then?" This sermon employs thirty-four questions, proceeds via experience, remembering and giving examples as it seems to grope toward his firm conclusion: "Be of good cheer, my brother, for I feel the bottom, and it is sound." In "The Clash of Age and Youth" Gossip asks forty-three questions after an opening 107-word sentence. Four of his five printed sermons each employ more than thirty questions besides using experience and examples to lead inductively toward conclusions, rather than asserting propositions at the outset in a deductive format.

Henry Sloane Coffin is deeply involved in the social and theological issues of his day. He insists on biblical sermons with picturesque, uninvolved sentences. "Shields of Brass" cites thirty-four questions, rests solidly on Scripture, and refers repeatedly to life, but his format is not strictly inductive.

Volume 9. Harry Emerson Fosdick advocates the Dewey problem-solving method, but he does not use it in his life-situation preaching. He does employ some elements of induction, but full-orbed inductive arrangement with delayed conclusions and assertions seems foreign to him. He seems eager to declare his conclusions early in the sermon, following the traditional homiletical deductive format from a position of assumed authority.

Fosdick's person-centered approach to preaching lends itself to respect the hearers and to seek their acceptance, agreement, approval and the adoption of the preacher's principles. He does accent the importance of human experience and learning from life—two key concepts of the induction process. He averages twelve to fifteen illustrations, and they vary from personal, biblical, literary, imaginary, biographical or contemporary.

He does not begin with either questions or traditional propositional assertion, but with background, biblical setting or example leading into the message. His references to experiences and examples tend to carry the movement of sermons along, rather than depending upon logical format per se.

Joseph Fort Newton urges inductive preaching rather than deductive, thus leading via examples to both the text and the conclusion at the end of the sermon. He cites Jesus as a "distinctly inductive preacher," beginning with facts from the life around him and by a series of illustrations, then progressing to the authority of the Scripture. "We may wish it otherwise, but we must face the facts," he says in *The New Preaching*. He speaks of bringing the listener to say, "Why, this is true!" as the unspoken verdict when the truth of the text is approved not only as on divine authority which has been accepted by the preacher, but as a truth of experience now accepted by hearers.

Newton's innovative view of preaching is theory in his mind—not fact in his practice. He is never able to map out a program, a structure, a format for inductive preaching. He does accent examples, he defers assertions, but he doesn't show how to involve hearers via questions and full inductive process.

Clarence Macartney uses biblical material in an interesting, convincing way in his attempt to escape from "dull expository sermons." His skillful biographical messages show greatest creativity with varied inductive approach. Narrative, questions, illustrations and experiences begin his sermons in induction and lead to strong Bible usage too. His famous "Come Before Winter" shows several inductive ingredients—comparison, contrast, stress on experience and illustrations, all leading to strong biblical content, but without significant use of questions.

Dick Sheppard states his personal warmth and friendly style in realistic preaching with its accent on the problems of modern life. He involves his listeners in "Taking Jesus Seriously" by using seventeen questions, strong use of pronouns (especially "we" and "us"), several references to experience and sharing.

William Temple is an excellent ecumenical communicator and social reformer, but his extemporaneous intellectual sermons give us few insights about induction.

Clovis Chappell preaches famous biographical sermons with a simplicity and significance touching all people. His vivid imagination, memory, narrative and homespun experiences lead listeners to his strong Bible conclusions. Examples carry much weight in his sermons as he lets his illustrations be pleasant substitutes for exhortations. He exhorts, he explains, he defines—all by examples rather than by hortatory preachments. That's inductive—to let life lead to conclusions.

G. A. Studdert Kennedy learns what people listen to, then he applies the gospel to social issues—war, poverty, labor, politics, home. He follows the "jewel" or one-point arrangement or a series of questions in a problem-solving approach. "He Ascended into Heaven" begins with a series of sixteen questions followed by two-point development. He often begins with personal experience and never concludes with summary. Called the "father of contemporary preachers," he uses simple language, abundant personal pronouns and questions. In the sermon mentioned above he asks fifty-five questions (twenty-one on page 1); but more often he allows the examples, references to experience and other content to lead inductively to the conclusion.

E. Stanley Jones says, "Christ must be interpreted in terms of Christian experience rather than through mere argument"—and that's induction! His sermons bear the marks of testimony, flowing naturally from experience to experience—rich in personal illustrations—not overly involved with organization or involved exposition (p. 315)—these too are qualities of inductive preaching.

Volume 10. Halford Luccock vividly illustrates his life-situation sermons with the concept that the preacher is a channel, not a source. While he seems steeped in Scripture, his sermons always start at sidewalk level with the problems people face. Recognizing the need and problem of involving his hearers, he usually begins with an arresting sentence. He shows relevance to modern life, illustrating from history, literature and current events of experience. His introductions average one-third of his total sermon—shades of induction.

He gives three general suggestions for sermons: (1) Use creative imagination to feel your way into the lives of people; (2) Collect a huge amount of sermon material before deciding upon structure or order; and (3) Probe yourself by asking questions to open doors into the meanings of the theme. He calls for both a sensible and psychological outline of the sermon. Thus he guides us in the direction of inductive insight for more effective preaching.

Paul Tillich says he finds it difficult to overcome "the impact of the authoritarian system on my personal life." In his "Method of Correlation" he seeks to explain the contents of the Christian faith. He says culture raises the questions and theology answers them in mutual interdependence as the preacher seeks to formulate the Christian message in the thought-forms of his generation.

Many who hear Tillich's biblical sermons are of non-Christian intellectual and cultural background; so he seeks "a language which expresses in other terms the human experience to which the biblical and ecclesiastical terminology point." Often his thesis statement is placed at the end of his sermon rather than at the beginning (inductive). He constantly relates his theme to the problems of his hearers. His sermons are "excellent presentations of biblical truth to the secular mind."

Karl Barth shows courage when he abandons the liberal position when it becomes obvious to him it is inadequate to cope with the issues of life. He becomes a homiletical fundamentalist, warning against the "excesses of irrelevant preaching through a vainglorious striving after relevance." He believes in stating his thesis in the introduction of the sermon—only biblical introductions are acceptable, and he thinks sermons need no conclusion, either summary or application. He does say sermons should be prepared with the Bible on one knee and a newspaper on the other. Four of his five printed sermons each ask two dozen or more questions.

Ronald Knox, one of the greatest Roman Catholic preachers in Christian history, shows a biblical approach to preaching—not merely technically, but also in a practical, personal way. Illustrations are the most striking feature of his manuscript sermons in spite of his heavy reliance upon Scripture. Often the thesis of the sermon in the opening paragraph betrays deductive approach. "The Gleaner," a biographical-type sermon on Ruth, asks twenty-three questions and incorporates more inductive approach than usual for him.

Ralph W. Sockman's sermons, crowded with illustrations, are models of contemporary relevance and practical application. He says: "When we start with life situations we start where men live, then lead the questioning soul to the doctrinal and biblical sources."

Martin Niemoller's pacifism doesn't extend to his preaching theory. Quite expectedly, defensiveness and deductive declarations describe some of his *Dachau Sermons*, but faith, hope and love join with joy in "Christmas Eve, 1944." Experience and narrative peek cautiously between the bars, but his traditional German view of life and preaching prevents much inductive sharing, search or story.

George Buttrick preaches without propositions, but with a surprising number of assertions from the very beginning of his sermons as preached in our seminary chapel services. He has been called "the preacher for the unconvinced congregation." His sermons average twenty-five to thirty illustrations, with skillful transitions, but he doesn't depend on examples the way Guthrie and Boreham do. He begins with some simple incident to enlist attention, but his illustrative conclusions aim at understanding only, instead of action. He combines emotional and intellectual appeals. Inductive elements also include an abundance of questions, many references to human experience, progressive involvement, and narrative, along with his varied and frequent examples.

Paul Scherer believes a sermon demands thirty hours of preparation besides the subtle contributions pastoral contacts give to preaching. An imaginative preacher, he demonstrates a deep social concern arising from his personal experiences and his own devotional life. In both his radio and his pastoral sermons he attempts to blend biblical proclamation with contemporary interpretation. He usually presents his text after a few sentences of introduction, but sometimes he places it inductively at the end of the sermon. He wants to "win the hearing God's Word deserves." Progress is easier to find than an outline in his sermons. Warning against a brilliant introduction lest the rest of the sermon seem lifeless, he urges arousing interest at once and providing a biblical foundation for the sermon in a relevant setting. Some of his sermons are casually inductive, using questions, narrative, reference to experience and memory to get hearers involved in the sermon process.

Reinhold Niebuhr, prophetic in his perceptive diagnosis of human need, bitterly opposes the 400-year drift toward individualism which has produced a rising tide of total secularism. He frequently turns from first one inadequate human explanation or solution to another, inductively moving at last to his assertions. His critics accuse him of being merely a dialectical critic with sharp analysis who only points at the gospel. His easy and informal sermons make no significant use of questions, but he does use dialectic pattern, some parable, experience, illustrations and narrative.

Volume 11. Walter Maier machine-guns the airwaves as the world's best-known radio preacher for twenty years. He preaches to five million each week, writes 800 pamphlets and nearly thirty books. His fan mail drops by 1,000 letters a day when he reduces his staccato rate temporarily at the urging of radio engineers. His sermons combine biblical, ethical and social accent. His preaching is vivid (verbs and description), varied, imaginative, narrative, emotive, direct, confrontive. He uses reference to experience, questions (as many as thirty), many examples and unsurpassed urgency. Some sermons lead by questions and a vivid rush of illustrations to the conclusion, but usually his urgent assertions pile up from the start of his vehement evangelistic messages.

Samuel Shoemaker makes preaching an exciting experience as he, too, pours his words out in the torrents of his individualistic sermons. Witnessing rather than arguing—that is his concept of preaching and his accent in a broad and balanced evangelism. People and human needs are central in his simple, pictorial preaching. He sees the pulpit as a point of involvement with his people. He seeks to lead listeners to deep involvement by shared experience through illustrations, questions (as many as sixteen or seventeen) and insightful directness growing out of his extensive counseling. Explicit use of inductive methodology is not evident.

Leslie D. Weatherhead relates psychology and religion in both his ministry and preaching. He urges: "Be relevant, be simple, be loving. The great preachers have been great lovers. Put arms around the whole congregation so no one feels left out." His sermons show vivid and abundant examples, frequent questions and general respect for listeners. Sometimes he seeks to build evidence to achieve his authority before he proclaims.

Fulton J. Sheen, gracious and skillful, is the first man to build such an extensive reputation as a preacher upon his regular use of both radio and television. His TV audiences reach nearly twenty million each week. He follows an inductive approach, beginning with the viewer, using material most acceptable to him—and proceeds only at the end of the sermon to those conclusions less easily accepted by the audience. He bridges the gap between the secular mind and Christianity with such reasonable, common-sense appeal he sweeps the people along until they willingly agree with his conclusions. His biographical "The Woman at the Well" uses obvious induction with perceptive commentary and powerful appeal in his strong finish.

James S. Stewart excels at painting descriptive word-pictures in varied formats as he preaches his biblical messages. Creative variety marks his differing sermon patterns: refrain (sixteen times in "Sacrifice and Song"), drama-type structure, many questions (up to fifty-seven) and imaginative replay. He begins with present-day experience where hearers are, trying to meet them on their own ground. Some of his sermons vary greatly from usual homiletical deductive approach.

Norman Vincent Peale distributes his extemporaneous twenty-five-minute pastoral sermons to a mailing list of over 400,000. His messages are developed logically without discernible outlines. He depends upon his illustrations to convey his thought. Usually illustrative material comprises about half of his sermon. He narrates many personal experiences, and five selected sermons each average nearly twenty questions. In inductive style, he attempts to bring listeners to his conclusions by the gentle pressure of cumulative human instances shared with his optimistic enthusiasm. Biblical content is sacrificed or overshadowed by strong but excessive, contemporary examples

Martyn Lloyd-Jones leaves medicine for ministry in preaching and succeeds G. Campbell Morgan at Westminster Chapel. Each of his forty- to sixty-minute-plus expository sermons is a cumulative argument delivered with unction, authority and power, thus creating an awesome impact. His deductive philosophy of preaching dictates a strong authority stance, with each sermon beginning solidly in Scripture. Preaching almost exclusively as he does to believers, he can start with the truth of God and only then go on to the immediate situation. Bible materials remain in the forefront (sometimes almost as an end in themselves), and illustrations function only as servants of Scripture. Despite his strongly Bible-centered sermons, he does a surprising amount of comparison and contrast and accents relevance, references to experience, many illustrations and questions (33, 22, 37, 20, 17 = 129 in five sermons or about twenty-six questions in each).

William E. Sangster, with his biblical perspective, uses life-situation preaching as a type of introduction or approach to a text. He sees a need to approach the sermon in this way to gain relevance in biblical preaching. He regards evangelism as the principal concern of Christianity, but includes social concerns too. The people flock to hear him. He refers to varied experiences often and sensitively seeks to steer his hearers to both intellectual and emotional involvement. His intensity and compassion are well-known.

Peter Marshall paints pictures with emotional brushes. Images are his tools to create visual portraits in his sermons as he turns ears into eyes. Visualization and imagery replace argument and objective evidence as he tries to move hearers to see and feel his message. Highly pictorial narration conveys his sentiment in popular format as his ministry propels him into the fore of our national life. Traditional exhortations and preachments are replaced by fast-flowing flicks in a sometimes syrupy sequence of shots from life as shared in his sentimental sermons. Some of his elements of induction include questions, references to experience, illustrations, deferred decrees, leading via examples to conclusions, his nonuse of propositions, and his use of Scripture more as example than as authority.

Robert McCracken steps into the breach at famous Riverside Church after Fosdick—during the decline of preaching influence in America. McCracken insists preaching is both careful preparation and "preaching instinct." He chooses the title early in the week so the subconscious can be working on the sermon. Letting his subjects call forth his texts, he compiles accumulated materials, sifts, systematizes and sketches out the outline. Then carefully writing and rewriting the introduction, he seeks to be first interesting and then quickly come to grips with his subject. Considering conclusions generally too short with too little application, he writes out and memorizes a conclusive wrap-up he thinks will conclude and confirm the entire message.

His functional format follows what he calls the "evolutionary principle" either in one great cycle or several times in the same sermon—explanation, illustration and application. In his question-type sermons, he answers obvious questions early and the more suspenseful inquiries he responds to at the end. Modified induction would be an accurate description of many of his messages.

Dietrich Bonhoeffer works hard at his preaching aimed at two objectives: missionary and edification accents. He warns against presupposing a mind-set in the congregation that is not there. His "Gideon" sermon, his first delivered after Hitler's takeover, shows great courage, but his forty-one questions, strong comparison and contrast in this inductive biographical sermon are most surprising.

Gerald Kennedy shows realistic optimism in his positive approach, trying early to get people to want to hear what he has to say. The chief element of inductive preaching he demonstrates is his strong and frequent references to experience and his gradual psychological approach to the conclusion. In "One Thorn of Experience," for example, in twenty-three paragraphs he makes at least twenty-six references to experience. He uses some Bible references, but frequently his sermons are without strong scriptural usage.

D. T. Niles, a lively preacher with long experience as a Christian evangelist, moves his sermon in response to the way the congregation moves. He summarizes his message with these four statements:

(1) There is a message—God acted and demands response.
(2) There is a messenger—the Church where the gospel is experienced.
(3) There is a story—the Church's witness to the gospel.
(4) There is a faith—the testimony of the Church.

Preaching must be in the present tense. "Preaching about a past event in the past tense is pure folly," he says. Parables provide basis for many of his creative, imaginative and inductive-type sermons. He skillfully uses questions and repeated references to experience, and seeks to intersect common life by his insightful background descriptions and applications. "Four Kinds of People," based on the parable of the sower, uses remarkable inductive approach and thirty-three questions.

Helmut Thielicke warns that theology must not overwhelm proclamation. He urges preachers to reflect their own experiences honestly in the unending dialogue with those to whom we must deliver our messages. "Every conversation becomes at bottom a meditation, a preparation, a gathering of material for my preaching," he says. Discovering his "well-ordered structure" in Thielicke's sermons is not easy. The progress of his messages follows a course not easy to chart, but it always seems inevitable and irresistible. The entire message is tied together by a strong theme with a definite movement toward a predetermined end. He establishes immediate contact with his hearers in his usually rather long introductions. He is skilled in the use of interrogation, organizing around a series of penetrating questions he gradually answers as the sermon progresses. Superb illustrations, contemporary experiences, dialogue, imagination and powerful descriptive language—these mark his sermons. "The Parable of the Prodigal Son" is biographical, descriptive, narrative, inductive— powerfully arranged, vividly portrayed in the midst of fifty-three questions (his five sermons average twenty-eight questions).

Billy Graham has grown from his almost formless sermons with few illustrations in his early ministry to a more inductive movement, mixing in each sermon Bible and life examples to reinforce the central facts of the gospel story. He may pound his palm and shout, "The Bible says," but he cites experience, uses narration, questions and other elements of induction far more. Many of his sermons are one-point messages with a series of various illustrations of his theme as found in different areas of human experience.

In his introductions he has moved steadily away from listing numbered sermon points. He often arouses audience interest in a problem from the human situation and introduces Scripture only when he is in the body of the sermon. Generally his crusade messages are loaded with illustrations. He uses as many as seven illustrations in a row, a total of 191 full-length illustrations in eleven sermons. While he does insist on positive immediate action, he lets the individual decide personal response on the basis of his message without cajoling or pleading during the invitation. The first four sample sermons use an average of thirty-seven questions and scores of references to experience with surprising inductive format in some of the messages.

Martin Luther King blends his vivid imagery with imaginative content and fine verbal skills. He draws illustrations from a broad range, his organization is simple, but logical, and he follows a tight-knit plan to develop his theme. While most of his listeners would grant him an authoritative posture, he seeks inductively to earn the right to make his declarations. He uses questions, experience, narrative and psychological approach to bring hearers to accept his considered conclusions.

Conclusion

So we see all ninety-six of the preachers in the series *Twenty Centuries of Great Preaching* show at least some use of induction. A few make only minimal references to experience, but others rely heavily on human instances and let examples, narrative and delayed assertion carry the sermon all the way to the conclusion before announcing their propositions.

Most who grasp inductive principles use the process to win listener involvement, then go beyond the established concepts to proclaim deductively their vital faith.

No, this inductive preaching is no novel idea, no innovation of recent days. From the earliest preacher, induction has blended with human creativity to help others learn from experience.

The most effective preachers combine inductive-deductive format. They first achieve authority by narrative, analogy, parable, biography, case study or human instances. *Then* they declare the unsearchable riches of Christ with confidence, compassion and courage.

Appendix 4
A Strategy for Making Traditional Sermon Structures Inductive

Some students of homiletics reading this book may say, "This inductive-deductive dichotomy of structure makes sense, but how does it relate to all the sermon structures I've already studied or used in my preaching?"

Any homiletic form can incorporate inductive elements and inductive movement by adjusting, modifying or simply delaying any assertive stance at the beginning of the sermon. Here I'd like to suggest simple ways to utilize some of the most common traditional sermon structures and transform them into inductive sermons. (All mention of preachers and specific sermons refers to material available for study in the 13-volume, *20 Centuries of Great Preaching*. See Appendix 3 for more details.)

1. One-idea sermons can accumulate representative examples, cases, experiences in inductive style to reach a reasonable conclusion.

2. Two contrasting ideas. Dialectic (F. W. Robertson, Bossuet, Fenelon) can develop via inductive examples and process as the listeners are involved and led to a resultant, recommended concept.

3. Three divisions. Maclaren and thousands since include as their divisions: (1) explain, (2) prove, (3) apply. By citing examples inductively to accomplish each of these tasks, this type could easily follow the pattern of induction. Inductive shift would improve this traditional format popularized since medieval preachers sought to honor the Trinity by their triple sermon points.

4. Four segments. Fosdick's box, James Stewart's "Christian Life" as happier, harder, holier, hopeful, or "Four Dimensions of the Love of God," four sides, four seasons, four directions—all of these could

defer assertions and lead inductively to a cooperatively derived conclusion.

5. Five points, like a star, can inductively trace various aspects of a subject to reach a strong conclusion on the basis of fivefold evidence.

6. Six divisions, as practiced by Fosdick, Ilion Jones and others, can incorporate inductive movement to explore various aspects of a topic.

7. Question-answer format, as often used by John Wesley and others, lends itself to inductive inquiry by respecting listeners and involving them in the quest for answers.

8. Ladder outline (James Stewart) can climb inductively rung by rung to explore the heights and reach an unstated goal in a nonthreatening, nonadversary route.

9. Classification (Joseph Fort Newton) can accumulate, analyze and let the particulars lead inductively to the conclusion.

10. Hegelian thesis, antithesis and synthesis format could postpone the thesis to form the conclusion, by posing the thesis as a problem or tentative theory and a search for verification by antithesis and synthesis. Or it can let the thesis serve as hypothesis or tentative base.

11. Cause and effect sermons—like Amos preached, or beginning with effect and seeking causes—use inductive movement. Some eager preachers have leaped from effect to consequent effect, abbreviating the process, but still intersecting listener experience and leading to involvement.

12. Chronological structure, common to Old Testament prophets, may inductively involve past, present and future, or *then* and *now, now* and *future*.

13. Motivated sequence. A cycle of attention, need, satisfy, visualize, action, as advocated by Allan H. Monroe, could appropriate induction at every stage.

14. Topical or subject development (Spurgeon's early sermons) lends itself to total inductive approach from beginning to end.

15. Text pattern (Spurgeon's later sermons) could incorporate inductive quest and movement in parts, if not in whole, to compare with other texts and to explore ramifications, implications and applications.

16. Expository sermons can incorporate the inductive elements by reference to experience, comparing and contrasting, delaying assertions, asking questions, employing narrative and other inductive elements, and leading listeners to conclusions.

17. A string of beads series of illustrations (many evangelists, "Acres of Diamonds"by Russell Conwell, Henry Ward Beecher

sometimes) often shows totally inductive approach as the sermon leads to a reasonable conclusion.

18. Peter Marshall's principle, illustration, application sequence appears deductive. But it can be modified so the propositional principle seems less a rigid, authoritarian decree. Narrative, biography, cases or questions could introduce the sermon as an introductory inductive porch of a now-revised four-part structure.

19. The parable pattern of Jesus and others stands as inductive because of its delayed assertions, narrative format, and its intersecting of experience, progressing from the known to the unknown and its nonadversary approach.

20. The need-remedy process roots down in common-life patterns to seek sensible answers, as we do in our daily experience. Involvement, interest and induction flow naturally from this format, as the preacher postpones personal pat answers until hearers come to reasonable agreement.

21. Narrative sermons involve imaginative description, drama and drawing conclusions from the inductive particulars.

22. A bull's-eye structure proceeds with a five-point format: Wake Up! This concerns you! Generally speaking. Examples. What to do? This modified inductive process can fit some subjects and some congregations.

23. The river sermon starts with particulars in the tributaries flowing forever toward the mainstream until the whole converges to flow into the conclusion—a classic inductive form.

24. Biographical sermons probably are the most common kind of inductive preaching. Life stories of Bible characters unroll inductively like a carpet, revealing, exploring, exposing, progressing to conclusions.

25. Flashback sermons can take cue from television drama, movies, novels. For example, Thornton Wilder in *The Bridge of San Luis Rey* begins with the tragic deaths of the five on the swinging footbridge. Then he traces the life of each victim up to the fateful day on the bridge. This can serve as an inductive variation for sermon structure, too, just as Wilder answers common questions about life, death and purpose in this indirect but graphic manner.

To the glory of God
and the help of preachers

INDEX